FLORENCE NIGHTINGALE

FLORENCE NIGHTINGALE
Reputation and Power

F. B. SMITH

CROOM HELM
London & Canberra

© 1982 F.B. Smith
Croom Helm Ltd, Provident House, Burrell Row,
Beckenham, Kent BR3 1AT
Croom Helm Australia, PO Box 391,
Manuka, ACT 2603, Australia
Reprinted 1983 and 1984; first paperback edition 1984

British Library Cataloguing in Publication Data

Smith, F.B.
    Florence Nightingale.
    1. Nightingale, Florence
    2. Nurse administrators – Great Britain – Biography
    I. Title
    610.73'0924   RT37.N5

    ISBN 0-7099-2314-7
    ISBN 0-7099-3320-7 Pbk

Printed and bound in Great Britain by
Biddles Ltd, Guildford and King's Lynn

CONTENTS

Preface

1.   Character and Public Life   11

2.   Miss Nightingale at Scutari   25

3.   The Campaign for Army Sanitary Reform   72

4.   India   114

5.   Nursing   155

6.   Reputation and Power   183

Select Bibliography   205

Index   212

To my daughters, Deborah and Laura

PREFACE

This is a study of some of Florence Nightingale's thoughts in action. It is not an attempt to retell the story of her life. There are already dozens of biographies and hagiographies of the Lady with the Lamp, beginning with the great biography by Sir Edward Cook. His two volumes form a monument worthy of their subject: they show his marvellous industry in combing through a huge archive which must have been largely unsorted when he began; he is accurate and has a keen sense of personality and period; his tact and fairness never falter when narrating the conflicts involving his redoubtable heroine; above all, he conveys the nature and force of Miss Nightingale's superb intelligence. These qualities together set his work on that rare plane with Morley on Gladstone, Maitland on Leslie Stephen and Forster on Dickens.

All subsequent works on Florence Nightingale, including Lytton Strachey's essay and the liveliest and perhaps least known study, that by Margaret Goldsmith, are recensions of Cook. The most pretentious and popular of them, the book by Cecil Woodham-Smith, is careless, often misleading, and ungrateful to Cook, from whom her work is closely derived. Instead of writing another biography, I have tried to discover from a fresh, close examination of the Nightingale Papers, and the manuscripts of some of her allies which were not available to Cook or Goldsmith, and not used by Woodham-Smith, why and how Miss Nightingale assumed the career of reformer, why and how she chose particular strategies and fought particular battles, and how she fared with them. I hope my accounts of these episodes will give the reader a clearer idea of Miss Nightingale's ambitions and beliefs than existing studies provide. I have tried, too, to place her in her context as a social improver and thereby to illuminate more widely the unofficial mind of reform in High Victorian England.

I am deeply grateful to my colleagues in the Research School of Social Sciences for their generous, expert and varied help with this book: Janice Aldridge shepherded my tangled drafts through the new technology; Cameron Hazlehurst supplied me with unlikely but profitable sources; Ken Inglis, Oliver McDonagh and Allan Martin criticised my drafts with marvellous acuity and forbearance; Pauline

Barratt, Jeanette Horrocks and Christine Woodland unearthed crucial facts.

Notes

I would like to clarify one or two points relating to the text. Parentheses within quotes are Miss Nightingale's own and square brackets contain my additions. I have also used square brackets within the notes to indicate my suggested names and dates for letters and memoranda where these are absent or uncertain in the original.

1 CHARACTER AND PUBLIC LIFE

Florence Nightingale's first chance to deploy her talent for manipulation came in August 1853. She then became resident lady superintendent of the Invalid Gentlewomen's Institution at 1, Upper Harley Street. This charity provided refuge for distressed ladies who paid for single rooms or 'compartments' at the subsidised but still formidable rates of 10/6 or one guinea a week. The Institution was a few years old; it was run down, and ill-managed by separate committees of ladies and gentlemen led by a half-hearted council; it had newly removed to the Upper Harley Street premises. The post was Miss Nightingale's first (though unsalaried) job, her first exercise of independent control. Her father made her an allowance of £500 a year. Her aunt Mai Smith secured her a flat in Pall Mall so that Florence could as she put it, 'clear off . . . at my *own* time' from the Institution.[1] The new superintendent had about five months' practical observation of hospital nursing. She was 33 years old.

Even while she was negotiating for the appointment, Miss Nightingale was insisting upon changes in the nursing arrangements and upon the installation of mechanical improvements at Upper Harley Street. Henceforth each nurse was to sleep next to her ward, and 'the bells of the patients should all ring in the passage outside the nurse's own door *on that story*, and should have a valve which flies open when its bell rings, and *remains* open in order that the nurse may see who has rung'. A piped hot water system and a 'windlass', a kind of tray hoist, were also to be built, to save the nurses' legs when serving meals, and their time in carrying water. The alterations were made. The superintendent-elect supervised the work by letter from Paris, simultaneously with mobilising biddable supporters in Lady Canning, Lady Inglis and Mrs Sidney Herbert to become more active on the committee.[2]

Within a week of her arrival at the Institution Miss Nightingale challenged the governing bodies with her decision to admit Catholics and even Jews. She let it be said that she would resign on the question. The governing bodies capitulated, in writing. There is no evidence that any Catholic or Jew ever sought admission or was admitted; but among the high-minded High Church aristocratic would-be tolerant membership of the committees, it was an inspired choice of issue. The new superintendent also dismissed the incumbent matron, an act which did not technically lie completely within her province, and introduced her own housekeeper, paid from her own pocket.[3] Within weeks of Miss Nightingale's installation the house surgeon resigned and she took a leading part in selecting his successor and defining his duties, once more exceeding her authority. She insisted, yet again upon threat of resignation, on accompanying the doctors on their rounds in order to ensure that orders were executed and that what she called the patients' 'legerdemain of Hysteria' should not prevail with the medical men. The young, zealous and personable Puseyite chaplain was forced out and, against the inclinations of the ladies' committee, the lady superintendent replaced him, with 'good, harmless Mr Garnier', older, physically and theologically nondescript, and tame.

These early victories confirmed Florence Nightingale in a strategy which she followed to the end of her career. She had discovered two great strengths in herself, necessary strengths in all reformers. She fed on an unyielding, unremitting drive to dominate her associates and opponents and to this end she defined issues and goals, distinct from theirs, in the pursuit of which she never faltered, regardless of the worth of her rivals' goals, the cogency of their arguments or the solidity of their facts. She had also an extraordinarily rich and firm imaginative grasp of the relations between individuals and the siting and working of things and of human beings' relations to them. This sense, which we might best describe as Balzacian —uncanny insight into both human obsessions, ambitions and delusions and the concreteness of 'things' − was to enable her to become a successful, indefatigable politician and disposer of persons and objects. Like a novelist drawing upon a month's visit to Bath or a few months as a governess, Florence Nightingale absorbed during her brief visits to hospitals sufficient ideas to sustain a lifetime of admonition, exposition and rule-making.

After three months at the Institution Florence Nightingale reported her successes in a long letter to her father:

> When I entered into service here, I determined that, happen what would, I never would intrigue among the Comtee. Now I perceive that I do all my business by intrigue. I propose in private to A, B, or C the resolution. I think A, B, or C most capable of carrying in Committee, and then leave it to them − and I always win.
>
> I am now in the hey-day of my power. At the last General Committee they proposed and carried (without my knowing

anything about it) a Resolution that I should have £50 per month to spend for the House, and wrote to the Treasurer to advance it me – whereupon I wrote to the Treasurer to refuse it me. Ly Cranworth, who was my greatest enemy, is now, I understand, trumpeting my fame thru' London. And all because I have reduced their expenditure from 1/10 per head per day to 1/-. The opinions of others concerning you depend, not at all, or very little, upon what <u>you</u> are, but upon what <u>they</u> are. Praise and blame are alike indifferent to me, as constituting an indication of what myself is, though very precious as the indication of the other's feeling . . .

Last General Meeting I executed a series of resolutions on five subjects, and presented them as coming from the Medical Men.

The new rules included in-house dispensing of drugs to save druggists' bills, new rules to enforce old provisions limiting each patient's stay to two months, new reduced diets, fixed by the superintendent, and a public advertisement for the Institution, also composed by Miss Nightingale.

All these I proposed and carried in Committee without telling them that they came from <u>me</u> and not from the Medical men – and then, and not till then, I showed them to the Medical Men, without telling <u>them</u> that they were already passed <u>in committee.</u>

It was a bold stroke, but success is said to make an insurrection into a revolution. The Medical Men have had two meetings upon them, approved them all nem-con – and thought they were their own – and I came off in flying colours, no one suspecting of my intrigue, which, of course, would ruin me, were it known.

Intriguers are often torn, as Florence Nightingale usually was, between savouring their triumphs in private and boasting of their victories to intimates. Florence was close to her father, her weak but indispensable ally against her mother, Fanny, and sister, Parthenope. Her revelation of her new powers seems to have been designed to fortify the faith William Nightingale showed in her when he backed her venture into pursuing a life independent of the family circle. The striking thing about Miss Nightingale's intrigues is their elaborateness, often amounting to elaboration for art's sake. At Upper Harley Street her reforms were easily accepted. No group, except the patients and servants, who were voiceless, was threatened by them. Patients and servants could only vote with their feet. Her rules on diet and restricting the sojourns of patients appeared to the doctors and some committee members to be rational and parsimonious, and not inhumane; her public measures promised to enhance the reputation of the Institution and its governors, and to improve the doctors' standing within it. Miss Nightingale chafed at the committee's dilatoriness and slack indulgence to patients rather than their indecisive opposition; by October 1853 she had overcome the 'treasurer who dealt with inexpedient principles and my Committee who dealt with unprincipled expedients . . . My Committee are such children in administration', she informed her father. This is a severe characterisation of men and women and medical men who most of them possessed many more years' experience of the charity arena than their lady superintendent. But none of them matched the force and ingenuity she brought to intrigue.

Miss Nightingale's urge to boast served yet another purpose which she seems not to have recognised. Her setbacks were numerous and glaring but she none the less recorded them, glossed them and laid the blame elsewhere. In November 1853, unprompted, she inaugurated a series of quarterly reports to the ladies' committee. The reports chronicle, jauntily and unaware, the decline of the Institution. During the three months after her arrival, she dismissed or lost one complete set of servants and nurses, with the exception of the cook and one nurse, and there are indications that she subsequently lost a second set. She also changed most of the tradespeople. Typically, she forsook the local grocer for Fortnum and Mason's. Within seven months she apparently was compelled to change several of the tradespeople again. She also started a frenetic bout of home-jam making, producing, on my estimate, many more pots than the patients could possibly consume. The charwoman had disappeared; this had permitted a great saving in money but 'the house has not now the advantage of efficient cleaning — the housemaids being two inexperienced girls, who, though willing and anxious to do all in their power, are unequal to the work without constant superintendence'. Miss Nightingale purchased and begged a great deal of new kitchen utensils, new linen and new furniture. Thereby she raised the capacity of the Institution to 27 beds, but from about March 1854 the average number of inmates was only nine. At this level the Institution's income from paying patients and subscriptions was falling £500 short of the running expenses which had jumped, under the new superintendent, from under £1,000 to £1,500 a year. The dismissals continued: 'I have changed one housemaid, on account of her love of dirt and inexperience, & one nurse, on account of her love of Opium & intimidation'[4]. The superintendent and her matron do not appear to have excelled in picking and training staff.

The shortcomings of the Institution were not, apparently, the lady superintendent's responsibility. She warned the ladies' committee that 'The fact of the deficiency of Patients calls for immediate attention. Otherwise, this Institution will degenerate into a luxurious piece of charity, not worth burthening the public with.' Meanwhile the furiously busy sewing, mending and jam making continued. By May 1854 the bedroom arm-chairs received spare covers made from the former curtains which Miss Nightingale disliked and discarded. The five bedroom sofas were all provided with spare covers, specially lined with calico. In addition, there were one dozen more dusters, two table-cloths, eight toilet-covers, four sand-bags, made out of 'old green baize', and two anti-macassars, together with extra dusters, old towels doubled into cloths (bringing the total to over 50 in six months — there is no indication of what they were used for, or if they were used), carpets repaired, counterpanes, pillow cases and towels mended. By August there were more sofa-covers, two more hassocks, more repairs to the linen, together with 30 more pots of red currant jam and six of jelly, at a cost of twopence per pot. The superintendent reported, in a single sentence apparently as an afterthought, that there was only one nurse left at the Institution. This development had saved £9 in wages for the quarter.

Miss Nightingale blandly concluded that the August report would be her last. She informed the Committee that she considered her work to be done, 'as far as it can be done' and that the Institution had 'been brought into as good a state as its capabilities admit'. 'Good order, good nursing, moral influence & economy' had all been satisfactorily implemented. She had not, she admitted, been able to effect her promised scheme of nurse training, but this was the committee's fault because they had allowed her too few patients. Moreover, the few they had introduced included too many of the wrong kind. Florence Nightingale always took a cool view of patients, and never wavered from her opinion, announced in the February report, that only the 'seriously ill' deserved hospital care. This classification excluded all 'trifling, hysterical or incurable cases'.[5] Such patients tended to press their individual needs and were difficult to control. The results of the superintendent's sharp way with patients shows in the final report. After less than a year of her ministrations only ten patients remained in the Institution, that is, only one-third of the beds were occupied:

five of the ten were dying, another was a child, and yet another was an apparently immovable 'spine case'. (The remaining three, who presumably were open to being discharged or to discharging themselves, included, in Florence Nightingale's judgement, '2 fancy-Patients' and a 'moral case'). About two years before the Harley Street episode Parthe, who was no fool, had confided to her and Florence's special friend, Madame Mohl, that Florence had 'little or none of what is called charity . . . she is ambitious − very, and would like to regenerate the world with a grand *coup de main*. . . I wish she could see that it is the intellectual part that interests her, not the manual. She has no *esprit de conduite* . . . she was a shocking nurse.'[6]

In her August report Miss Nightingale had given notice of three months, though adding that she might stay on for six; but she was already privately negotiating to transfer to King's College Hospital. But before the month was out she had moved without warning her committee to the Middlesex Hospital, she claimed, to supervise the admission of female cholera victims. Our knowledge of this episode comes from the vivid account Miss Nightingale gave Mrs Gaskell, the novelist, later in August while both were on holiday at one of the Nightingale country houses, Lea Hurst. Mrs Gaskell reported to Catherine Winkworth that Florence told her

> The prostitutes come in perpetually − poor creatures staggering off their beat! It took worse hold of them than of any. One poor girl, loathsomely filthy, came in, and was dead in four hours. I held her in my arms and I heard her saying something. I bent down to hear. 'Pray God, that you may never be in the despair I am in at this time.' I said, 'Oh, my girl, are you not now more merciful than the God you think you are going to?' . . . Then, again, I never heard such capital mimicry as she gave of a poor woman, who was brought in one night, when F.N. and a porter were the only people up − every other nurse worn out for the time. . . F.N. undressed the woman, who was half tipsy but kept saying, 'You would not think it ma'am, but a week ago I was in silk and satins; in silk and satins dancing at Woolwich' . . . She got better.

This story is not supported by the Middlesex Hospital archives. Miss Nightingale is not mentioned in the medical superintendent's detailed record of the Hospital's work during the cholera outbreak in late August and the first three weeks of September. He named many devoted workers, from senior physicians to general servants; it is inconceivable that he would have overlooked an exotic lady volunteer. There is no evidence that any of the female patients were prostitutes and the notably proper behaviour of both male and female inmates [the men were mostly 'respectable artisans' from a neighbouring piano factory] suggests that it is unlikely that the females were prostitutes or indeed that they would have been admitted had they been known as such. Moreover, the first female case diagnosed as suffering from 'undoubted [Asian] cholera' was not admitted until 5 September.[7] Miss Nightingale's account of her good works at the Middlesex Hospital constitute a memorable example of her powers as titillating fabulist.

By early October 1854 she was back at Upper Harley Street, preparing to leave for the Crimea. After Miss Nightingale's departure the Institution became moribund, presumably burdened with the debts she had incurred. It seems to have revived somewhat in the 1860s and to have lingered on, beset by financial troubles, into the present century. There is no evidence that Miss Nightingale ever revisited Harley Street or took any further interest in it.

Biographers from Cook to Woodham-Smith, even Strachey and the editor of the quarterly reports I have quoted, are unanimous in representing Miss Nightingale's sojourn at Harley Street as her first great triumph. Yet the evidence they quote is mostly from people like Mrs Gaskell, who never saw the Institution and knew of it only from hearsay from Mr Nightingale, Parthe and Fanny, whose acquaintance with it was equally remote and whose information derived from Florence's own self-justifying letters. Each was gradually enfolded in Florence's great plans. 'Our vocation is a difficult one', she confided in January 1854 to her cousin, Marianne Galton, who had no vocation, 'as you, I am sure, know; and though there are many consolations, and very high ones, the disappointments are so numerous that we require all our faith and trust. But that is enough. I have never repented nor looked back.'[8] The sheer oddity of her enterprise beguiled her relations, as it beguiled the ladies and gentlemen of the committees, underpinned as it was by her insouciant explanations of her failures with staff, patients, tradesmen and accounts and her generalising of the blame; and biographers have been beguiled ever since. Her superbly assured epigrammatic Byronic prose by a process of stylistic legerdemain turns small gains with linen and jellies into mighty personal feats and big set-backs into everybody's moral shortcomings. By style and instinct she was a consummate politician.

The ladies and gentlemen of the committees were the more easily beguiled by Florence Nightingale because she was one of them. Her name represented enormous wealth, expressed in two large country estates and easy membership of the best circles – yet with a difference, quite apart from her superb intelligence. Miss Nightingale came of a politically radical Unitarian dynasty which had become in her parents' generation wealthier, probably, than many of the titled families whose members graced the committees. As her reports reveal, she stood a little apart, unresponsive to the claims of birth.

There is no need for the purposes of this revaluation to recount her childhood and early adulthood. What can be assumed and indeed rather more than can be proved has been delicately told by Cook and splendidly over-dramatised by Strachey and Woodham-Smith. Nearly all of the evidence about Florence Nightingale's conflicts with her mother and Parthe derives from Florence herself, as does her largely retrospective account of her religious travails as an adolescent and young woman. As I shall show later, Florence Nightingale's uncorroborated accounts of her troubles cannot be trusted. The only points that are clear are that William, her father, Fanny and Parthe realised very early that they had a very brilliant obstinate being to cope with and that at every crisis, whether in Florence's foreign travels, her impulsive ventures into local village nursing and other charitable works, her interest in Egyptology, music and natural history, or Monckton Milnes's proposal of marriage, they were supportive. Typically, it was Parthe who took over caring for the owl Florence brought back from Athens. Occasionally Fanny's and Parthe's sympathy wore thin, as when the latter diagnosed Florence as 'a poseur', but in general they appear to have been discerning about Florence's moody egotism and extraordinarily patient in coping with it.[9]

Her father, a clever, amiable dilettante, taught Florence and Parthe fluent Italian, French, Latin and Greek and mathematics. He also required his daughters to write essays on philosophical and historical themes. Both he and Fanny wrote easily and aphoristically and Florence probably acquired her style from them. Parthe's prose is more novelettish and wordy but it is still effective. Florence, unlike Parthe, was blessed with a prodigious memory for anecdotes and quotations from a huge range of reading, from Aristotle, Shakespeare and Milton to Spanish mystics such as St Teresa. It is a measure of the family's intellectual and fashionable standing, and their confidence in their conversational resources, that they knew not only the best of the English intelligentsia but also cultivated such foreign luminaries as

Sismondi, de Tocqueville, Thiers and Élie de Beaumont.

The family's sceptical intellectualism and wealth made them the less ready to give in to Florence's threats to express her capabilities in hospital work or superintending a religious sisterhood. Yet outside conducting a London salon or presiding over charities, controlling a sisterhood was the one avenue to power open to ambitious single women of the upper classes.

Florence's private estimates of her parents and sister did not reciprocate their tolerance. Her father she unsparingly yet accurately characterised as wanting in the strenuousness she found in herself. He was 'a man who has never known what struggle is . . . & having never by circumstances been forced to look into anything, to carry it out'. Had he succeeded in entering Parliament in 1835 he might have found a focus for his abilities but he lost the election because he refused to bribe the voters, and never tried again. On hearing of his death in 1874 Florence noted privately that he was a weak, inexpressive man: 'It was his utter indifference to me – he never cared what I was or what I might become.' A little later on a second slip of paper she added that 'he never had a[n]. . . office of his own'. But she kept up appearances. On about the same day she told at least one close friend, probably Benjamin Jowett, the master of Balliol College Oxford, that her one consolation was that 'my Father cared for my work'.[10] 'Parthe', she privately assured herself in 1851, 'was a child'. Child or not, Parthe was a formidable rival who, as Florence knew, often saw through her, but who nonetheless exemplified a feminity which Florence sought to dismiss as trivial. 'Parthe says I blow a trumpet – that it gives her indigestion – that is alas true – Struggle must make a noise – & every thing that I have to do that concerns my real being must be done with struggle.' Parthe's interests in music, art and dress, and her attempts to reform her sister's dowdiness, Florence rejected as petty and womanish.[11] Parthe had a sharp literary intelligence, too, as her subsequent five novels, essays on agricultural and landholding questions and invaluable *Memoirs of the Verney Family during the Civil War* [vols. I and II] were to prove. Rather than the nonentity depicted by Florence's biographers, she was a considerable competitor. Florence reserved her sharpest comment and keenest resentment for her mother. Fanny was intelligent and formidable. Florence noted that her mother had a 'genius for doing all she wants to do & has never felt the absence of power'. She had 'organized the best society' for her daughter, who did not want it. 'I felt insane at her disappointment.'[12] Her family's ready acknowledgement of Florence's talents made her revolt the harder to sustain. About 1851-2 she wrote, 'There is scarcely anyone who cannot, within his [sic] own experience, remember some instance where some amiable person has been slowly put to death at home — aye, and at an estimable & virtuous home.' Only when Fanny's health broke in the mid-1860s did Florence accept her: 'I don't think my dear mother was ever more touching or interesting to me than she is now in her state of dilapidation', Florence told Madame Mohl in 1866. By 1869 Fanny's memory was 'almost gone', but Florence confided to Dr Sutherland that she found her 'far more respect=able than ever she was before'. Even so, after her mother became completely senile and blind Florence visited her rarely and then only under protest at being, as she told herself in 1872 during her first visit for about six years, 'turned back into this petty, stagnant stifling life'. Florence kept to her room at Embley; her mother was wheeled in to her each day at 12.30 for a brief meeting. Two years later, at the time of her father's death even this meeting with the helpless old woman stopped, 'on account of my [Florence's] weakness'.[13]

Occasionally, as in the preceding note from 1851-2, Miss Nightingale referred to herself in the male gender. She apparently believed, reasonably enough, that her parents would have preferred her, their second and last child, to have been a male, in order to inherit the estate and continue the new family name, changed from Shore with a fresh accession of wealth in 1815. Her father liked to praise his daughter as the possessor of 'quite a man's mind', while Florence in one of her imaginary conversations with her mother in 1851-2 informed her that 'with my "talents" & my "European reputation" ' she was not 'going to stay dangling about my mother's drawing-room . . . I shall go out and look for work . . . You must look upon me as your son . . . You must consider me married or a son.'[14]

Her parents had encouraged her to marry Richard Monckton Milnes, the rising Liberal social reformer and literary man, during his nine-year-long courtship during the 1840s. But their hopes that Florence would thereby realise her talents for conversation and philanthropy in becoming a great London hostess foundered on her resolve not to marry and perforce subordinate her career. As she remarked in her anonymously published *Suggestions for Thought* (first drafted 1851-2) 'Marriage is the most selfish of all ties . . . as Milton put "He thy God, thou mine".' 'Can one man or woman', she added, 'be more interesting to us than mankind? I know that I could not bear his life — that to be nailed to a continuation & exaggeration of my present life without hope of another would be intolerable to me.' John Stuart Mill, whom she subsequently bullied into reading her manuscript, noted that her Milton quotation was incorrect: 'Milton says worse than this: he says He thy God, I his.'[15] Mill, theoretically a more thoroughgoing egalitarian feminist whose correction was even more egregiously inaccurate, prudently did not draw the implications of Miss Nightingale's slip. Her emotional attachments were directed to her own sex and from adolescence onwards she engaged occasionally in sentimentally effusive protestations of love for various female relatives and acquaintances. These sudden outbursts, during which Florence lost her usual steeliness and even her curt prose-style, were to continue into her old age.

Miss Nightingale's struggles to reconcile her egotism with her unfixed, non-Biblical, non-sacerdotal religiosity were equally explosive. When she reached her early twenties she had learned to exist with her dilemma by imagining herself a victim of special persecution and as destined endlessly to re-live Christ's crucifixion. Thereby she mortified her narcissism. Whilst travelling in Egypt in 1849 she experienced a severe crisis of suffocated ambition. She recorded in her diary that Christ appeared to her on five occasions, two of them on successive days. At each apparition she heard Him ask her the same general question: 'Would I do good for Him, for Him alone without the reputation?' (7 March 1849). A week later, at Thebes, 'as I sat in the large dull room waiting for the letters, God told me what a privilege he had reserved for me . . . & how I had been blind to it. If I were never thinking of the reputation how I should be better able to see what God intends for me.'[16]

Soon after this visitation Florence Nightingale accepted an instruction she heard from God to proceed, against the wishes of the family, to Kaiserswerth, to sample the communal nursing and reformative duties of the Lutheran evangelical deaconesses gathered there by Pastor Fliedner. Her visit may have satisfied her urge to defy the family but she found Kaiserswerth nursing grubby and ineffectual and the devotions of the community profoundly anti-intellectual; although she never ceased subsequently to praise Kaiserswerth and Fliedner in public. Indeed Kaiserswerth was a valuable experience for her: it provided a living lesson in what to avoid both in the shape of high-minded, affected spirituality and in stupid nursing routines which ignored common cleanliness, rational comfort, and punctuality.[17] Miss Nightingale determined that nurses should serve their Creator by helping patients physically and morally and not by worshipping while their charges died in their own filth. Still, the dedication and obedience of the deaconesses impressed her. They were 'consecrated' by the pastor after probation, but did not take religious vows. Florence Nightingale approved this compromise. She distrusted Catholic and High-Church sisterhood vows because they enjoined obedience to a supernatural regime which deflected commands issued by rational mundane authority and provided an excuse for non-compliance. Nurses should nurse to meet God's purposes and to advance their personal quest for selflessness, but under human direction – as it turned out – Nightingale direction. Moreover, vows entailed a self-abased striving for the humblest office, whereas, Miss Nightingale wrote in 1851-2, 'we should strive for that we can best do and what is most attractive & thereby find our duty'.[18] She formed this view of nursing, like her other beliefs, early in her career when she knew little of their results in practice, but she never wavered from her formulas. Her approach was *a priori* all her life.

There is another element, rather less obvious, which must be added: the narcissistic quality of her personality. Throughout her career there is abundant evidence to attest to this strand in her behaviour. Florence Nightingale's diaries and hundreds of letters and private memoranda show her to have been an untiring watcher of herself. She observed every play of her intelligence and weighed it, fluctuating between self-admiration and self-contempt. Her self-regard was never stable. In public she was gracious and ingratiating, immensely productive and politically effective. In private she indulged in bouts of self-depreciation, scorn of others, and guilt for her passion for fame and her destructive use of her allies. Within the family her father, her mother and Parthe were too easy and yielding, and emotionally inaccessible, to supply the tensions and gratifications that Florence craved. Her mother's retrospective accounts of Florence's essays on keeping pets, sick nursing in the village and management of her dolls all indicate, however falsified and toned down they were in memory, that from childhood Florence was alternately unpredictably wilful and petulant, and a docile seeker of adult approval. Her mother's remarks also indicate that neither she nor her husband was very interested in Florence's enthusiasms. As Florence reminded herself in the *Suggestions* of 1851-2,

'God makes the family' . . . Perhaps it is just the contrary. God makes attractions – & the principle of the family is <u>not</u> to go by attractions . . . In an amiable family, the common cause of things is for everyone to give up just enough to prevent such a 'row' as would make it intolerable.

— Good for us to practise self-denial & forebearance — But if God
wants us to do what we like — we overturn the family. Man is born
into the world — woman into a family. Woman must be born into
world to find joy — to exercise their powers. People are 'robbed &
murdered' by their families & no one notices — their <u>time</u> to do
original <u>thought</u> is murdered.[19]

Outside the family Miss Nightingale used auxiliaries to obey her orders
and reinforce her self-esteem; she dropped them when they rebelled
or lost their ability to service that esteem. She yearned for intimacy,
to fuse herself with idealised others, yet she retained a profound sense
of her psychological distance from other human beings, a contradiction,
as I shall outline later, that permeated her dealings with such confidants
as Sidney Herbert and Mary Jones, the superintendent of a High Church
nursing sisterhood. Florence Nightingale's sexual relationships remained
infantile. She never permitted herself to become unguardedly close or
unreservedly dependent upon anyone. Throughout her career she made
public emotional investments in others, in shared great plans and
objects, and when the others' commitment wavered or their
contribution disappointed her, as invariably they did, she ostentatiously
withdrew the outlay and reinvested it in herself. In all her ventures
she played by turns the role of trusting acolyte and the only begetter
who was always let down. Ultimately she had made a mystic marriage
with God's work: 'real mothers & fathers of the human race', she told
her soul mate Jowett about 1865, 'are <u>not</u> the males and females,
according to the flesh'.[20] They were instead spiritual heroines and
heroes consecrated to spirituality. In this scheme of things there was
little place for earthly competitors, as the Crimean adventure was to
show.

Notes

1. Sir Harry Verney (ed.) *Florence Nightingale At Harley Street,* (London, 1970), p.viii.
2. F.N. to Madame Mohl, 8 April 1853, Sir Edward Cook, *The Life Of Florence Nightingale* (2 vols., London, 1913), vol. I, p.130.
3. F.N. to Lady Canning, 29 April [1853], BL Add.Mss 45796 ff.17-28.
4. F.N. to William Edward Nightingale (her father), 3 December 1853, BL Add.Mss 45790, ff.152-6.
5. Verney, *Harley Street,* p.28.
6. Quoted in Margaret Leland Goldsmith, *Florence Nightingale. The Woman and the Legend,* (London, 1937), p.97.
7. Mrs Gaskell to Emily Shaen, 27 October 1854, in J.A.V. Chapple and Arthur Pollard (eds.), *The Letters of Mrs Gaskell* (Manchester, 1966), p.318;

'Report on the recent outbreak of Cholera near the Hospital; and the means adopted to meet the influx of patients, 23 September 1854', Admission Books for 1854, Middlesex Hospital Archives. I am indebted to Mr W.R. Winterton, FRCS, FRCOG, for help with these sources.

8. Cook, *Nightingale*, vol. I, pp.137-8.

9. Goldsmith, *Nightingale*, p.112.

10. F.N. memoranda, BL Add.Mss 43402 f.79 [1851?]; 'My Father', BL Add.Mss 45845 ff.136, 139 [January 1874?]; F.N. to [Benjamin Jowett?] draft with first page missing [January 1874?], Nightingale Collection, Greater London Record Office, SU 214.

11. F.N. memoranda, Whit Monday, 8 June 1851, 15 June [1851?], BL Add.Mss 43404 ff.72-6.

12. F.N. Memorandum [1851?] BL Add.Mss 43402, f.80.

13. F.N. Draft for 'Stuff' (later partly incorporated into 'Suggestions for thought') [1851-2?], BL Add.Mss 45843 f.18; Goldsmith, *Nightingale*, p.259; F.N. to Sutherland [1869?], BL Add.Mss 45754 f.61; Memorandum, Embley, 7 August 1872, BL Add.Mss 45844 f.18; F.N. to Lizzie Herbert (copy), 8 January 1874, BL Add.Mss 43396 f.220.

14. 7 December 1851 quoted in Goldsmith, *Nightingale*, p.99.

15. F.N. draft for 'Suggestions, vol. II', BL Add.Mss 45840 f.126.

16. F.N. Diary 7, 16 March 1850, BL Add.Mss 45846 ff.23-5.

17. F.N. to Sutherland [December 1864?] BL Add.Mss 45751 ff.250-1.

18. F.N. 'Suggestions', draft [1851-52?] BL Add.Mss 45838 ff.220.

19. F.N. 'Suggestions', draft [1851-2?] BL Add.Mss 45838 f.171.

20. F.N. to Jowett, draft [1865?] BL Add.Mss 45783 f.68.

2 MISS NIGHTINGALE AT SCUTARI

Miss Nightingale's expedition to the Crimean War had no British precedent. She was free to make her own rules. When she decided to go, her first steps were to oust competitors and secure sole authority.

The idea that women should help nurse the British wounded, as the Sisters of Charity helped nurse the French, was first propounded by W.H. Russell, *The Times* special correspondent at the front. It had not occurred to anyone at home. Russell's despatches from Constantinople at the end of September 1854, after the casualties from the Battle of the Alma had arrived, were published in London on 9 October. He passionately described the collapse of the army nursing system and the agonies of the common soldiers. Such collapses and neglect had accompanied the army through centuries, but for the first time the mismanagement and suffering were recounted at middle- and upper-class breakfast tables. Russell's reports aroused two early volunteer leaders of nurses: the Rev. Mr Hume, a former chaplain at the Birmingham General Hospital with seven years' experience of the army, undertook to bring his two daughters and twelve paid nurses; Lady Maria Forester, a philanthropic widow of Evangelical persusasion, offered herself to lead nurses from the Low Church Fitzroy Square training institution. Miss Nightingale apparently decided to head an expedition on 11 October, after she learned of Lady Maria's move.[1]

Unlike Hume and Lady Maria, who applied only to the War Office and to Dr Andrew Smith, the head of the Army Medical Department, Miss Nightingale sought personal backing at the highest level. The Home Secretary, Lord Palmerston, a neighbour in Hampshire, agreed to ask the Foreign Secretary, Lord Clarendon, to write on her behalf to the ambassador at Constantinople, Lord Stratford de Redcliffe. She also saw Dr Smith and secured an introduction to the Chief Medical Officer at Scutari establishing her right to nurse in his hospitals. By 14 October she had, according to Parthe, persuaded Lady Maria Forester that she would 'not have been of the slightest use' at the Crimea, and Miss Nightingale had accepted the £200 Lady Maria had raised for her venture.[2] All these transactions were concluded before Miss Nightingale received any official invitation to lead a party at Scutari. Only on 14 October did she charge Mrs Herbert with obtaining her severance from the Harley Street Institution, of which she was still nominally head, and with securing specific authorisation for the expedition from Sidney Herbert and the War Secretary, the Duke of Newcastle. In an artful postscript she put the onus on to Lizzie Herbert and tightened the web of personal allegiances: 'Perhaps it is better to keep it quite a private thing, and not apply to Govt qua Govt.' On the morning of that same Saturday 14th, before she announced her intentions to the Herberts, Miss Nightingale sent her uncle Sam Smith to her parents to obtain their consent.[3]

Then follows one of the dramatic set-pieces of Victorian history. Miss Nightingale's biographers, even sceptical Strachey, agree that her announcement of her readiness to go to the Crimea and Sidney Herbert's invitation, written on Sunday 15 October, crossed in the mail. Thereby a charming coincidence is revealed and two great minds and hearts are shown as one. The story was popularised by Lord Stanmore's *Sidney Herbert* (compiled from about 1890 and published in 1906), using letters selected by Miss Nightingale. The episode is worth scrutiny because it exhibits Miss Nightingale's *modus operandi* and the hagiographical temptations of even the best biographers. The first oddity is that Miss Nightingale's letter was not addressed to Sidney Herbert, but to his wife. Moreover, Miss Nightingale asked specifically about applying for official sanction for her venture to the Duke of Newcastle, the Secretary for War, within whose province the issue lay. Sidney Herbert had no proper standing in the matter and no authority to invite anyone to help nurse the army. His remark about the Bracebridges – old friends of the Herberts and Nightingales with whom they had travelled in Rome in 1847 and whom Florence had accompanied to Egypt – that he was certain they would go with her; his assurance that Lizzie was writing to Mrs Bracebridge about the mission and the need to have the consent of the Nightingale family, together with the shelving of Lady Maria Forester and the other early volunteer, Mr Hume – 'the difficulty of finding nurses who are at all versed in their business is probably not known to Mr Hume' – despite his seven years experience – imply an appreciation of the situation that came from coaching by Mrs Herbert, coached in turn by Miss Nightingale. The unusual briskness of Herbert's letter and its remarkable confidence that Miss Nightingale would accept such an extraordinary commission from the War Office and place herself instantly at its disposal allow us to infer that Herbert's letter was the formal product of a prior understanding. This inference is strengthened by Parthe's private account of the affair, written on Monday 16 October, to Richard Monckton Milnes, whom she had no reason to deceive. Parthe explained that all was resolved on Friday 13 October, that is, before Miss Nightingale wrote to Mrs Herbert. On that day the Bracebridges, indomitable travellers both, decided to go and the Nightingale family then immediately adopted the venture.

The underlying purpose of Miss Nightingale's formal approach to the Herberts also emerges in Parthe's letter to Monckton Milnes:

> There has been but one feeling tho' in all the Institutions, they have given up their rules, the 10 Sisters of Mercy wished to take a head, Miss Sellon wished to go herself with her 8, St John's Home wanted to send a chief with their 6, but all gave way & Florence is sole leader.[4]

Sole leadership was a *sine qua non* with Miss Nightingale. The War Office and Sidney Herbert found it easiest to allow this imperious, unstoppable woman to lead. Within the pertinent areas of hospital experience and proven ability to select and manage nurses her claims were insubstantial. She did not emphasise them in her letters to Mrs Herbert; instead, she begged Mrs Herbert 'or some one of my Committee [to] write to Lady Stratford [the Constantinople ambassador's wife] to say, "This is not a lady but a real Hospital Nurse", . . . "And she has experience"'.[5] Quite apart from Rev. Mr. Hume, the superioress of the Sisters of Mercy had much more nursing experience and knowledge of handling women, while Miss Sellon was a proven charismatic, creative, dominating person with six years' experience of directing nurses. The chaplain of St John's House was also used to commanding women whose vocation was nursing. But their Catholic, Puseyite and High Church affiliations, amidst the febrile bigotry of the early 1850s, put them all beyond consideration. Miss Nightingale had the advantage in the government's view of being safely Protestant but otherwise religiously neuter.

Miss Sellon, who had offered herself and eight of her followers, without telling them, acquiesced with uncharacteristic meekness when Miss Nightingale took over her followers but rejected her. Miss Sellon enforced austerities on her communities which she never observed herself.[6] The Crimea promised a hard life. The St John's House chaplain, Rev. C.P. Shepherd, proved more obdurate. He had applied on 13 October to his bishop, Blomfield, for permission to head a party of seven nurses. A letter in *The Times* of that day, opening a Crimea fund with £200, 'removed', as one of Shepherd's female coadjutors observed, 'all hesitation on the score of Funds'. Miss Nightingale had to use Sidney Herbert to direct the Bishop of London to squash him.

On 17 October Herbert informed the Bishop that:

> Miss Nightingale has consented to go out to Scutari to undertake the
> whole management of the female nursing – Her great hospital
> experience & skill & courage in surgical treatment together with her
> administrative capacity peculiarly fit her for the undertaking and in
> a military hospital where subordination is everything, without some
> recognized head with ample authority, there [?] will be no chance
> of success. She is in communication with the nurses of St John's
> House & I have no doubt will take them with her.

Blomfield, who had already on 14 October told Shepherd that he 'quite
approve[d]' of his proposal and had commended it to Herbert, now
apparently accepted Shepherd's exclusion, for we hear no more of him.[7]
The Evangelical Protestant communities at Fitzroy Square and
Devonshire Square, suspicious of the Puseyite-Papist ambience of the
Nightingale contingent and, probably, piqued by the rejection of Lady
Maria Forester, refused to surrender control of their nurses to Miss
Nightingale who thereupon refused to have them. None went to the
Crimea.

This rebuff was the more damaging to Miss Nightingale because she
had been forestalled in the race to Scutari by a group of Catholic nuns.
Bishop Thomas Grant of Southwark had seized the opportunity to
counter anti-Roman feeling by making his nuns into conspicuous
patriots. He unhesitatingly made his nuns subject to Miss Nightingale's
general superintendence and got ten of his contingent, Sisters of Mercy
from Bermondsey, to France within 24 hours of informing them that
they were going. Thereby they took a four day lead on the official
party, but Miss Nightingale ensured that Grant ordered them to wait
in Paris until she caught up.[8] Their rushed travel arrangements were so
incomplete that they would hardly have been able to proceed without
her anyway. The Bermondsey sisters were experienced nurses. Grant
had rashly promised ten nuns: Bermondsey refused to supply more
than five. He finally unearthed five others at the Convent of the
Daughters of the Faithful Virgin at Norwood, where they conducted
an orphanage. They were members of a high caste French order, with
no tradition of nursing. Bishop Grant signed on their behalf Miss
Nightingale's tightly worded agreement subjecting them to her
authority. Miss Nightingale had composed the agreement and had it
lithographed within four days of deciding on the expedition. Like the
Anglicans, the Catholic nuns went without a chaplain.[9]

Bishop Grant had also sought nuns from Ireland but was brusquely rejected by the Irish bishops. Now the despatch of the Bermondsey sisters, chaplainless and subject to a Protestant superintendent, provoked a reaction. Father Henry Edward Manning, Miss Nightingale's and the Herberts' erstwhile religious mentor in Rome in 1847, now a Catholic and as always an astute, compulsive politician, moved to ensure that the Catholics contingent retained its identity. The expedient way of doing this was to gather a party of Irish nuns reinforced by their own chaplains. Manning wanted to drive the point home: he envisaged at least 20 Catholic nurses, all religious – 'we shall not do well to take any seculars'.[10] Sister Evelyn Bolster gives the details of his negotiations to obtain an offer of Irish nuns and there is no need to recount their devious course here. The salient moves in the challenge were, first, the offer to the War Office on 18 October by the Vicar-General of Dublin, Dr Youl, of twenty Irish Sisters of Mercy, to be accompanied by a chaplain, all to be paid for by the government. The first move nearly misfired because the Irish bishops still proved obstructive (many of them were in Rome for the promulgation of the doctrine of the Immaculate Conception and found it easy to hinder the Manning initiative by dilatory letter-writing). In the event only eleven Sisters of Mercy came from convents in Ireland and the final total of fifteen was made up with nuns from Liverpool and Chelsea. Meanwhile, despite Manning's desperate pressure, Herbert and the War Office had still not agreed to the chaplain.[11]

The second part of the challenge was the selection of Rev. Mother Mary Francis Bridgeman to head the Irish contingent. She was less senior than Rev. Mother Mary Clare of the Bermondsey sisters and she had less experience in dealing with the sick and with English authorities, but Rev. Mother Clare was mild and Rev. Mother Francis was the opposite. Indeed she was the analogue in beefier form of Florence Nightingale. Mother Francis was born in 1813 into an ancient Irish gentry family, with a rakehelly father. Her mother died when she was five and she was brought up by a maiden aunt who devoted herself to rescuing prostitutes and visiting the sick in Limerick. They nursed together during the cholera epidemic of 1832. Miss Bridgeman joined the new and rapidly growing Sisters of Mercy in 1838, and soon emerged as a forceful organiser and administrator, used to being heard and obeyed. Father Manning found her 'ardent, high-tempered and . . . somewhat difficult . . . but truly good'.[12]

Rev. Mother Francis collected her nuns together in Dublin while Manning worked to win the chaplaincy issue. Led by Mother Francis, the nuns acceded to a written code. This code assumed the presence of a chaplain; it subtly transgressed the War Office ruling against proselytism; it ignored the existence of the other nurses in the Nightingale contingent, even the London nuns; it set aside Miss Nightingale's authority by not mentioning her and instead interposed Rev. Mother Francis as sole head of the nurses and intermediary with the hospital authorities. The relevant clauses run:

> They shall not discuss religious topics with those outside the Catholic Church. If a desire for knowledge of Catholic doctrine is evinced, they shall inform the chaplain ... Any notable difficulties which the Sisters may experience in the discharge of their hospital duties, are to be mentioned to the Superior, who if she deems it expedient, shall refer the matter to the administrator of the hospital.[13]

By 30 October Manning had still not prevailed with the War Office. Afraid that the Irish nuns would disband and return to their convents, he wrote to John Henry Newman to tell them that the War Office had agreed to the nuns having a chaplain attached at the hospital, chosen from among the six or seven Catholic chaplains already with the army, and that the party would be permitted to form a separate community under their own superior in distinct quarters. Manning presented this as a major concession from the War Office but it was only what had already been promised to the Bermondsey and Norwood nuns. It is even uncertain whether it was a specific concession: I have been unable to find it in the War Office papers. (I did not obtain access to the Manning Papers.) Concession or not, Manning was resolved that the Irish party should go: 'I do not know', he warned Newman, 'what would do us more harm or injustice than to be backward at this moment.' Newman did nothing: he kept clear of the intrigue.[14]

Rev. Mother Francis finally sought to force matters by journeying to London and confronting Manning and Herbert on 3 November. Herbert gave ground. He agreed that the Bridgeman party might be accompanied by a chaplain of their choice, but the priest was to be unofficial and not their 'chaplain'. He also acknowledged Rev. Mother Francis's standing as superior of her group, although there is no evidence that Herbert saw this arrangement as more than the equivalent recognition accorded the heads of the Bermondsey and Norwood contingents with respect to their duties as religious. This point gained, Rev. Mother Francis spent the next fortnight visiting London convents and hospitals in a new move to increase her contingent by 20. Effectively, she was enlarging the outsiders' challenge into an insiders' take-over bid.

This transformation was furthered by Rev. Mother Francis's new-found disciple, Mary Stanley. They were introduced to one another by Manning, who had been Miss Stanley's spiritual director since at least 1847, when she had been yet another of the Nightingale party of pilgrims in Rome. She was the daughter of the Anglican Bishop of Norwich and sister to A.P. Stanley, the future Dean of Westminster, with whom she appears to have had an unusually close relationship. Mary Stanley was a gawky, short-sighted woman, plodding through life aspiring to parish visiting and other good works, successively attaching herself to more powerful personalities. In 1852 she had exhibited a short devotion to Florence Nightingale. Now, after her attachment to Manning, she immediately came under the thumb of Rev. Mother Francis. Miss Stanley was to announce her conversion to Catholicism at the Crimea. In the three weeks to 1 December Mary Stanley's High Anglican contacts and Rev. Mother Francis's drive through the London convents (she finally had to go as far as Liverpool) yielded 15 Catholic nuns, 22 nurses and nine 'ladies', a contingent more than double the size of Manning's original offer.

Sidney Herbert and the War Office took fright and ordered absolutely that no priest should travel with the nuns. With what must have been deliberate provocation, midst the anti-Catholic furor of the early 1850s, Rev. Mother Francis had already equipped herself with a Jesuit, made available by the Vicar General of Westminster.[15] It seems that the Irish hierarchy refused to release any secular Irish priests. The Jesuit, Father William Ronan, justified his selection: he emerged in the Crimea as an unrelenting bigot who fostered Rev. Mother Bridgeman's worst tendencies.

The news of Father Ronan's appointment and Herbert's new-found resistance put Manning in a fresh dilemma. Using Mary Stanley as go-between, he tried to placate Herbert and compel Rev. Mother Bridgeman to shed Father Ronan:

> I have from first to last understood that the chaplain is not to travel with the Sisters. I have said so and written ten times. If power of mine can hinder it, it shall not be. Say this to Sidney Herbert in my name, and tell him I have borne many censures on this point, and will do so to the end for his sake.[16]

Father Ronan promised Manning not to travel with the nuns.

Rev. Mother Bridgeman completed her challenge by refusing on her own behalf and forbidding her sisters to sign the agreement, endorsed by the British cabinet, acknowledging Miss Nightingale's headship of the mission. She took her stand on the document agreed among the Irish nuns establishing her own headship of her nuns which was a private agreement among the volunteered nuns; it had no standing with the War Office or the Nightingale contingent. Sidney Herbert gave way and Rev. Mother Bridgeman signed a copy of the sisters' agreement for his benefit. The final irony of Manning's offer and the Irish challenge was the admission that the sisters could not afford the outfitting and incidental expenses of the journey to Scutari. Manning scraped £200 together:[17] at over £14 a head they cost the equivalent of a common nurse's wages for five months.

Miss Nightingale, after the rebuff from the Evangelical institutions and the contretemps with Rev. Mr Shepherd, had made the confirmation of her authority a cabinet matter. On 19 October she secured from Sidney Herbert official notification of her headship. The nature of the authority conveyed in the letter bespeaks Miss Nightingale's instigation, but the loose drafting suggests that Herbert composed it:

> Having consented at the pressing instance of the Government to accept the office of Superintendent of the Female Nursing establishment in the English General Military Hospitals in Turkey, you will, on your arrival there, place yourself at once in communication with the Chief Medical Officer of the Hospital at Scutari, under whose orders and direction you will carry on the duties of your appointment.
>
> Everything relating to the distribution of the nurses ... their allotment to particular duties, is placed in your hands, subject, of course, to the sanction and approval of the Chief Medical Officer ...
>
> I feel confident that ... you will impress upon those acting under your orders the necessity of the strictest attention to the regulations of the Hospital, and the preservation of that subordination which is indispensable in every Military Establishment.
>
> And I rely on your ... vigilance carefully to guard against any attempt being made among those under your authority, selected as they are with a view to fitness and without any reference to religious creed, to make use of their position in the Hospitals to tamper with ... the religious opinions of the patients ... and at once to check any such tendency and to take, if necessary, severe measures to prevent its repetition.[18]

The reference to Turkey, rather than to the seat of war in the Crimea, shows that the Nightingale mission was conceived, sensibly, as a minor ancillary aid in the general base hospitals away from the front. Herbert and possibly Miss Nightingale at this stage did not envisage the whole war area as a field to be subjected to her ministrations. Miss Nightingale, as head of her nurses, was made responsible to the Chief Medical Officer at Scutari, Dr Duncan Menzies; implicitly, this made her subject to the Chief Medical Officer at the Crimea, Dr John Hall, but apparently Herbert and Nightingale saw no need to define this relationship. It might be thought that omission of the Crimea reveals a careful limitation on Miss Nightingale's ambitions: but that entails a prevision on Herbert's part which he does not otherwise display. In the result both omissions were to cause trouble.

While preparing the mission Miss Nightingale concentrated upon establishing her authority with government and heads of religious houses. She left the recruitment of nurses to loyal busybodies like Mrs Herbert, Lady Canning and Mrs Bracebridge. Nurses proved as scarce as nuns: there was no rush to the colours. Their wages had to be raised to about double the going rate: 12 shillings to 14 shillings a week plus keep and uniform, rising to 18 shillings to 20 shillings a week after a year's good conduct. Selina Bracebridge, Florence Nightingale's dearest 'E' during the Egyptian tour, was especially haughty to the candidates she inspected. During the preparation week she travelled to Oxford to look over the potential recruits assembled by Miss Felicia Skene, another High Anglican lady active in the prison visiting and prostitute rescue business. Miss Skene, who seems to have resented her supercession by Mrs Bracebridge as recruiting agent, recalled the lady as acting like the Duchess (recte − Queen of Hearts?) in *Alice in Wonderland*. She lined the postulants along a wall and fired 'sudden questions' at them. If the questions were not answered immediately and to her satisfaction she barked, 'She won't do; send her out.'[19] No 'ladies' were accepted for the mission, apparently by Miss Nightingale's decision. The exertions of Lady Canning, Mrs Herbert and Mrs Bracebridge, after the impossibly old and blatantly dissolute had been excluded, yielded 38 nurses, only 14 of whom were 'seculars'; the rest comprised six St Johnites and eight Sellonites and the ten Catholic nuns.[20]

Mr Bracebridge, a veteran of the Greek War of Independence, also secured his role in the drama. He assumed the management of the accounts for the trip and attempted to take charge of protecting the nuns' and nurses' virtue. Once in Turkey he also set up as a propagandist for the mission, with bad results for the standing of the party. Irrepressible, on his return from the war he adopted the cause of Shakespeare's innocence of deer-stealing, and of protecting the Bard's house at Stratford. He also promoted reformatories, and garotting as tidier than hanging, especially for female and other subjects deficient in weight.[21]

Miss Nightingale and her party had a wretched journey. Their ship, the *Vectis*, was ill-found and they ran into heavy storms, which continued almost throughout the eight days of the voyage. Like most of the group, Miss Nightingale suffered badly from prolonged sea-sickness. Her cabin and the Bracebridges' room were separate from the rest who were huddled in the airless fo'castle, awash with vomit. Even so, she arrived exhausted. The terrible journey weakened her, as it weakened others in the party, even before they reached their work. The delicate Norwood nuns proved feeble at Scutari and Miss Nightingale sent them home within the month. Sister Ethelreda, one of the Sellonites, also never recovered from the journey and could not eat the coarse Scutari food. She went home shortly after the Norwood sisters, together with four of the nurses from St John's Home who rejected the discipline and privations of Scutari life.[22]

The poor, skimpy food and the sordid living conditions were army routine. The new element, unique in the history of war, was that some of the human beings involved could choose to leave the shambles and report them, unpunished. Miss Nightingale quickly diagnosed the weaknesses in the army hospital system and their consequent limitations upon her ambitions. From hindsight the weaknesses are glaring, but no military man or minister for war had done anything about them; melioration meant money. The fundamental difficulty was the subordination of the medical officers to their military colleagues. Medical officers were inhibited from taking decisions and implementing plans to ensure optimal sanitary safety and hospital comfort for their charges. Decisions about the siting and management of camps, the ordering of the soldiers' food and dress and the organisation of regimental and base hospitals were the side results of military officers' choices of ground and disposition for tactical and display purposes. The men drafted as orderlies in the hospitals were ne'er-do-wells or the walking sick: the military officers retained the ablest men for the fighting and as camp servants; there was no separate trained orderly corps. Soldiers' wives sho had traditionally done some nursing and washing around the hospitals had been eased out in 1832. There had been a move to revive female nursing when the army left for the East, but it had been rejected because, as the Duke of Newcastle explained, 'it was not liked by the military authorities'.[23] Within the hospitals authority over medicines, food and furniture for the sick was divided between the medical officers who ordered the items and the purveyors who were supposed to supply them, and the ill-supervised orderlies who were supposed to administer them to the patients. The outside transport of wounded and supplies was yet another distinct authority; the men in the corps were notorious, even in the army, for their slovenliness. At best, in times of peace and in benign weather, the routine was inefficient and callous. The death rate from disease and gangrenous wounds was heavy and steady. Disasters — typhus and dysentery outbreaks, severe battles, lost supply ships — all of which occurred immediately before and after the Nightingale party assumed their posts in the two Scutari hospitals, overwhelmed the system and men died in their hundreds. Two thousand wounded and sick men were unloaded into the Scutari hospitals in the month after the battles of Balaclava (25 October) and Inkerman (5 November). During that same month about 330 men died in the hospitals from scurvy, dysentry, typhoid and other diseases. During the worst of the winter the death rate was to climb to about 46 per cent of all admissions.[24]

Under the direction of the surgeons, Miss Nightingale's sisters and nurses were set to prepare the prescribed diets and extras such as beef tea and wine for the patients, dress their wounds, make up palliasses — these were almost non-existent when the Nightingale party arrived — cajole the orderlies into caring for their patients, and write letters for the illiterate, the dying and the dead. They also distributed fresh clothes and bedding from Miss Nightingale's stock, supplied by *The Times* and other patriotic relief funds.

Miss Nightingale believed that only the 'really sick', those unable to help themselves, and the dying required nursing. Nursing comprised watching, giving medication under doctors' orders, feeding under doctors' orders, and washing patients and bed linen. Her belief prevented her from using the nurses of both contingents to the best advantage. The 43 nurses who were to help nurse a projected 500 patients at Koulali in May 1855 she regarded as dangerously numerous. 'The greater the number the harder they are to manage.' Ultimately they endangered the army too; unsupervised nurses 'over indulged' soldiers who were unused to cosseting and thereby had their discipline 'spoilt'.[25] As at Harley Street, Miss Nightingale failed to win the allegiance of subordinates or to allocate tasks efficiently. The nuns and nurses engaged in the kitchens and the administration of the extra comforts were overworked, while the nurses detailed to wash, feed and solace patients were underemployed, especially as they were forbidden to speak with their charges and prevented from attending convalescents who, the Lady Superintendent believed — perhaps rightly — should help themselves. Moreover, such attendance led to intimacies which were 'obviously objectionable'.[26] The male orderlies, dressers and soldiers continued to do the bulk of the work in the hospitals. The nuns' and ladies' delicacy, reinforced by the men's modesty, generally inhibited them from dealing with the men's evacuations and with wounds to their abdominal regions. Emma Fagg, an experienced St John's nurse, complained from 'Scrutaria' Barracks Hospital in early January 1855 that she and her colleagues found it a 'great *disappointment* . . . we are not fatigued with our duties'.[27]

The slackness of the orderlies, apothecaries and purveyors, the filth and muddle, the general unfitness of affairs, affronted Miss Nightingale. Her resource was her independent store of medicines, food and clothing and her headship of her nurses. Her lever on the doctors and the military authorities was her link with Sidney Herbert reinforced by her role as the lady of mercy. She placed her housekeeper, Mrs Clarke, in charge of her kitchen stores, the superioress of the Bermondsey nuns, Mother Mary Clare Moore, was appointed to direct the kitchen cooking at the Barracks Hospital and other Bermondsey nuns were set over the stores. They drudged devotedly throughout the war. Miss Nightingale's response to her powerlessness to influence lazily inflexible purveyors like Mr Ward and tough old army doctors like Dr Menzies was to inveigle Sidney Herbert into acting on her behalf. She essayed this in a flow of nagging, half resentful, half conspiratorial letters that ran throughout her time in the East. The first that survives dates from 25 November 1854, within three weeks of her arrival. The purveyors held up soap and bathing utensils because, Miss Nightingale explained, they considered the washing of the men and the linen 'a minor detail . . . though our remonstrances have been treated with perfect civility, yet no washing whatever has been performed . . . except by ourselves & a few wives of the Wounded . . . we are organizing a Washing Establishment of our own'. This she did, and she ended by developing the specifications of washing and drying machines specially devised for the Crimea, paid for from *The Times* fund.

> Your name, [she told Herbert], is also continually used as a bug-bear — they make a deity of cheapness here . . . The cheese-paring system, which sounds unmusical in British ears, is here identified by the officers who carry it out with you.

The requirements are, unity of action [that is, ending the division between doctors' requisitions and purveyors' supplying them] & personal responsibility . . .

All the above is written in obedience to your private instructions. Do not let me appear as a Govt. spy here.'[28]

This was consummate web-spinning. Florence Nightingale gradually entangled Herbert in her concerns. He was to act, as inferentially instructed in this letter, to realise Miss Nightingale's designs but never to betray his leading strings. Herbert seems to have tamely accepted his subjection. Beginning with his mother, a strong-willed Russian aristocrat, then Caroline Norton, the much-wronged blue stocking, and then the devout Lizzie O'Brien, Sidney Herbert was habituated to acquiescing in the plans of handsome, determined women.

This letter also signals a new development in Miss Nightingale's statecraft. A woman in a man's world, she was adopting a secretarial mode of gaining her ends. Secretive, purposeful, she was to satisfy herself with manipulating persons having executive powers whilst she remained unseen and unsung, savouring the private knowledge of the process. Occasionally, as the boasting episode at Harley Street revealed, she could not resist the craving for reputation and published her secrets, but for the remainder of her life she was to relish supplying ideas, data, schemes for others to propagate and carry forward. Long before H.G. Wells's piercing evocation of the Webbs, she personified the new Machiavelli.

As part of the programme of capturing Sidney Herbert, Miss Nightingale essayed to neutralise the influence of the local British ambassador and his wife, Sir Stratford and Lady de Redcliffe. He was a pompous, lazy aristocrat who patronised Miss Nightingale; his lady was a gushing, High Anglican snob who had begun to interfere with Miss Nightingale's relief stores. Lady Stratford was doubly dangerous because she was an intimate of Lizzie Herbert's. The ambassador's wife was an incompetent 'impediment', Florence Nightingale warned Herbert; ten days after this, on 5 December, she protested to Herbert that Lady Stratford had wrecked her plans for rebuilding unusable parts of the Barrack Hospital. Indeed, Lady Stratford had had the impertinence to place herself 'as my correspondent . . . [but] I don't want her'. Yet Miss Nightingale had used Lady Stratford to persuade her husband, whose authorisation was necessary, to allow the expenditure for the work. Initially 125 Turkish workmen were engaged. They struck for higher pay. Miss Nightingale had them dismissed and recruited 200 Greeks. Lord Stratford disclaimed responsibility. Miss Nightingale claimed that she had paid for the rebuilding out of her own pocket, assisted by *The Times* fund, although her report is very unclear. In fact, although the War Office never published it, the government paid all the bills. Miss Nightingale had only guaranteed 70 sovereigns from *The Times* fund. None of her own money was guaranteed or spent. The 70 sovereigns were never needed and presumably remained in the fund. Long after the War Miss Nightingale continued to let it be known that she had paid for the hospital and had never been reimbursed by a pinch-penny government.[29] It is equally unclear that Lady Stratford was to blame: she had helped when asked and seems not to have meddled too deeply. If anything she too easily allowed her mean-spirited husband to wash his hands of the job. But then neither she nor her husband could before have encountered a young woman who expected deference and who independently possessed funds for public purposes.

In the midst of coping with 715 sick and wounded in the Barrack Hospital and 650 wounded in the General Hospital, her building operations and her clash with Lady Stratford, Miss Nightingale was faced with a mutiny among the St John's nurses. Several of them were Irish and some others were about to go over to Rome. One who did convert was Mrs Lawfield who protested in mid November against having to wear her thick ungainly nurse's cap. Miss Nightingale quashed Mrs Lawfield, temporarily at least, and she became, Miss Nightingale reported, 'quite a different person, and she is now, though not skilful (she does not know a fractured limb when she sees it) one of the most valuable nurses I have from her great propriety of conduct & kindness'.[30] On 4 December a St John's nurse – she forgot to sign her indignant note – informed a superior in London, probably Miss Jones, that at 'Scutariar Baricks . . . We are treated With the greates disrepect and unkindness by Miss nightingale and her housekeeper [Mrs Clarke from Harley Street] she all but starves us an it is very hurtfull to our feelings . . . she picks out all the wirst side Sortes(?) of meate and We Cannot get our teeth through and the Magets get out on our plats'.[31] Miss Nightingale, the Bracebridges, and the nuns and sisters got better fare, although meat, eggs and milk were always short. This must have been a special privation to Florence Nightingale who, in later life at least, took a keen interest in good meat and bread. But at Scutari sisterhood in service did not mean equality. Miss Nightingale and her entourage, the Bermondsey nuns, Sellonites and St John's nurses all dined separately. Miss Nightingale was too little interested in other people to discover in herself the art by which she might unite and lead.

Moreover, she made no effective allocations of authority. Mother Mary Clare ruled her nuns, but the anomalous roles of Mrs Bracebridge, and Mrs Clarke her housekeeper and personal servant, were never defined and each was allowed to play the tyrant. There was a second complaint from a St Johnite, Mary Ann Coyle, on the day following the first letter:

> wee are all so very unappey Miss Nightingale have sum spite against us but for wat cawse wee know not: and Mrs Brasebridg has treated us with Contempt ever since the day Mr. Sheperd left us: I woold not mind minde wat harde ships wee had to incaunenter with if they woold be kinde to us: thay treate us worse than the Coman low wimon thay brate oute. I was never so unappey in My life, and wee are truley sorey that wee ever came oute withoute some one to care for us: wee do the thing that is rite and if good be for us wee nead not feer . . . Mrs Clarke the housekeeper Is A Compleate tirant she insults us every time she sees us Maryann in particular.[32]

Mary Ann Coyle went on to allege that she and her colléagues were kept in ignorance of the progress of the war. Newspapers were, she said, sent out for the nurses 'but they will not lett us see them'. But the St Johnites had their pride too. Mrs Bracebridge and Mrs Clarke might domineer over them, but they would 'not Mix with those Low womin Miss Nightingale braught out [Mrs Bracebridge's chosen nurses?] and for that reason they are so invitered against us'.[33] It was the first time in British history that women of diverse classes, regional origins and religions were brought to work together for a common secular cause in a foreign land. Rather than notice that the mission was fragmenting, we should marvel that it achieved anything at all, let alone its eventual successes in deaths eased and lives saved.

The mission survived partly because Miss Nightingale must have intercepted these two letters. They remain among her papers. The likelihood of seizure — rather than their having been duly posted and received and then entering the Nightingale collection later — is increased by the existence of a draft of a letter from Miss Nightingale to Miss Gipps, a lady superior at St John's House in London, dated the following day, 5 December, denouncing four St Johnites as 'flibberty-gibbet'. 'They do not command the respect imperatively necessary where forty women are turned loose among three thousand men. They do not keep the rules which I have made to ensure female decorum.' They visited the wards at nights, they fed patients without first obtaining medical orders. They dressed wounds carelessly. They would 'not take a hint except from me — I have consequently employed them less in nursing & more in making Stump pillows ... with the view of protecting them — And they said, which is very true, that they did not come out for needlework — They have consequently done little or nothing.' Miss Nightingale never learned how to deploy and handle nurses. Sewing, as at Harley Street, was a safe diversion. Miss Nightingale concluded by asking, indirectly, that Miss Gipps recall the errant four, 'because you want them, rather than because I don't.[34] They sailed by the first available ship, before a recall could have been received at Scutari. By Christmas 1854, Miss Nightingale had dismissed — on my estimate, because the evidence is ambiguous — 13 of her original contingent, leaving her with 25 nuns and nurses to help about 11,000 men admitted to the hospitals rotten with disease — only about 100 had war wounds. The total was to rise to its peak in January 1855.

Miss Nightingale's narrow but effective notion of nursing was adjusted to these constraints. It consisted of caring for the seriously ill with unremitting attention to the patient's comfort, cleanliness, quiet and mental solace, and the administering of medicines and plasters under medical direction. She herself did little actual nursing at the hospitals. By day she negotiated with doctors, drove orderlies, and inspected stores, the nurses' work and hospital maintenance. She was like the new owner of a run down great estate. The Bracebridges, Aunt Mai and Sister Mary Clare were her agents, Mrs Clarke her housekeeper, the nurses and orderlies were her labourers, the patients her tenantry. The evidence is contradictory about her manner. One Catholic nun recalled years later that she was never heard to raise her voice — she had a peculiarly soft, clear intonation. (Even in old age the Edison recording of her voice displays a precise enunciation and an effortlessly resonant actressy voice.) But nearer the time, that is on 20 November 1854, Mr Bracebridge boasted to the family that 'She scolds sergeants and orderlies all day long; You would be astonished to see how fierce she is grown.' One old transport orderly recalled that she asked him sharply whether he carried his patients gently, admonished him to do so even after he averred that he did, and gave him a plug of tobacco as a reminder. Thereafter, he said, he revered Miss Nightingale and tried especially to be gentle.[35] By night she broke her own rule about walking the wards alone and glided in her peculiarly beautiful floating walk, her tallish slight figure erect, carrying her Turkish lantern, inspecting the patients and the wards, noting the dying. Then she returned to her room in the corner tower of the hospital to write: letters of condolence, answers to enquiries about the missing and above all orders, insinuations and recriminations in 10-30 page repetitive private letters to Sidney Herbert. She and her ladies constituted a proto-army welfare branch, long before the Army established a system of its own:

> I grieve to be obliged to inform you, [she wrote to Mrs Maria Hunt in a letter typical of many others, dated September 1855 from the General Hospital, Scutari] that your son died in this Hospital on Sunday last. . . His complaint was Chronic Dysentery — he sank gradually from weakness, without much suffering. Everything was done that was possible to keep up his strength. He was fed every half hour with the most nourishing things he could take, & when there was anything he had a fancy for, it was taken to him immediately. . . He spoke much of his mother, & gave us the direction to you in his last moments. . . His great anxiety was that his Mother should receive the pay due to him, & should know that he had not received any since he had been Out. . . You may have the satisfaction of knowing that he had the most constant & careful care from the Doctors and the Nurses. . . The Chaplain and myself saw him every day . . .

From 'Catforth near Swillbrook near Preston' Elizabeth Kellett wrote in a struggling copperplate to Miss Nightingale, the soldiers' friend, one of a dozen similar letters which survive among the Nightingale Papers:

> Dear madam
> it is with reagret that inow persume to adress these few lines to you Beging won kind favour from you will you pleas dear madam to wright and let me no if hever my son Robert kellet has Been in this hospital they last account I herd of in he had Been Brought to they ospital iashure you that I have rote several times But has recived no answer from im dear madam they acount that iherd was that he was Brought to scutarion ospital in they later end of genuary and idoo ashure you that ifeel verry unapy about im and if he Bee dead pleas to let mee know what was is complaint I will now give you they discriptions of im he his a streight nice clean looking light complexioned young youth near twenty so now imust conclude with hevery kind regards towards you and Belive mee to Be yours affectionetley frend John and ElisaBeth kellet. . .
> > privat Robert kellet
> > No 3510 34th Rigiment
> > Light Division[36]

No wonder the common people regarded Miss Nightingale as a saint. She depended on their gratitude. They, for the first time in war, had a great person who made it her business to console them in their deepest distresses.

Her letters to Sidney Herbert were her safety-valve. She rarely wrote to her family. That task she left to the Bracebridges and to Aunt Mai Smith after she replaced them at Scutari in August 1855. Throughout her time at the Crimea, apart from the period of her illness, Miss Nightingale allowed herself but a few hours sleep in the early hours of the morning. Had she been prepared to delegate authority and create a chain of command she might have been able to cope with more than 25 women and enjoy more rest. But there is no evidence she ever entertained that choice.

She first learned that more women were on their way to Scutari on 9 or 10 December, a week after the second party had left London. Fearing her reaction, Sidney Herbert had not used the telegraph to warn her, nor did he write. After his ordeal with Manning and Rev. Mother Bridgeman and his knowledge of Miss Nightingale's temperament, his evasion is understandable. His more ingenuous wife finally conveyed the news by writing to Mrs Bracebridge on 23 November, leaving it to the latter to inform Miss Nightingale.[37]

Immediately upon reading the letter Miss Nightingale enrolled the deputy Inspector-General of hospitals, Dr Menzies, 'under whose order I am', in her 'private' remonstrance to Sidney Herbert. The pliant, cautious Menzies, who secretly disliked having women in his hospitals, 'considers', Miss Nightingale reported, that as large a number are now

> employed ... as can be usefully appropriated & as can be made consistent with morality and discipline − [Privately, she had warned Herbert that Menzies was weak on discipline] And the discipline of 40 women, collected together for the first time, is not trifling matter − under these new and strange circumstances.
>
> He considers that, if we were swamped with a number increased to 60 or 70, good order would become impossible and in all these views [and here Miss Nightingale finally emerges in her own persona, having nowhere earlier indicated that Menzies had authorized her to report his views, if indeed they were his views] I so fully concur that I should resign my situation as impossible, were such circumstances forced upon me.
>
> For our quarters are already inadequate to preserving one tenth

our number. More quarters cannot be assured us ... With regard to taking a house in Scutari the Medical Officers considered it as simply impossible. Regularity could not be preserved, where the Sisters & Nurses were living from under our eye.

Miss Nightingale went on to argue that 40 nurses for 3,000 sick were 'sufficient'. Indeed, she added that the party would have done better with 20: 'The work has really been done by 10 − the rest "get under our feet".' The letter continues over 19 pages.[38]

The threat of resignation presumably was meant to compel Herbert to recall the Stanley-Bridgeman party by telegraph at their next land fall. This Herbert could have done, because their ship, the *Egyptus*, called in for repairs at Navarino and Athens before arriving at the Dardanelles; but Herbert did not take the hint. Miss Nightingale's threat also gave her the option of sending the new party packing the moment they arrived at Scutari. Certainly the hospital quarters were extremely crowded and certainly the sisters, at once delicate ladies and religious zealots, could not be trusted unsupervised as the Norwood nuns and Sellonites had proved, while the nurses, as their sorry tale of drunkenness and insubordination showed, could not be trusted either. But there was no great difficulty in securing houses in Scutari if money was available for the exorbitant rentals, as the venturesome Lady Alicia Blackwood had demonstrated. She had arrived at Scutari ready to join in the nursing, but Miss Nightingale had adroitly steered her outside to nurse soldiers' wives and camp followers in two dwellings Lady Alicia privately rented.[39] The notion that 40 nurses could cope with 3,000 patients, especially cholera and dysentery victims, and that ten − in another letter at this time Miss Nightingale put the number at eighteen and five in successive sentences − would really suffice, throws a startling light on her views on management. It also highlights the fact, which Miss Nightingale − followed by her biographers − managed to obscure, that the greater part of the nursing was done, as it always had been done, by male medical orderlies. She commandeered about 300 more of them than the army normally allowed, most of them near able-bodied. She and her ladies supplied essential norms of gentleness and concern and harried the orderlies into doing their duty; they also raised standards of cleanliness, cookery and promptitude − although meals were often six hours late even near the end of the war − and, perhaps most vital of all, Miss Nightingale was the agent who supplied large quantities of food and clothing to debilitated men.[40] In this last aspect of her work, as in the rest, nursing was for Miss Nightingale merely a form of applied housekeeping — a view she retained all her life.

Without waiting for Herbert's reply or news that the second party had been stopped, Miss Nightingale wrote again on 15 December, eleven pages of harangue, not counting the repetitive postscripts. Some of her remonstrances were dubiously grounded. She claimed that she undertook the mission only on

> the distinct undertaking (expressed both in your hand-writing and in the printed announcement . . .) that nurses were to be sent out at my requisition only, made with the approbation of the Medical Officers here.
>
> You came to me in your distress, and told me that you were unable for the moment to find any other person for the office, and that, if I failed you, the scheme would fail. I sacrificed my own judgment and went out with 40 females.

The first paragraph refers to the original agreement, which I suggested had been generally inspired at least by Miss Nightingale. The agreement refers to the allocation of nurses in Turkey and does not mention any further party, which was apparently not envisaged at the time. But implicitly, the document does confirm Miss Nightingale's supremacy in all matters relating to female nurses, subject only to the medical officers. Similarly, the second paragraph is a rearrangement of the truth. I have suggested that Miss Nightingale set up the approach from Sidney Herbert, but even if that interpretation is false, it is at least indisputable that his written invitation and her written offer were made simultaneously. There is no indication that she set any limit on the number of nurses in the mission, or that the 38 she took exceeded her notional optimal number. Here, as she was increasingly to do throughout her life, Miss Nightingale was moralising upon a fantasy of her own creation. After repeating the assertion that the doctors could not and would not employ the extra nurses, she added, inconsequentially,

> you have sacrificed the cause, so near my heart — you have sacrificed me, a matter of small importance now — you have sacrificed your own written word to a popular cry.
>
> I will not say anything of the cruel injustice to me.

She then raised the questions of where the newcomers were to be housed and the shortage of space in the hospitals. She would, she supposed, have 'to take a house in Scutari'. Five days earlier this choice had been 'impossible'. There they were to wait until 'you can employ them at Therapia [the Embassy compound, where there was nothing to do], or elsewhere – or till you recall them. Of course these unoccupied women will "go to the Devil".'

The climax of this letter was a consummate mingling of inferential blame and adumbrated threat:

> You must feel that I ought to resign, where [sic – when?] conditions are imposed upon me which render the object for which I am employed unattainable – and I only remain at my post till I have provided ... for these poor wanderers ... I must again refer to the deficiency of knives and forks here.[41]

When the Stanley-Bridgeman party arrived on 17 December Miss Nightingale, true to her threat, packed them off to Therapia. The nurses in the party rebelled that evening when they discovered they were to act as servants to the ecclesiastical ladies rather than minister to wounded soldiers. Rev. Mother Francis, bent upon establishing her independence from the outset, separated from the Therapia group and took her fifteen nuns across the Bosphorus to an already crowded French convent in Galata. The second Therapia house was apparently not considered. The nuns could indeed have been squeezed in at the first Therapia house. They stayed at the Maison de Providence until after Christmas, yet to meet Miss Nightingale. With characteristic inappropriateness Rev. Mother Francis confided in her diary: 'It was the best Christmas we ever spent ... replete with spiritual joys and conformity to Him who came unto His own and His own received Him not.'[42] Until she and her party moved, the French nuns could not re-open their boarding school, on which their income depended.

Miss Nightingale tackled the interlopers by crushing Mary Stanley. After leaving her to stew for four days in the midst of the nurses' rebellion, she summoned her on 21 December. Miss Nightingale, clad in her black merino, spotless linen collar and cuffs, white apron, white cap with a black hankerchief tied over it, sat working at a small unpainted deal table in a small room, the door of which was screened by a heavy curtain. It was post day. Miss Nightingale kept Miss Stanley waiting through the morning while a stream of visitors entered before her. The crushing was easy. Miss Nightingale opened with a direct challenge, made in the presence of Mr Bracebridge and Dr Cumming.

She formally resigned and requested Miss Stanley to succeed her immediately. Miss Stanley, duly flustered, demurred and gabbled out 'every reason'. Miss Nightingale confirmed her victory by lending a suppliant Miss Stanley £90, to be followed later by another £90. That foolish, sybaritic Lady Bountiful and her party had spent all she had upon the best hotels and fare en route, and they had arrived penniless. The grants came from Miss Nightingale's private funds, that is, publicly subscribed monies which she controlled. Her sharp sense of legal niceties ensured that Miss Stanley and her people were given no 'official' money and Miss Nightingale saw to it that Dr Cumming made no official payments either. Stratford de Redcliffe, who was empowered to disburse official funds for good causes also refused Miss Stanley, but whether from reasons of fear of Miss Nightingale, inherent meanness, or prudence, or all three, I have not discovered.[43]

In the circumstances Miss Stanley's vague suggestions for the allocation of her people stood little chance with the lady superintendent. Miss Stanley hoped to place her ladies, under the chaplains' direction, as visitors to the sick and dying. They were not to 'nurse' the soldiery. The Catholic nuns were equally to be set under their chaplain, Father Ronan (who was yet to arrive after the Manning/Herbert/Bridgeman contretemps), 'supposing', Miss Stanley ventured, 'that Father Ronan ... should approve and wish it'. The common nurses were not considered; presumably, until Miss Nightingale should change her mind, they were to continue to cook, sweep and wash for the ladies at Therapia. One among them, Jane Harding, who had served under Miss Nightingale at Harley Street, was expressly forbidden to communicate with her.[44] Irrespective of Father Ronan's likely views, Miss Nightingale rejected the plan. The British evangelical press — Miss Stanley noticed that Miss Nightingale's sofa was bestrewn with English newspapers — was already replete with lurid speculations about Puseyite and Papist sisters whose only object at the war must be to pervert British soldiers. Miss Nightingale could simply have ignored the abuse, as she had done hitherto, but it served her now to allege the practical and 'moral impossibility' of employing more females with dangerous religious labels.[45]

Four days later, on Christmas Eve, the lady superintendent summoned Miss Stanley again. Miss Nightingale was now equipped with a memorandum signed by Dr Cumming, cast in the now distinctive Nightingale format of close argument and secretarial mien. He formally requested the lady superintendent to select a total of 50 ladies and nurses, 'the number which you, in agreement with myself, have deemed sufficient for the proper working of the establishment, and beyond which you do not think yourself capable of managing as best to carry out the objects in view'.[46] This concession was Miss Nightingale's best option. It enabled her, with Miss Stanley's and Dr Cumming's acquiescence, to take women from both the Stanley and Bridgeman groups and thereby split them. Miss Nightingale chose thirteen of the ladies and nurses for Scutari. Another seven of the 31 in the Stanley party were sent in January 1855 to the General Hospital at Balaclava. The remaining eight apparently were left at Therapia.

Miss Nightingale offered to take five of the fifteen Bridgeman nuns. They were to replace the five Norwood sisters whom the lady superintendent planned to dismiss, thereby keeping the number of nuns constant. The Norwood sisters, apart from Miss Nightingale's complaints about their genteel ineffectiveness, had offended by flaunting their distinctive white habits. On joining the contingent in London they had arrived in discreet black, but once in France they blossomed in their normal white.[47] Miss Nightingale hated being tricked.

Rev. Mother Bridgeman proved a harder case than Miss Stanley. On 22 December Miss Nightingale had invited her, in writing, to place five of her nuns in the Scutari hospitals under the spiritual direction of Rev. Mother Clare, the Bermondsey superioress. Rather than negotiate on paper, Rev. Mother Bridgeman sailed over the Bosphorus to confront Miss Nightingale. This procedure had, after all, succeeded with Mr Herbert and Father Manning. Mother Mary Clare met the interloping superioress with icy formality. The lady superintendent duly kept her visitor waiting and then offered her lunch: 'a small remnant of musty cheese, a scrap of dirty butter in a bowl, some sour bread and some cold potatoes'. Rev. Mother Bridgeman, whose bulk implied a hearty appetite, was sufficiently piqued by this tactic to record it at length in her diary. None the less, Miss Nightingale failed to gain her point. Rev. Mother Brickbat, as Miss Nightingale henceforth called her — in reference to her complexion and manner — cited her agreement among her nuns confirming her headship and asserted the moral impossibility of setting part of her contingent under Rev. Mother Clare and thereby under Miss Nightingale.[48]

Rev. Mother Brickbat's behaviour and claims were impudent and legally unfounded. Father Cuffe, the senior Catholic chaplain, hinted that she should go home. Father Manning, writing a few days later, was fearful that the Irish contingent might indeed return in high dudgeon and warned them to stand fast. Rev. Mother Bridgeman, who neither needed nor heeded advice, decided to stay and fight. With Nightingalesque cunning she informed her nuns that anyone who wished to transfer to Rev. Mother Clare might write home for permission. Given the delays of the post, this move gave her three more weeks for parley. She must have been shocked when four nuns actually sought permission: but their temerity went unrequited; permission was refused for two of them and time ran out before permission arrived for the others. On Christmas Eve, two days after their initial encounter, Miss Nightingale renewed her offer to take five Bridgeman nuns and to house the remainder at Therapia. Rev. Mother Brickbat riposted by offering herself to go with four of her party to work under Rev. Mother Clare on condition that the lady superintendent separately housed the surplus ten nuns. The French nuns at Galata urgently wanted their rooms. Miss Nightingale's offer had explicitly excluded the Brickbat. Their confrontation continued until 5 January 1855 when the lady superintendent gave way and admitted Rev. Mother Bridgeman as an 'ordinary nun', like her four sisters, at the hospitals. Rev. Mother Clare put two of the Irish party into the kitchens, two to sort linen and left Rev. Mother Bridgeman unemployed and ignored. But by mid-January cholera had begun to ravage the overcrowded wards and all five Bridgeman nuns were finally enlisted as nurses.[49]

The Scutari female nursing venture rested on a fragile sectarian truce. Miss Nightingale, who had no firm denominational allegiance, was justifiably wary. But her predictions that the Irish sisters would proselytise in the hospitals were not borne out. The nuns were ostentatious in rounding up dying Irishmen, ostentatious enough to earn a rebuke from Rev. Mother Clare, and on one occasion they baptised a delirious terminal case whose affiliations were unknown, but they did not seek to convert known Protestants. Watchful Protestant chaplains and nurses would have remonstrated had they tried. The nuns for their part were quick to warn nominal Catholics to reject the ministrations of Protestant ladies, thereby provoking hitherto indifferent men into welcoming the ladies. The Anglican Sellonites were equally assiduous, if less officious, in mustering their nominal co-religionists. Presbyterian Scots and Irish were poorly supplied with both chaplains and nurses of their persuasion and some of them complained about the flaunting of Popery and pseudo-Popery in the wards, but the absence of overt sectarian conflict among the soldiers can be explained by their easy-going scepticism about the religious zeal of their betters. In December 1854 a dying man was given a medal by a Catholic chaplain. The man was idly fingering the medal, whereupon the chaplain accepted an offer of a piece of red tape from a hovering Sellonite and tied the medal around the patient's neck. Embarrassed, the man remarked to the Sellonite: 'I am what is called a Roman Catholic; I know no better. I would as soon be a Protestant if I knew how.' Near him lay Sam Gregg, aged 17, bereft since the Battle of Inkerman of his right arm and left hand, but described as 'cheerful'. He whispered smilingly to the Sellonite, Sister Terrot, 'I don't think much of that gammon! What good can a medal do to a dying man?'[50]

Had Miss Nightingale been able to coax rather than bully she would have defeated the Bridgeman challenge. Her remoteness from other human beings, her strident dealings with doctors, orderlies and ladies, their well-founded suspicions that she both saw through their inefficiencies and reported them home, all prevented her from cultivating useful friends and isolating the Irish nuns. Instead, the medical and purveying fraternity adopted Rev. Mother Bridgeman and her following as a weapon against their interfering, overbearing enemy. Miss Nightingale could neither risk the uproar if she sent the Irish party home nor cope with the Brickbat while they stayed. She could however, blame Sidney Herbert. She used Christmas Day to pen an eleven page reproach:

> You have not stood by me, but I have stood by you. In this new situation, I have taken your written instructions as my guide ... Had I not done this, we should have been turned out of the Hospitals in a month, and the War Office would have borne the blame of swamping the experiment.

Aggrieved self-justification merged imperceptibly into outright threat:

> Such a tempest has been brewed in this little pint-pot as you could have no idea of. But I, like the ass, have put on the lion's skin, and when once I have done that (poor me, who never affronted any one before), I can bray so loud that I shall be heard, I am afraid, as far as England.[51]

The Nightingale family had already begun to bray. They were practised in it, at least since October of that year, when Fanny and Parthe had told Mrs Gaskell several otherwise unsubstantiated anecdotes of Florence's childhood precocity as nurse and saint. Mrs Gaskell immediately broadcast them. Parthe's repertoire included a richly circumstantial story of Florence's devoted nursing, seven years before, of a dying child of a village woman. Mrs Gaskell recounted it, yet she observed, although the observation only half registered, that

> the father of this dead child – the husband of this poor woman – died last 5th of September, and I was witness to the extreme difficulty with which Parthe induced Florence to go and see the childless widow once ... and though the woman entreated her to come again she never did.[52]

The intimacy between the famous Unitarian novelist and Florence Nightingale, which the family ardently desired, never developed after this episode. Within weeks of Miss Nightingale's arrival at Scutari the family propagandists were in spate. In November 1854 Parthe informed Monckton Milnes that 'in one week F has gained the confidence of all, the Doctors do her will, & the fund has poured ... into her lap, tin pots, saucepans, jars, basons, sherry, combs, shirts, socks, sheets, coal, wooden spoons.' She also warned him, with the implied instruction to take counter measures among his political friends, that 'Dizzy is making trouble with (?) the RC and High Ch nurses.'[53] (No written evidence survives to substantiate this accusation. But it is consonant with Disraeli's character.) By the second week of December news reached the family from the Bracebridges of the flooding in of wounded and diseased soldiers from the Battle of Inkerman (which had occurred on 5 November, the day after Miss Nightingale's landing at Scutari) and of the loss of lives, provisions and hospital stores in the terrible Black Sea storm of 14 November, together with the first disclosures of strains between the lady superintendent, and unfeeling doctors, orderlies and nurses. 'The difficulties of her path thicken upon her', Parthe told Lizzie Herbert, '[but] ... her heart does not quail.' 'May we', Parthe added, 'spread the Queen's letter a little?' Queen Victoria had informed Mr Herbert, in a letter written to Mrs Herbert, that she wished 'Miss Nightingale and the ladies would tell these poor, noble wounded and sick men that *no one* takes a warmer interest or feels *more* for their sufferings or admires their courage ... *more* than their Queen'. This recognition was a triumph for the family; the Nightingales' dissenting, radical parvenu origins made it the more delectable. Florence saw to it that the Queen's message was read in the wards and placarded throughout the hospitals. She reported that the men said, '"She thinks of us", (said with tears)' and '"To think of her thinking of us"'. Burns, an Irish soldier, the only man from whom we have an identifiable verbatim report, expressed a more mundane view: 'It's very pleasant and proper, but I hope the good folks at home won't spend all their kindness in words, but will keep it up, and give us enough to keep the pot aboiling when we come back to them.' True to the family gift for evocative anecdote, Parthe ended her letter to Lizzie Herbert with 'a little story – Flo sat up all night with 5 Inkerman men – given up by doctors – she nursed them through – "saved by her" the Doctors say'.[54] This story is uncorroborated. Letters to William Nightingale from his friends at the Crimea praising Florence were copied by Parthe and distributed through their circle.[55] By mid-February 1855 the cheap serial *Illustrated History of the Expedition To The Crimea* contained the first portrait of the new heroine, although she was still too little known to compel the authors to mention her in their text. Their engraving is not a precise representation of its subject, but rather a generalised picture of an early Victorian, Frenchified young lady, plump-cheeked, with hair coiled around her ears like the young Queen, a cross on a chain encircling her neck, sitting reading a devotional work. By April 1855 such portraits were appearing in the soldiers' huts at the Crimea, cut from home papers. The sceptical young Protestant Irish medical man, Joseph Samuel Prendergast, who resented Miss Nightingale as a meddling Puseyite – perhaps even a secret Papist – yielded to the sentiments of his sisters at home and began, half-heartedly, to regard Miss Nightingale as a female martyr to duty. He duly pasted up in his mess hut the woodcut portrait they sent him and read the *Life Sketch of Miss Nightingale* they posted with it. But he was a conventionally-minded man and remained unconvinced: 'everyone . . . gives favourable accounts of her . . . I am certain I never said anything against her . . . [but] there is something in these Protestant maidens proceedings repugnant to some men's ideas of morality, decency & refinement'.[56]

The patriotic canonisation proceeded with the Rev. Sidney Godolphin Osborne's racy, opinionated glorification of Miss Nightingale in his reports to *The Times*.[57] He worked in the Scutari hospitals as a volunteer chaplain and medical helper. Osborne, was a knight errant who spent his life questing for objects to love and reform. Like Cobbett, whom he resembles, not least in his robust, compelling prose, he wrote on Tory-radical political reform, class mutuality, agricultural improvement, famine relief, sanitary reform and the Heroine of the Crimea. He was the first of a line of forceful men who found in her their Lady. Osborne, Russell the war correspondent,

A.W. Kinglake the historian, and other critics created The Lady with the Lamp as the living counter to the muddle and national shame of a war that failed public expectations of early glory. Russell's despatches brought direct to middle-class homes the horrors and mistakes of war and aristocracy's and officialdom's contempt for their common soldiery. Miss Nightingale projected herself and was projected by others as a mature, maternal symbol, the embodiment of common-sensical housewifely virtues, in contrast to infantile male parliamentary and military blundering. She became a neutral, safely non-political diversionary focus for the discontents that might otherwise have been concentrated by J.A. Roebuck, Augustus Stafford, Charles Dickens and other radical critics in their attacks on aristocratic dominance and mismanagement.

Resentment at Miss Nightingale's high-handedness festered throughout the winter of 1854/5. She was saved from an open rebellion by the drafting of the unemployed Therapian ladies and nurses, and the remaining Bridgeman nuns, to the Koulali hospitals (a few miles East from Scutari) which opened in January/February 1855, and the despatch at the request of the Commander in Chief, Lord Raglan, of ladies and nurses to two hospitals at the Crimea. Dissatisfied nurses also moved, when they could, beyond her reach. The lady superintendent opposed all these deployments, seeing in each a diffusion of her authority. Publicly she shed responsibility for them, privately she kept control of their funding.[58] Meanwhile she pressed Sidney Herbert and Lord Panmure, the new War Secretary, for a stronger statement of her powers, and suppressed mutinous nurses. In January the St Johnites complained about unequal work loads, the rules forbidding speaking with patients and reading to them without the chaplain's permission (the chaplains were especially wary of novels and High Church poetry), and 'the want of due consideration towards themselves' from the aloof lady superintendent, the haughty Mrs Bracebridge and the nagging Mrs Clarke.[59] The novelty of the enterprise and the frightful environment of its work demanded qualities of leadership and experience which no woman of the 1850s could have possessed. It is fair to remind ourselves that Miss Nightingale saved the mission from religious catastrophe and the ladies' fatuities. But she never won loyalty and instead met her subordinates' complaints with a mixture of unforgiving authoritarianism and tortuous self-justification. On learning of the complaints she issued instant 'letters of recall', which meant loss of wages, bonuses and 'characters'. She told the St Johnites' superiors that 'had they given me any opportunity of setting matters right, I might have convinced them of the impropriety of lightly taking offence', and then remarked that she was 'wholly unable to enquire into trifles', which in turn allowed her to conclude that the nurses' allegations were 'unfounded'. The council of St John's House acquiesed.[60]

On 27 April 1855 Miss Nightingale received from the War Office part of her much sought extended authority. She was named as almoner of the free gifts in all the British hospitals in the Crimea war zone. Within the week she sailed for Balaclava on the Crimean Peninsula, accompanied by an entourage which included Mr Bracebridge and Alexis Soyer, the great chef come to reform the soldiers' cooking.

Miss Nightingale's first act was to make an official visit to Lord Raglan. It happened that the Commander in Chief was absent from headquarters but her reception there none the less proclaimed her standing to the army. She spent the following days investigating the hospitals, especially those housing the Stanley ladies and St John's nurses. Thanks to the capable, hard-working nurses, and medical officers, helped by the lull in the fighting, the improvement in the weather and the enlarged supplies of food and clothing, affairs were less chaotic than accounts of the ladies' antics would have led her to expect. Miss Clough had left to follow a romantic whim to preside, uninvited, at the Highland Brigade Hospital on the heights above Balaclava. The Sellonite Mother Eldress at the General Hospital had suffered a mental collapse and spent her time praying while the nurses, orderlies and Turkish labourers made hay among the free gifts. Her successor, the tearful dithering Miss Wear, trailed around the hospital cradling a King Charles spaniel. Miss Nightingale's worst predictions about the Stanley party were being borne out.[61]

While at the Crimea Miss Nightingale established her credentials with Sir John McNeill, a distinguished civil administrator and medical man, the joint leader, with Colonel Alexander Tulloch, of the official inquiry into the commissariat of the army. She also strengthened her links with Dr John Sutherland and Mr Robert Rawlinson, the civil engineer, members of the second commission inquiring into the sanitary conditions of the army. Sutherland, one of the first sanitary inspectors appointed to the Board of Health in 1848, had already met Miss Nightingale when he inspected the Scutari hospitals. He was to become her devoted ally for the rest of his life. Sutherland was always more rigid in his thinking, more hardworking and more single-mindedly dedicated to sanitary improvement than Miss Nightingale. He was to subordinate himself to her and endure her slights and tantrums in the realisation that she had access to power to do good that he could never hope to tap. He brought a steadiness to their partnership that immeasurably strengthened its effectiveness.

Not surprisingly, McNeill, Sutherland and their colleagues found much to criticise among the unsuitable buildings used as hospitals, the collapse of primitive sanitary arrangements under the pressure of numbers and epidemic disease, and the dim, complacent timidity of overtasked doctors and purveyors sheltering behind regulations. Miss Nightingale cultivated the commissioners' esteem and fed them information. She was building for herself a defence against detractors and a means of publicly punishing those who stood in her way. Her alliance with the commissioners, themselves outsiders among the army men, was none the less an astonishing feat for a female with no official standing in the army.[62]

Miss Nightingale's powerlessness in the Crimea in relation to the ladies and nurses, imposed by the terms of her letter of appointment which specified only Turkey, was quickly exposed. Miss Wear and another zealot, Miss Fanny Taylor, especially, ignored Miss Nightingale's remonstrances. She ordered the ebullient Welsh cook, Elizabeth Davis, to cease cooking for the officers, but Davis, a survivor of trading voyages and shipwreck in the Pacific in the 1820s and 1830s, who relished the badinage of gentlemen of large fortune as they clustered around her cookhouse, boldly ignored the lady superintendent.[63] Miss Nightingale never wavered from the belief that her mission was to the common soldiery. With true wealthy upper-class Radical disdain, she declared that officers could look after themselves.

Within a fortnight of her arrival Miss Nightingale collapsed. The doctors were said to have diagnosed her sickness as 'Crimean fever', probably a form of typhus. This episode is mysterious. The date of the onset of the illness is not recorded and there are few records of its progress. Yet her illness was a public event. Soon after her collapse Miss Nightingale was conveyed in procession from her stateroom in a ship in Balaclava harbour up the hill to the Castle Hospital. Relays of soldiers carried her litter, Dr Anderson, Chief Medical Officer at the General Hospital, and her maid, Mrs Roberts, walked beside her, Soyer's secretary held a white parasol above her head and her uniformed message-boy, Robert Robinson, marched at the rear. The cortege launched rumours of her illness throughout the Crimea and evoked great sympathy among the troops. Officers like young Joseph Prendergast, who hitherto in his letters to his family had been facetiously dismissive of the lady superintendent and her female entourage, now became interested in her fate. Telegraphic bulletins about her illness reached the Queen and Lord Raglan, who paid Miss Nightingale a belated visit on 24 May, after she began to recover. Miss Nightingale is not recorded as showing the usual symptoms of fever whether of the typhus or typhoid varieties; that is, there is no record of diarrhoea, constipation, bleeding or pinkish spots. But she was delirious and unusually active for a person stricken with fever. Her hair was cut off, the normal treatment to reduce the heat of the brain in delirium. While at the Castle Hospital she wrote coherent-seeming notes about engines pounding in her head, persecutions from people crowding into her room demanding supplies, and the deceits of friends. The surviving letters do not mention nursing problems or the sufferings of the soldiers. On 21 May she wrote to Sir John McNeill to warn him that

> Last week a Persian adventurer appeared to me like a phantom, shewed me papers by which Mr Bracebridge seemed to have drawn upon me for £300000, I sent for him – He said very little, neither denied nor assented . . . but said nothing (?) would even (?) that I had seen (?) the papers there for the first time . . .
>
> Have you any advice to give? I come to you because you have shewn me much kindness.[64]

McNeill apparently returned the letter unanswered.

After about three weeks of illness Miss Nightingale's doctors decided she was sufficiently recovered to travel and they advised her to return to England to convalesce. She refused. About four months later, in October 1855, she alleged to the family, knowing they would spread the story,

> that Drs. Hall and Hadley sent for a list of vessels going home & chose one, the Jura which was <u>not</u> going to stop at Scutari . . . and put me on board of her for England . . . And that Mr Bracebridge and Ld. Ward took me out, at the risk to my life –. to <u>save</u> my going to England, though unconscious all the time.[65]

There is much confusion about this episode, not least in the presentations by recent biographers who muddle who said and did what. But a few salient elements are clear. Miss Nightingale was not 'unconscious all the time': she was sufficiently alert to reject the doctors' advice. Dr John Hall was devious — we know nothing about Hadley — but he was also cautious and punctilious. He was not the man to risk the uproar the lady superintendent would have aroused had he shanghaied her. There is no evidence that the officious, indiscreet Bracebridge made any allegations about the episode, as he would surely have done had he been involved as Miss Nightingale claimed. There is no record of Lord Ward remarking on it. I have been unable to discover whether the *Jura* did bypass Constantinople, but it seems inherently unlikely that a ship could not at least pause to allow important passengers to disembark. It is thinkable that Miss Nightingale, a poor sea-traveller, preferred to sail on Lord Ward's fast, well-appointed steam yacht rather than on a tub like the *Jura*. Finally, the story first appears to have been told in October, four months after the event, by its central character who was 'unconscious' during its unfolding. October was the month when Miss Nightingale first clashed with Dr John Hall. The real oddity is the ready acceptance by historians, without conclusive evidence, of such an implausible accusation. Its real significance is its testimony to Miss Nightingale's novelistic imagination and her resolute effrontery in propagating stories to gain her ends.

After her return from the Crimea in Lord Ward's yacht Miss Nightingale took about six more weeks to recuperate and apparently did not return to the Scutari hospitals until about the middle of July. The feeding of the soldiers and the washing of the linen seems to have proceeded smoothly in her absence but the work of the nuns and nurses must have become even more peripheral to the daily regime of the hospitals because by the end of June only about five of the original 14 nurses, two of the six St Johnites and two of the five Stanleyites remained on the job. The others had proved to have 'unsuitable characters', a St Johnite confided to her chaplain.[66] Only the dedicated and disciplined contingent of Catholic religious remained undiminished. Although there had been a sudden rise in admissions in June due to another cholera outbreak, the overall number of patients in the Bosphorus and Crimean hospitals had fallen fairly steadily after January 1855 from 4,176 per 1,000 strength to 2,832 per 1,000 strength in July, while the death rate had diminished even faster.

Upon her return to business in mid-July Miss Nightingale used this decline as a new argument for asserting her overt control over the Stanleyites, escapee St Johnites and Bridgemanites at the Crimea hospitals. She opened negotiations with Dr John Hall, their nominal chief at the Crimea, to have them returned to the Scutari hospitals. The hot Crimean summer would damage their health, she suggested, and if Hall's reported intention to convert his Crimean hospitals into convalescent and staging depots was true, there was no need for female nurses. While seeking Hall's agreement and the exercise of his authority to return the nurses to Scutari, Miss Nightingale approached him as one commandant to another: 'I ... hasten to apply for your advice on this subject — & trust that you will have the goodness as soon as possible to examine the question.'[67] The nuns and ladies were not to be consulted. But without their return to Scutari, the Nightingale mission would have virtually no presence. Hall's reply to Miss Nightingale was a cool, polite sidestep. Clearly he was under pressure from the Crimean ladies, Miss Wear especially, not to order them back to Miss Nightingale. He pleaded the necessity of the General Hospital, half-filled with seamen and other non-army patients with nowhere else to go, but he left it to the lady with the powerful friends to make the decisive move: 'If two nurses could be kept there it would be a convenience [Hall's idea of female nursing was as limited as Florence Nightingale's], but if you wish to withdraw them altogether we must endeavour to make some other arrangement.' The lady superintendent, outmatched by Hall's pliability, grudgingly agreed to leave Miss Dean and a nurse at the General Hospital.[68]

Miss Nightingale's return to business and the fall in the number of patients in the Kulali hospitals — there were now less than 50 — proved the last straw for Rev. Mother Francis. After obtaining permission from her bishop in Ireland she told Father Woollett, SJ, a chaplain at the front, on 2 September 1855 to advise Hall that she was ready to transfer her contingent, together with additional nuns whom she would bring from Ireland, to the Crimea to work 'under his direction'. In fact, Woollett had already sounded Hall, very likely at her instigation, and had found him cautiously compliant. Rev. Mother Francis now completed her entrapment of Hall with an ultimatum: 'I would not undertake again *to work with Miss Nightingale*.' Not that she had ever done so, but Hall plumped for the lesser of two inescapable rows.[69] Rev. Mother Francis alleged that she could no longer stand Miss Nightingale's low standards of hospital management, but after all, the Kulali nuns had been free for months to run their hospital in their own way. Given their advantage of a superior building and a much smaller press of patients, such reports as we have suggest that they had done little better than their colleagues at Scutari. The real precipitating cause of this secession appears to have been the proselytising forays of the recently converted Mrs Lawfield who was pressing her family during August 1855 to come over to Rome. Miss Nightingale found time to join the tug of war: 'I got her to talk to me as much as possible . . . as she otherwise falls into the hands of a silly little Priest here [Duffy?] & an unprincipled R. Catholic nurse whom I have dismissed'. [Nurse Wagstaff?] [70]

Hall accepted the Bridgeman offer, without informing the lady superintendent. She, after all, still had no official control over the allocation of female nurses outside Turkey. Rev. Mother Francis curtly informed Miss Nightingale of the new plan after receiving Hall's acceptance. 'I shall . . . be obliged to withdraw the Sisters from the General Hospital, Scutari . . . We hope to sail for the Crimea at the beginning of next week.'[71] This was more Bridgeman impudence. Miss Nightingale alone had the power to dispose of nuns and nurses at Scutari.

Miss Nightingale immediately sought to reinforce her authority. She approached Stratford de Redcliffe, who shied away and redirected her to General Storks, the newly appointed commandant at Constantinople, and to Rear-Admiral Grey. She also reiterated her demand to the War Office that her control over the female nurses should be extended throughout 'the East'. Storks, like the rest of his colleagues, tried to keep clear of the warring women. He ignored, as he was able to do in the absence of specific instructions, Miss Nightingale's call for extended powers. But he made a conciliatory gesture, within his and Grey's sphere of authority, by mildly rebuking Hall for requisitioning shipping berths for the nuns without obtaining permission. Yet Storks did not forbid the nuns' removal to the Crimea, although he added a warning that Miss Nightingale had decided to 'conduct' them to the Crimea in person. Hall returned a rather flippant, unrepentant note pointing out that Miss Nightingale had given the impression that she had washed her hands of the Irish nuns and the Crimea and 'if proselytism is what is dreaded, this is the very field for the poor nuns, as the greatest portion of their patients will be Turks, Jews, Greeks, & I fear, Infidels'. None the less, Hall was not a fool. He remarked that the contretemps was 'a very simple affair, tho' much I see, will be made of it'. After the row about Miss Wear and now this, he was coming to appreciate what he was up against. He would have been even more worried had he known that Storks would immediately supply Miss Nightingale with a full copy of his letter.[72]

The long sought strengthening of Miss Nightingale's mandate throughout the hospitals of the East arrived from Lord Panmure, the new Secretary for War, on 15 October, in the midst of these dissensions. It was less than she wanted: the permanent officials at the War Office were awake to the lady's pretensions. The order recognised Miss Nightingale 'as the General Superintendent of the female nursing Establishment of the Military Hospitals of the Army' and repeated that she was subject to the Principal Medical Officer, who was to give his directions through her. But the document left ambiguous her powers over the allocation of nurses outside Turkey. Such transfers were now subject to 'consultation' with Miss Nightingale but she had no absolute control. Disappointing though it was, Miss Nightingale brandished the document at her new enemy Hall on the day she received it, and she immediately set about establishing her version of the sequence of events, thereby warning Hall that the War Office was already informed of where the blame lay:

In September 1855 Mrs Bridgeman . . . who came out to serve under my orders in December 1854 . . . offered the services of herself & Sisters, without the knowledge or consent of [General Storks] . . . or my own, to you – which you accepted for the General Hospital Balaclava. that you had written to me (referring to a letter of mine dated some months previous proposing to withdraw the Nurses then there, a proposition at that time negatived by you) – desiring that this proposition should now be carried into effect, which I acceded to . . . that I immediately communicated with our Ambassador, who gave it as his opinion that I should be fully justified in calling upon Mrs Bridgeman not to undertake her intended voyage & upon Dr Hall not to receive her at Balaclava without my 'consent & permission' & that I 'should be entitled to the support of Brigadier-General Storks and Rear Admiral Grey in giving effect to my determination'. that, conceiving it to be injudicious to take such a measure and thus produce a breach between the Roman Catholic and Protestant elements, I consulted with . . . Storks . . . and came to the determination to bring Mrs Bridgeman and her sisters . . . to Balaclava myself. that, finding you of opinion that it was better for the arrangement to stand – viz. that the General Hospital . . . should be served by Roman Catholic Sisters alone, because the Patients in that Hospital at present consist chiefly of Roman Catholics, Jews, Turks, infidels and heathens – and referring to my instructions from the War Office placing me 'under the direction of the Chief Medical Officer' . . . I considered it to be my duty to acquiesce in your arrangement.[73]

Every sentence of this letter contains, as the reader will have perceived, a half-truth, lie or threat. Rev. Mother Francis did not come to serve under Miss Nightingale. The second sentence, refers to Miss Nightingale's proposal of mid-July to remove Miss Wear and her nurses, at which Hall temporised, and to her letters of 21 September repeating her proposal, to which Hall had explicitly replied: 'I do not want to get rid of Miss Wear and her nurses.'[74] Miss Nightingale's account of Stratford de Redcliffe's opinions is inherently improbable, given the ambassador's evasiveness and Storks's refusal to forbid the Bridgeman nuns' removal to the Crimea. It is equally improbable that consultation with Storks was needed to persuade Miss Nightingale to travel with the Bridgeman party. The quotation about the 'Jews and Infidels' from Hall's private letter to Storks was a nasty piece of bullying. And if Miss Nightingale was to hand over the Bridgeman nuns to Hall, as she protested that her War Office instructions impelled her to do, her journey to the Crimea was unnecessary.

Despite having surrendered the Bridgeman party to Hall, Miss Nightingale three days later besought Stratford de Redcliffe to cancel their permission to leave. 'What do I do – what do you direct? – I think you [must?] communicate to Hall and Bridgeman the instructions under which I act.' But the Ambassador was not to be inveigled. He duly undertook to advise the War Office to extend her authority, but he did nothing to forbid the Bridgeman venture.[75] Miss Nightingale's efforts to collar the Brickbat also failed. The latter coolly informed the lady superintendent that she 'never gave up the right to withdraw my Sisters from Scutari or elsewhere ... Were I about to place any of my Sisters in a hospital under your control, I should, of course, have referred the matter to you; but it is not so'.[76]

After a voyage of two days the *Ottawa* hove to off Balaclava in the midst of a storm. Bridgeman was determined to be first ashore. The rough seas did not permit a tug to approach the *Ottawa* but Rev. Mother Francis hoisted herself into a rocking small boat. Miss Nightingale was in her cabin. Immediately upon hearing that the Brickbat had got off, she rushed on deck and insisted upon plumping into a second small boat. The ladies landed at Balaclava together.

Miss Nightingale set about an inspection of the hospitals, looking for dirt and decay. Hall, with icy courtesy, regretted that he was unable to attend her. Miss Wear, who had signified her determination to stay at the Crimea, out of the superintendent's clutches, was now made to pay for her tenacity. Miss Nightingale removed Miss Wear's two allies – in reality they dominated her and did as they liked – nurses

Davis and Sheridan, and ordered Hall to replace them with 'two women', presumably soldiers' wives.

> As both your followers have alas! deserted you . . . I fear it cannot be very comfortable for you to remain at the General Hospital with the 'monks'.
> Would you not think it better to come up here . . . [the Castle Hospital — FN's temporary headquarters] And knowing as I do the Characters of your successors and of many of those with whom you have to do, I think it would be far pleasanter for you, better for your dignity, and might [avert?] much that may be and will be said both about our being spies . . . and of our pampering 'the monks'.

Miss Wear passed on to Hall Miss Nightingale's tormenting letter. He copied it. That canny man had begun to collect evidence for the defence. Miss Wear did not budge. Miss Nightingale was further incensed by discovering that she had taken up with the Brickbat and was sheltering behind her. The lady superintendent, after further futile badgering, at last requested Hall to order Miss Wear to the Castle Hospital. He politely offered to ask Miss Wear what she preferred. She preferred to stay.[77]

During this second visit Miss Nightingale established extra diet kitchens, saw that insulation felt was put in to the hospital huts to protect the inmates from the looming winter and besought the military authorities to set aside rooms as rest and reading rooms for the men. She had begun to look to the moral well being of the troops as well as to their care when physically disabled. She also closeted herself with each of the nurses, seeking private information about the behaviour of their colleagues.[78] Rev. Mother Francis and her nuns meanwhile set about stirrring up the orderlies to clean the General Hospital and run it efficiently.

In early November there arrived at Balaclava, while Miss Nightingale was in the midst of her battles at the Crimea, copies of *The Times* containing an extravagant attack on the army medical and purveying services, delivered in England as a public lecture by the newly returned Mr Bracebridge. Miss Nightingale was furious with him. She took to her bed alleging sciatica. Hall, too, was furious. He believed, wrongly, that Bracebridge's diatribe had been inspired by the lady superintendent. Miss Nightingale saw that Bracebridge's indiscretions also provided openings for the Irish Bridgeman faction. While in bed she wrote to scold Bracebridge and to warn him against launching into public denunciations of the Irish nuns. After all, she remarked, '"they can lie & I cannot". If you see well to tell this to Manning — I have no objection.'[79] She also primed Lizzie Herbert: 'Dr Hall does not think it beneath him to broil me slowly upon the fires of my own Extra Diet kitchen . . . Remember, please, that this is quite private, that I do not wish to complain of Dr. Hall, who is an able & efficient officer in some ways'. She went on to note incidentally that Hall had countermanded her order to supply eggs to non-officer patients.

> And, if Mr Herbert saw no impropriety in it . . . a private letter from some high authority to the Commander in Chief [Raglan had died — his successor, Codrington so far had ignored her] . . . to the effect that this work is not a silly display of feminine sensibility but an authorized set of tools.

Miss Nightingale also advised Mrs Herbert to press the War Office to send out more Bermondsey nuns 'to counterbalance . . . the Irish . . . who hate their soberer sisters with the moral hatred which, I believe, only Nuns and Household Servants can feel towards each other'.[80] The additional nuns were never sent.

Three weeks before this letter Miss Nightingale had had a final row with Rev. Mother Francis. Sister Mary Winifred, one of the Bridgemanites, although recruited from Liverpool, died of cholera at Balaclava. Miss Nightingale joined the group at her bedside and prayed with them. While praying she had also dispatched with her umbrella a large rat attempting to get at the dying nun. Miss Nightingale then joined the funeral procession to a prominent site on the Balaclava hills, and offered to build a cross upon the grave. Rev. Mother Francis delayed her reply until she had received and accepted a similar offer from the 89th Royal Irish Regiment. Miss Nightingale told Sidney Herbert: 'Mother Brickbat's conduct has been neither that of a Christian, a gentlewoman, or even a woman.' Miss Nightingale returned to Scutari, embattled on all fronts.[81]

Miss Nightingale had now reached the limits of the possible in her contributions to the internal working of the hospitals. Increasingly she looked beyond to the general management of army medical services. Her views on compelling the purveyors to work within a framework of standard issues of food, clothes and furniture and to make regular daily rounds to monitor the flow of their supplies, and on appointing house stewards and hospital commissaries on the French model, were all adopted by the War Office. Her scheme for the revision of the duties and pay of medical officers was adopted in the Royal Warrant of September 1855. She also conceived the idea of a school of army medicine early in 1855 and one was begun in a small way at Scutari.

On Good Friday 1856 (21 March) she returned for her third inspection of the Crimea. Her long awaited rescript proclaiming her full jurisdiction over 'the East' had finally arrived some days earlier.[82] Very likely Lord Panmure and the War Office had held it up until the end of the war was imminent. The peace conference had already begun. She was now equipped to stop Hall placing nurses without consulting her – she alleged that he had installed two nurses from Smyrna in the Crimea hospitals – and to stop Rev. Mother Francis extending her sway over the two Land Transport hospitals which hitherto had had no female nurses. Cholera had broken out there. Hall had invited Miss Nightingale to send nurses, but she was afraid that the Brickbat would preempt her. When Herbert sent news of the forthcoming rescript he counselled Miss Nightingale against wielding it too heavily upon Hall and the Brickbat; this would only provoke a 'damaging public row'. 'You need not be afraid that I shall molest the "Brickbat"', Miss Nightingale jauntily assured him through Colonel J.H. Lefroy. 'Above all, I am afraid of their resigning, & making Martyrs of themselves.'[83]

The row would have indeed been damaging. Hall, who had learned to deal carefully with Miss Nightingale's letters, supplied General Codrington and the War Office with copies of letters proving that she had offered the Smyrna nurses and that he had accepted them in good faith. As Miss Nightingale's future enemy at the War Office, the Deputy Secretary, Benjamin Hawes, remarked, 'Sir J. Hall has met the charge.'[84] She then adverted to an episode which her biographers have accepted as proving petty persecution from an aggrieved purveyor and Bridgeman ally at the Crimea:

As a practical woman, I think it a pity to give Mr Fitzgerald [Deputy-Purveyor at the Crimea] the pleasure either of refusing my Requisitions or of falsifying them to the W.O. I shall therefore take up everything with me which my Hospitals will want, leaving it to the Queen to supply such things only as bread & meat etc which I cannot make.

Had this man been one of our persuasion, he would have been brought to a Court Martial – But it is enough for a man to be a Roman Catholic for the Government to say 'Oh! do pray be quiet, don't tell of his lies'.[85]

David Fitzgerald had in December/January 1855/6 been deputed by the War Office to report secretly on the nursing arrangements at the Crimea. Although I have found no evidence to this effect, his commission might well have been part of a Hawes — Hall-Andrew Smith plan to counter Miss Nightingale. Fitzgerald commended the Bridgeman party for their efficiency and devoted service. He criticised Miss Nightingale for meddling, intriguing, and pretensions to dominate the whole hospital system.[86] In all, the report, which I could not find in the War Office papers — probably it was never officially filed — appears to have been a shrewd and fairly accurate survey, if unduly kind to the Bridgemanites, whose hospitals were as dirty and cholera-infested as the rest and whose impact on the orderlies was apparently about as marginal as the Nightingale party's. Fitzgerald gave a copy of of his report to Rev. Mother Francis — possibly she had helped with it because some of the detail in it could have come only from her (this also explains the strange survival of a copy in a Kinsale convent). Miss Nightingale knew by hearsay of the report but she had been unable to obtain it, even from Sidney Herbert, who very sensibly had refused her demand that he move for its tabling in the House of Commons. So, on Miss Nightingale's third visit to the Crimea, Fitzgerald was a marked man.

Within days of her arrival Miss Nightingale alleged to Sidney Herbert and other important people that Fitzgerald had refused food and shelter to the Bermondsey nuns whom she had brought with her. For over ten days she had to feed them and supply fuel from the special stores she had brought with her.

I tell you this not because I ask you to do anything. It is merely because I wish to leave on record some instance of that which nobody in England will believe or can ever imagine . . . You don't know what it is to have your 'children' short of food and warmth and to doubt whether you are not sacrificing them . . . for the good of the work.[87]

There is a novelist's perverted irony in these paragraphs. Miss Nightingale was beguiled by her own effrontery in playing the great power game. Astute Dr Hall had instructed his subordinates in writing to provide Miss Nightingale with everything she asked for; all was to be supplied according to rule by countersigned requisitions. But even this precaution was insufficient to thwart Miss Nightingale's outrageous stratagem which was, as she exulted, unimaginable at home – but only too believable to Hall. Dr Taylor had instantly agreed to place her contingent on full rations by requisition as things were required. She led him to believe that only part of the contingent had arrived and that he would be informed when the remainder from Scutari disembarked. He was never told that they were all at the Crimea. He never received a complaint about inadequate supplies. Moreover, he learned that potted meat supplied to the 'half'contingent had not, on Miss Nightingale's orders, been used. The ten obedient Bermondsey nuns, devoted to the lady superintendent in her struggle with the Brickbat, had fasted in silence. Miss Nightingale also drew upon her arrival a full allocation of tea, sugar and food from the purveyor's store but when the assistant purveyor asked her servant if they wanted more, the servant replied 'the Nurses had a sufficient quantity to last for a few days longer, and when necessary he would draw them altogether'. These further supplies were never requested. The assistant purveyor's statement was attested by three of his men. Miss Nightingale continued to broadcast the story throughout April: to Uncle Sam, to Parthe, to Sidney Herbert, to Sir John McNeill with the understanding that McNeill would bypass the War Office and Horse Guards and convey its gravamen to Prince Albert and the Queen. Parthe made copies and distributed them. In the Crimea, Hall finally countered by threatening to hold an open inquiry, but at home the lying went on.[88]

Miss Nightingale's arrival with her general order confirming her power throughout 'the East' brought the final collision with the Brickbat. Miss Nightingale wanted the Irish nuns to acknowledge her chieftainship and stay. She refused to accept Rev. Mother Francis's refusal and gave her twenty-four hours in which to submit. The Brickbat, backed by four Catholic chaplains, tendered her resignation to the newly knighted Sir John Hall. Miss Nightingale then tried to move Sidney Herbert to press Manning and the hierarchy to order them to stay, and pleaded hysterically with the Brickbat at a final interview, but the Brickbat and her nuns went home, leaving the key to their storeroom with Mr Purveyor Fitzgerald. Miss Nightingale posted herself outside the storeroom until an orderly gave in and fetched the key.[89]

After their departure Miss Nightingale brought four more Bermondsey nuns to staff a hospital rapidly emptying of patients and now containing only 98. Such aid as was needed was required at Scutari, caring for seriously ill men invalided from the Crimea. But Miss Nightingale had a point to make. She set about telling important people that the General Hospital held twice the number of patients which it had really held when she arrived, and that the numbers remained large long after they had in fact diminished. By May, Hall was able to close the hospitals, for want of patients. Her story was to become enshrined in official narratives. Something of the virulence of intra-Catholic hatreds shows in the treatment accorded the Bermondsey nuns by the Crimea chaplains. The chaplain to the Irish party, Father Michael Gleeson CM, declared that the Bermondseys' submission to Miss Nightingale was not 'for the good of religion'. He refused to visit them. Father Duffy SJ, refused them confession and holy communion. And lest Manning and the Irish bishops admonish the Bridgemanites for not standing to their post, Rev. Mother Francis saw to it that the four chaplains endorsed her decision to leave the Crimea.[90]

Miss Nightingale's private vilification of the Irish nuns began even before their departure. 'Your pig-sty is cleaner than ... the Hospital, as left by Mrs Bridgeman — The patients were grimed with dirt, infested with vermin, with bedsores like Lazarus (Mrs Bridgeman, I suppose, thought it holy)'. This letter, to Uncle Sam Smith, was copied by Parthe and sent to Sir John McNeill and Monckton Milnes, among others. Florence sent similar accounts to Lady Cranworth and Colonel Lefroy, one of the commissioners who investigated the hospitals at the Crimea. Lefroy, despite professing admiration for her work, refused to incorporate in his report her allegations against Fitzgerald and her charge that the Bridgeman hospital had squandered abnormally large amounts of rations. But he did imply that the Irish nuns fed their charges larger portions than the patients received at the Scutari hospitals. Hall privately denied to the War Office that the Bridgeman hospital was unusually dirty and, indeed, suggested the opposite. Miss Nightingale had spread the notion that he had been 'disgusted with the state of the Hospital'.[91]

The letter to the Puseyite, philanthropic Lady Cranworth contains a vivid example of that fine-toned double-bluff which had now become characteristic of Miss Nightingale, and of that distancing which issued in contempt for the pawns in her game:

> I almost consider it a duty to add that, upon comparing the dirt, disorder, extravagance & carelessness which ... this Hospital, when

just left by Mrs Bridgeman & her 11 nuns exhibited – with the working of our poor, despised & (I am sorry to admit it) too often exposing – themselves – to – be – dispised Nurses, I think that everybody who understands Nursing, must say 'rather one Nurse than 5 Irish nuns'.[92]

To other correspondents Miss Nightingale was, as we have seen with Mrs Lawfield and others, almost entirely dismissive of the common nurses.

Yet it was this passion to succeed, this assertion of the right to command, exemplified both in Miss Nightingale and Rev. Mother Francis, which did compel the doctors to exert themselves and the orderlies to improve their work. While the British hospitals consistently reduced their disease death rates after the crisis of the first terrible winter of 1854/5, the death rates in the French hospitals continued high and finally topped the worst British rates. The fifty French sisters of Charity were lowly, semi-literate drudges in the hospitals, unable to command anybody, and shared the insanitary habits of their patients and doctors. British doctors, none too fastidious themselves, were appalled at the filthiness of French hospitals, at the overflowing chamber pots which lay about uncovered and unemptied, at the soiled, reeking beds, at the typhus, scurvy and diarrhoea which ravaged the wards unchecked.[93] Miss Nightingale went to Scutari to emulate the French sisters, but she quickly surpassed them. It was a splendid achievement for her thin red line which only numbered 142 altogether and never more than 49 at any one time, constantly beset by illness and breakdowns.[94]

Miss Nightingale returned from the Crimea as the ministering angel, recognised by her sovereign. She had made valuable, influential friends in the Crimea, McNeill, Lefroy, and Tulloch. She had won the allegiance of able, biddable disciples, Drs Parkes, Sutherland, Alexander and Balfour, and Rawlinson the engineer. The Nightingale Fund, soon to rise beyond £40,000, was at her disposal. Sidney Herbert's political fortunes were now intertwined with her reputation. Lord Panmure could procrastinate, but ultimately was unable to withstand the political pressure she could mobilise. She was poised to make a new career in reforming the sanitary state of the British army to avenge the 11,000 men who, she believed, had died of disease and ill-attended wounds. Henceforth her enemies, Sir Benjamin Hawes, the prospective Permanent Secretary in the War Office who had seen through her tactics and had suffered from them, Sir John Hall, the generals at the Horse Guards, and the Commander in Chief, the Duke of Cambridge, would have to take extraordinary measures to stop this unleashed free-lance elemental force.

Notes

1. F.N. to Mrs Herbert, 14 Oct. 1854, quoted in Sir Edward Cook, *The Life of Florence Nightingale* (2 vols., London, 1913), vol. I, p.152.

2. Ibid., pp.148, 151.

3. F.N. to Mrs Herbert, 14 Oct. 1854, BL Add.Mss 43396, ff.11-12; Cook, *Nightingale*, vol. I, p.151.

4. S. Herbert to F.N., 14 Oct. [1854], Cook, *Nightingale*, vol. I, pp.150-1; Parthe Nightingale to R. Monckton Milnes, 'Monday' [16 Oct. 1854], Houghton Mss 18/158, Trinity College, Cambridge.

5. Cook, *Nightingale*, vol. I, p.151.

6. Margaret Goodman, *Experience of an English Sister of Mercy* (London, 1862), pp.57-60; Thomas Jay Williams, *Priscilla Lydia Sellon* (London, 1965), p.134.

7. Charlotte Willoughby Moore to C.P. Shepherd, 12, 15 Oct. [1854]; S. Herbert to Bishop Blomfield, 17 Oct. 1854; Blomfield to Shepherd, 14 Oct. 1854, GLRO HI/ST/NC3/SU/4, 2, 3, 5.

8. Evelyn Bolster, *The Sisters of Mercy in the Crimean War* (Cork, 1964), pp.17-21.

9. 'Memorandum of Agreement' GLRO HI/ST/NC3/SU/1; Grace Ramsay, *Thomas Grant first Bishop of Southwark* (London, 1874), pp.136-7; Sister Bolster quotes in *Sisters of Mercy* (pp.62-3) what seems to be a variant version of the 'Agreement' held in the Bridgeman Crimean War collection at the Convent of Mercy, Kinsale. I was not permitted access to this collection.

10. Bolster, *Sisters of Mercy*, p.27.

11. Ibid., pp.27-33.

12. Ibid., p.52.

13. Ibid., p.38.

14. Ibid., pp.49-51.

15. Ibid., pp.58-60.

16. Ibid., p.60.

17. Ibid., p.64.

18. Sidney Herbert to F.N., 19 Oct. 1854, BL Add.Mss 43393, f.1.

19. E.C. Rickards, *Felicia Skene Of Oxford* (London, 1902), p.111.

20. Cook, *Nightingale*, vol. I, p.158.

21. C.H. Bracebridge to T.B. Murray, 5 Nov. 1854; Selina Bracebridge to 'Dear Sir' [C.P. Shepherd?], 22 Jan [1855], GLRO HI/ST/NC3/SU/24, 7; C. Holte Bracebridge, *Shakespeare No Deerstealer* (London, 1862); C.H. Bracebridge, 'On the Mode of Inflicting the Punishment of Death', *Transactions of the National Association for the Promotion of Social Science*, 1866. (Hereafter *Transactions NAPSS*.)

22. F.N. to Sidney Herbert, 25 Dec. 1854, BL Add.Mss 43393, f.51; Mary Jones to F.N., 22 Dec. 1854, GLRO HI/ST/NC3/54/17.

23. Cook, *Nightingale*, vol. I, p.167.

24. Florence Nightingale, *A Contribution to the Sanitary History of the British Army during the Late War With Russia* (London, 1859), p.2; Return showing the Number of Officers and Men ... in the Military Hospitals at Scutari ... October and ... November 1854, *H.C. Papers, 1854-55*, vol. XXXIII, pp.256-7.

25. F.N. to Sidney Herbert, Private, 10 Dec. 1854, BL Add.Mss 43393, ff.22-5; 1 May 1855, GLRO HI/ST/NC8/14d.

26. Elizabeth Davis, *The Autobiography of a Crimean Nurse*, ed. Jane Williams (2 vols., London, 1857), vol. II, pp.102, 128; F.N. to [Duke of Newcastle?] 10 May 1855, GLRO HI/ST/NC8/14d.

27. Emma Fagg to Madam [Mary Jones?] 4 Jan. 1855, GLRO HI/ST/SU/22; *Nurse Sarah Anne* [Terrot] *With Florence Nightingale at Scutari*, ed. Robert G. Richardson (London, 1977), p.88.

28. Elspeth Huxley, *Florence Nightingale* (London, 1975), pp.101-3; F.N. to Sidney Herbert, 25 Nov. 1854, BL Add.Mss 43393, ff.13-14.

29. Ibid., f.17; Dr A.J. Cumming to Sir John McNeill, 5 Nov. 1856 (copy); Sir John McNeill to F.N., 8 Nov. 1856, BL Add.Mss 45768, ff.21, 33-4; Stanley Lane-Poole, *The Life of . . . Stratford Canning* (2 vols., London, 1888), vol. II, p.383.

30. F.N. to Miss Gipps, 5 Dec. 1854, GLRO HI/ST/SU/14; Bolster, *Sisters of Mercy*, quoting Fanny Taylor, p.121.

31. Unknown correspondent to 'Dear Madam' [M. Jones?], 4 Dec. 1854, GLRO HI/ST/SU/15.

32. Marey Ann Coyle to Dear Madam [M. Jones?], 5 Dec. [1854], GLRO HI/ST/SU/16.

33. Ibid.

34. F.N. to Miss Gipps, 5 Dec. 1854; Mary Jones to F.N., 22 Dec. 1854, GLRO HI/ST/SU/14, 17.

35. Cook, *Nightingale*, vol. I, pp.182, 186; Sidney Godolphin Osborne, *Scutari and Its Hospitals* (London, 1855), p.25; William Usher to F.N., 24 Feb. 1895, GLRO HI/ST/NC2/V/1/95.

36. F.N. to Mrs Maria Hunt, 6 Sept. 1855; Elizabeth Kellett to F.N., n.d., GLRO HI/ST/NC1/55/4, NC/V10.55.

37. F.N. to Sidney Herbert, Private, 10 Dec. 1854, BL Add.Mss 43393, ff.22-5.

38. Ibid.

39. Alicia Blackwood, *Narrative of personal experiences . . . During a Residence on the Bosphorus throughout the Crimean War* (London, 1881), p.233.

40. Lord Stanmore, *Sidney Herbert* (2 vols., London, 1906), vol. I, p.365; F.N. to Sidney Herbert, 3 April 1856, BL Add.Mss 43393, ff.231-2; Sir Anthony Sterling, Assistant Adjutant-General of the Highland Division, complained that Miss Nightingale used far too many orderlies in the hospitals, Sir Anthony Coningham Sterling, *Letters from the Army In The Crimea* (privately printed 1857), pp.227, 314-5.

41. F.N. to Sidney Herbert, 15 Dec. 1854, BL Add.Mss 43393, ff.34-40.

42. Bolster, *Sisters of Mercy*, p.75; Helena Concannon, *The Irish Sisters of Mercy in The Crimean War* (Dublin, 1950), p.13.

43. Mary Stanley to Lizzie Herbert, 21 Dec. 1854, quoted in Stanmore, *Herbert*, vol. II, p.374; F.N. to Sidney Herbert, 21 Dec. 1854, 12 Feb. 1855, BL Add.Mss 43393, ff.40, 142-4.

44. Bolster, *Sisters of Mercy*, p.90; Jane Harding to F.N., 15 Aug. 1856, GLRO, HI/ST/NC2/V10/56.

45. F.N. to Sidney Herbert, 15 Dec. 1854, 25 Dec. 1854, BL Add.Mss 43393 ff.37, 46, Joseph John Gurney, *The "Record" and Miss Nightingale* (London, 1855).

46. A.J. Cumming to F.N., 22 Dec. 1854, BL Add.Mss 43401, f.23.

47. A Lady Volunteer (Fanny Taylor) *Eastern Hospitals and English Nurses* (2 vols., London, 1856), vol. I, p.66; Bolster, *Sisters of Mercy*, pp.99-100.

48. Bolster, *Sisters of Mercy*, pp.96-8.

49. F.N. to Sidney Herbert, 25 Dec. 1854, BL Add.Mss 43393 ff.47, 54; Bolster, *Sisters of Mercy*, pp.94-5, 99-101, 110.

50. [Terrot], *Nurse Sarah Anne*, pp.98, 115-6; [Sarah Terrot] *Reminiscences of Scutari Hospital in Winter 1854-55* (Edinburgh, 1898), pp.86, 89, 98.

51. F.N. to Sidney Herbert, 25 Dec. 1854, BL Add.Mss 43393, f.45.

52. Mrs Gaskell to Emily Shaen, 27 Oct. 1854, J.A.V. Chapple and Arthur Pollard (eds.) *The Letters of Mrs Gaskell*, (Manchester, 1966), p.319.

53. Parthe Nightingale to Monckton Milnes, n.d. [Dec. 1854?], Houghton Mss, Trinity College Cambridge, 18 149(2).

54. Cook, *Nightingale*, vol. I, p.215; [Terrot] *Nurse Sarah Anne*, pp.146-7; Parthe Nightingale to Lizzie Herbert, 9 Dec. 1854, (copy) BL Add.Mss 43396, f.14.

55. e.g. Dr Wallis to W.E. Nightingale, Jan. 10 1855, BL Add.Mss 45790, f.164.

56. Anon., *Illustrated History of the Expedition To The Crimea*, issue of mid-Feb. 1855, p.16; Joseph Samuel Prendergast to Frank Prendergast, 15-17 Feb., 4-6 March, 25-28 Apr. 1855, BL Add.Mss 59849, ff.35, 50, 82.

57. Osborne, *Scutari*, p.25.

58. F.N. to Sidney Herbert, Private 14 Jan., 22 Jan. 1855, BL Add.Mss 43393, ff.95, 105.

59. Elizabeth Woodward to [M. Jones?] 3 Jan. 1855, GLRO HI/ST/SU/20; F.N. to Sidney Herbert 15 Feb. 1855, BL Add.Mss 43393 ff.154-9. Bolster, *Sisters of Mercy*, p.156; [Terrot] *Nurse Sarah Anne*, p.133.

60. F.N. to Council of St. John's House, 11 Jan. 1854 [recte 5] GLRO HI/ST/SU/18.

61. Cook, *Nightingale*, vol.I, p.255; Davis, *Autobiography*, vol. II, p.136; Sidney Herbert to F.N., 10 Apr. 1859, BL Add.Mss 43395, f.155.

62. Cook, *Nightingale*, vol. I, pp.220-1.

63. F.N. to Aunt Mai Smith, 19 Oct. 1855, BL Add.Mss 45793, f.106; Bolster, *Sisters of Mercy*, pp.123, 147; Davis, *Autobiography*, vol. II, p.164.

64. Joseph Samuel Prendergast to John Prendergast, 31 Dec. 1855, BL Add.Mss 59849 f.1; F.N. to Aunt Mai Smith, 19 Oct. 1855, BL Add.Mss 45793, f.106; James S. Taylor, *Alexis Soyer A Chivalrous Chef* (Washington, 1921), p.15; Cook *Nightingale*, vol. I, pp.258-9; F.N. to Sir John McNeill, 21 May 1855, BL Add.Mss 45768, f.1.

65. F.N. to Aunt Mai Smith, 19 Oct. 1855, BL Add.Mss 45793, ff.108-9.

66. Mrs Mary Sansom to Rev. C.P. Shepherd, 28 June 1855, GLRO, HI/ST/SU/33.

67. Florence Nightingale, *A Contribution to the Sanitary History of the British Army during the Late War With Russia* (London, 1859), p.14; F.N. to Dr John Hall, 14 July 1855, BL Add.Mss 39867, ff.17-19.

68. Dr John Hall to F.N., 20 July 1855; F.N. to Hall, 24 July 1855, BL Add.Mss 39867, ff.20-22.

69. Rev. Mother M.F. Bridgeman to Father Woollett, SJ, 2 Sept. 1855; Woollett to Dr John Hall, 3 Sept. 1855; Hall to Rev. Mother Bridgeman (copy) 27 Sept. 1855, BL Add.Mss 39867, ff.27-9.

70. F.N. to Rev. C.P. Shepherd, 21 Aug. 1855, GLRO HI/ST/SU/36.

71. Bolster, *Sisters Of Mercy*, p.196.

72. General Storks to Hall, 8 Oct. 1855; Hall to Storks, 'Private & Confidential' [copy] 11 Oct. 1855, BL Add.Mss 39867, ff.42-3.

73. F.N. to Hall, 15 Oct. 1855; Copy to War Office instructions 155656/193, BL Add.Mss 39867, ff.44-6, 43401, f.11.

74. F.N. to Hall, 21 Sept. 1855; Hall to F.N., 27 Sept. 1855, BL Add.Mss 39867, ff.31-7.

75. F.N. to Lord Stratford de Redcliffe, n.d. [18 Oct? 1855]; Stratford de Redcliffe to F.N., n.d. [19 Oct.? 1855], BL Add.Mss 43401, ff.86-7.

76. Bolster, *Sisters of Mercy*, p.199. Sister Bolster gives no date for this letter.

77. A Lady Volunteer, *Eastern Hospitals*, vol. II, pp.163-7; Hall to F.N.,

19 Oct. 1855 (copy); F.N. to Mary Wear, 6 Nov. 1855 (copy); Hall to F.N., 28 Oct. 1855; F.N. to Hall, 7 Nov. 1855; Hall to F.N., 7 Nov. 1855 (copy), Mary Wear to Hall, 9 Nov. 1855; BL Add.Mss 39867, ff.52-63; F.N. to Hall, 27 Oct. 1856 [recte 5] PRO WO1/383/109.

78. Davis, *Autobiography*, vol. II, pp.185-6.

79. F.N. to C.H. Bracebridge, 4 Nov. 1855, BL Add.Mss 43397, ff.171-5.

80. F.N. to Lizzie Herbert, 17 Nov. 1855, BL Add.Mss 43396, ff.40-4.

81. Bolster, *Sisters of Mercy*, pp.212-14.

82. Cook, *Nightingale*, vol. I, pp.292-3.

83. Sidney Herbert to F.N., 4 Mar. 1856, F.N. to Sidney Herbert, 20 Feb. 1856, 21 Feb. 1856, BL Add.Mss 43393, ff.211-22; F.N. to Colonel J.H. Lefroy, 16 Mar. 1856, BL Add.Mss 43397, f.225.

84. Hall to General Codrington 12 Mar. 1856 (copy); minutes by Lefroy, J. Peel and Hawes, early Apr. 1856, PRO WO1/383, ff.105-16.

85. F.N. to Lefroy, 16 Mar. 1856, BL Add.Mss 43397, ff.225-6.

86. F.N. to Lefroy, 11 Jan. 1856, BL Add.Mss 43397, ff.205-6; David Fitzgerald to Hall, 23 May 1856, BL Add.Mss 39867, ff.156-8.

87. F.N. to Sidney Herbert, 3 Apr. 1856, BL Add.Mss 43393, ff.224-8.

88. Hall to F.N., 26 Mar. 1856 (copy); F.N. to Hall, 19 Apr. 1856; Dr G. Taylor to Hall, 21 Apr. 1856, Henry Powell (Acting Purveyor) to Fitzgerald, 23 Apr. 1856, Hall to F.N. 23 Apr. 1856, BL Add.Mss 39867, ff.100-28; S.M. Mitra, *The Life and Letters of Sir John Hall* (London, 1911), pp.441, 459-63; F.N. to Uncle Sam Smith, 17 Apr. 1856, BL Add.Mss 45792, ff.28-30; Parthe Nightingale to Sir John McNeill, n.d. [late Apr. 1856?] GLRO HI/ST/SU64; Parthe to ? with extracts from F.N.'s letter to Uncle Sam, 17 Apr. 1856, BL Add.Mss 45768, ff.14-5.

89. F.N. to Sidney Herbert, 3 Apr. 1856, BL Add.Mss 43393, f.229; F.N. to Uncle Sam Smith 17 Apr. 1856 and copy by Parthe, BL Add.Mss 45792, f.28, 45768, f.6.

90. F.N. to Lefroy, 5 Apr. 1856, BL Add.Mss 43397, ff.228-30; Bolster, *Sisters of Mercy*, pp.281-2.

91. F.N. to Uncle Sam Smith, 17 Apr. 1856, BL Add.Mss 45792, f.30; Parthe Nightingale to Monckton Milnes, [late Apr. 1856]. Houghton Mss., Trinity College, Cambridge, 18, 152 (A,B); Lefroy to F.N., 10-22 May 1856, BL Add.Mss 43396, f.231; Sir John Hall, 'Observations', (Oct. 1856) PRO WO33/3B.

92. F.N. to Lady Cranworth, 19 May 1856, BL Add.Mss 43397, f.109.

93. F.N. to Sidney Herbert, 28 Dec. 1854, BL Add.Mss 43393, f.58; F.N. to Douglas Galton, 5 May 1863, BL Add.Mss 45761, f.3; Charles Bryce, *England and France before Sepastopol, looked at From a Medical Point of View* (London, 1857); C. Shrimpton, *La Guerre d'Orient, L'Armée Anglaise et Miss Nightingale* (Paris, 1864), pp.4, 57; A.W., Kinglake, *The Invasion of the Crimea*, 8 vols., Edinburgh, 1883, vol. VII, pp.157-63, 440-3.

94. Lady Volunteer, *Eastern Hospitals*, vol. II, p.269.

3 THE CAMPAIGN FOR ARMY SANITARY REFORM

War is the opportunists' festival. Miss Nightingale's appointment had been a minor political expedient. She had seized the chance to enlarge her authority, but her relation to the army and War Office remained anomalous and insecure. With the ending of the war her career was in jeopardy. At 36 she was now a national heroine, the compeer of Grace Darling and Mrs Fry. The 'Lady-in-Chief' enjoyed the sentimental reverence of the nation and the palpable reward of the Nightingale Fund, together with a brooch from her sovereign, being the first woman to be so decorated for public services. The War Office, however, was resolved to end this meddle: ~me coadjuvancy. Moreover, the Nightingale family reported that her hea.th was impaired. It seemed that her great public work must conclude and that she would retire, or return eventually, like any ordinary good woman, to the redcurrant jam of hospital management.

But Miss Nightingale had savoured the political game at the highest level. The commanding of others, the access to privileged information, the making of secret decisions, the entrapment of enemies and promotion of friends, canonisation by the public, had become the foci of her will, the pabulum of her imagination. She had to find a way of continuing in the power game. Her strength was her public standing and the admiration of some important persons; her resource was her capacity for indefatigable intrigue; her justification was the abolition of insanitary muddle in the army and the identification and punishment of those who had blundered. Within limits – the great personages who had per custom declared a war in which they themselves did not fight, who had mismanaged it, and who had botched the peace – they remained beyond Miss Nightingale's censure. She was no radical critic or leveller. She kept clear, for reasons both of faith and prudence, of patriot-agitators in the House of Commons like J.A. Roebuck and Augustus Stafford.[1] They wanted to stigmatise, rather than reconstruct. She, more than they, saw that it was a question of power. To join their campaigns, as a woman in their male parliamentary world, would entail oblivion. Her target comprised the men in the army and War Office who threatened her own reputation and the continuance of her secretaryship: doctors, purveyors, army officers, War Office officials, ministers of the crown. Many of their blunders had already been documented by

Sutherland's Sanitary Commission which had begun ordering improvements early in 1855 and by the McNeill-Tulloch reports on the commissariat in June 1855 and January 1856. All the commissioners found administrative confusion, laziness, timidity, callousness and stupidity. There had been shortages of food, clothing, animal fodder and shelter, but fundamentally the catastrophe of the first winter resulted from a breakdown in distribution ensuing from the High Command's unpreparedness to cope with a prolonged campaign in extreme climatic conditions. In terms of absolute numbers of dead the Crimean losses of 16,300 from disease and 13,000 invalided – compared with 1,760 dying from wounds and 2,660 killed in action – about 46 per cent of the 94,000 men who embarked for the East, amounted to a disaster comparable in modern times only with the calamitous campaign in the Netherlands in 1794-5. It was small consolation that the French losses, at about 70,000 dead and 65,000 invalided were absolutely and relatively greater, and that the uncounted Russian losses were probably larger still.[2] Miss Nightingale had much to be angry about. 'I stand at the altar of the murdered men, and, while I live, I fight their cause', she jotted in a private note of 1856.[3]

Her return to England in July 1856 coincided with the release of a report from the Enquiry of the Chelsea Board of General Officers which had been concocted by the Horse Guards to rebut the findings of the various commissions, especially the severe but balanced reports by McNeill and Tulloch. The Chelsea Board, composed of men who had never seen the Crimea, exonerated staff and regimental officers. 'Nobody was to blame.' The military Barnacles, abetted by ministers who wanted to extinguish a dangerous issue and a public become weary of yesterday's war, joined to bury the problem. Even McNeill and Tulloch, both at the end of their careers, were disposed to give up.[4]

Not so Miss Nightingale: within a fortnight of her homecoming she had wangled an invitation to visit the Queen and was busily prodding McNeill and Tulloch. She needed royal backing for her move to compel Panmure to institute an enquiry into the sanitary condition of the army, as a front for her work. The Queen was a ready tool, but Prince Albert proved difficult. He was, Miss Nightingale found, 'predisposed in favour of the Horse Guards'. She specially equipped herself with details, supplied by McNeill, about Mr Commissary Filder's false excuses about the want of transport to bring fresh meat to the Crimean soldiers, but Albert remained unconvinced. Panmure acquiesced, and then did nothing about it for six months, until March 1857, probably in the ill-founded expectation that Miss Nightingale would drop the matter. Miss Nightingale privately diagnosed him for her friends as possessing 'no courage or conscientiousness' and as 'the most bully-able of mortals'.[5] More accurately, he was a politician in a shaky coalition ministry, committed to reducing expenditure on the army now that peace had come, and adept at lying low on contentious questions. Moreover, Miss Nightingale's demands were extraordinary. She confronted Panmure as a private person with no official standing beyond that of public heroine, and a woman to boot, to demand official sanction for a commission of enquiry, the membership of which would be nominated by her, the procedures of which were to be determined by her, the objects of which were to be defined by her. The whole affair was to be independent of the War Office and Horse Guards, and yet it was to be paid for by government. Only a national heroine who could not imagine limits to her presumption, supported by a queen blind to the implications of that presumption, could have brought off such a coup.

Meanwhile Miss Nightingale was counter-attacking on other fronts. She learnt that Mary Stanley and other ladies were circulating rumours about her high-handedness. She arranged to see Lord Murray, 'amongst several other prominent persons', to tell him 'the truth'. 'You are the very person with whom I should like to make an exception to my rule of silence when attacked, yet I believe that you would be the very person who would advise me not to do so.' None the less, Miss Nightingale repeated that she was not going to enter into public controversy: by implication Lord Murray and other recipients of the truth were to do her fighting for her.[6] She had also heard that Dr Peter Pincoffs, a civilian who had served at the Barrack Hospital and whom she had lately snubbed, was contemplating writing a history of hospital services in the Crimea. Now, in October 1856, she sent him a long, warm invitation to visit her.

> I will mention to you, <u>in confidence</u>, that I am under orders from the Queen, Lord Palmerston, and Lord Panmure to do the same thing in the form of a Précis to be presented to the Government . . . I expect that the consequences to me and the Service will be . . . great harm to my means of usefulness . . . But truth is truth & I shall tell it − my own object in thus writing to you, is to say that it is evidently of great importance that the Reformers should not appear to contradict each other − & therefore, if you would allow me a sight of your manuscript . . . with a hearing of your . . . explanations of it I should esteem it . . . a matter of great value to the Service.

Pincoffs's *Eastern Military Hospitals* is a well-informed account solidly based on the personal experience of a decent man. But several assertions in it, notably that Miss Nightingale won the confidence of most doctors, and that the high quality of the tiny medical school at Scutari owed everything to her, together with the vague hagiographical declarations which intrude into the narrative, suggest that Pincoffs belatedly revised his manuscript to please his new found patroness.[7] It also happens that these dubious assertions are just the ones used by Cook and repeated since by most biographers.

In November Panmure came to Miss Nightingale to settle the membership of her commission. He was now alert to her alliance with the Queen, her general support from Palmerston, the Prime Minister, and her hold over Sidney Herbert who was now out of office and ready to interfere. Panmure was well briefed by the War Office and the army medical authorities. They had equipped themselves with a long memorandum by Sir John Hall which refuted Miss Nightingale's wilder accusations about neglect, dirt and conspiracy.[8] There is no evidence that she knew of the existence of this document although she doubtless expected that Dr Andrew Smith and the War Office would look to their defences. Sidney Herbert was subsequently to use his position as head of the commission to supply Miss Nightingale with as many of Hall's letters as he could extract from the War Office. 'I send you Hall's correspondence. You know the matters treated with all the dates which I do not, and will see in them what I should not.' The proceeding was quite improper. Miss Nightingale relished it: 'I return your stolen goods. Pray keep them carefully. If ever we have to besiege the Army Medical Department, no Lancaster gun could be more formidable than this document.'[9] She took the initiative, confident that she could use the Queen, Palmerston and Herbert. Her list for the commission began with Herbert as president, and included General Storks, Dr Sutherland, Colonel Lefroy and Dr T.G. Balfour, assistant-surgeon to the Grenadier Guards, but a reformer, and former colleague of Tulloch's and already a distinguished medical statistician. Each was an ally, from the Crimea. She had been briefing some of them, at least, for almost a year, letting them think that the ideas were theirs.[10] It was a blatant exercise in packing but the quality was first-rate. Panmure, himself not averse to seeing the army medical service smartened up, proposed only Dr Andrew Smith, and vetoed only two of Miss Nightingale's more outrageous and costly suggestions. During their three hour meeting Miss Nightingale extended the scope of her proposed operations. As she noted afterwards in a triumphant personal memorandum on the interview:

Instructions: general and comprehensive, comprising the whole
Army Medical Department, and the health of the Army, at home
and abroad ... Smith, equal parts lachrymose and threatening,
will say, 'I did not understand that we were to inquire into this'. . . .
    You must drag it through. If not you, no one else.

Herbert now glimpsed glory in his prospective headship of the
commission and busied himself with preparing for it. Miss Nightingale
perceived her danger: 'My master jealous. Does not wish it to be
supposed he takes suggestions from me.' She countered by ignoring
him when issuing her orders to Panmure:

(1) Col Lefroy to be instructed by Lord P. to draw up scheme
and estimate for Army Medical School . . . I won.
    (2) Netley Hospital [the projected new military hospital near
Southampton] plans to be privately reported on by Sutherland and
me to Lord P. I won . . .
    (5) Sir J. Hall not to be made Director-General while Lord P. in
office. I won.
    (6) Colonel Tulloch to be knighted. I lost.[11] [Tulloch was sub-
sequently knighted and McNeill made a Privy Councillor after the
government had blundered early in 1857 by trying to buy them off
with £1000 each. They indignantly refused the offer and, egged on
by Miss Nightingale, they made a public fuss, Herbert raised the
matter in the House of Commons and the government gave in.]

In the event she also gained her two unacceptable nominees: Dr
Thomas Alexander, another Crimean reform ally, specifically recalled at
much expense from Canada; and Sir James Clark, the Queen's
physician, whom Miss Nightingale wanted because it was 'Agreeable to
the Queen to have him – just as well to have Her on our side'.[12]
    Although she had no direct experience of high politics Miss
Nightingale moved effortlessly into the political game. Her forte was
annexation. In an age when ministers could be isolated from their
civil servants and, in a spirit of *noblesse oblige*, cajoled into entrusting
public business to high-born meddlers, her standing and determination
enabled her to gain ill-defined mandates over areas that ministers
deemed peripheral to national concerns. Once gained, the mandate
became the justification for further annexations embodied in particular
reform programmes launched without effective ministerial or financial
control. These she enlarged until she tired of them or until the costs

became so great that government became interested enough to override her. She was not an original thinker. She rarely was first to see what needed amendment and equally rarely did she foresee how the amendment was to be effected. But as a reformer she had four brilliant, unusual gifts. First, she repeatedly discovered and enlisted people with the skills to define problems and formulate solutions. Second, once briefed by her aides she could state the case with compelling clarity and marshall tremendous personal force and persistence in the ensuing battle with officialdom. Third, she possessed an unfailing alertness to the distribution of power and to the ambitions of others, although sometimes this sense was negated by her own ambition and her desire to boast. Finally she acted in the faith that whatever she believed and whatever she proposed to do was practically and morally right. Her memorandum of her interview with Panmure indicates her strengths and limitations. Only one of the main items on the list was her original contribution — the veto on Sir John Hall. Drs Pincoffs and Alexander and Colonel Lefroy, amongst others, had developed the idea of an army medical school and improved conditions of service for army doctors. Dr Sutherland did the critical work on the Netley Hospital designs. Even Tulloch's knighthood was a subject of dinner-table controversy before she took it up. Among her subsequent memoranda on the medical school, the projected courses on ambulance work, field surgery, sanitary reporting and climatology, amongst an impressively thorough list, were, with one notable exception, devised by Sutherland and Alexander. Their ingenuous exception formed the subject of Miss Nightingale's paper to the exclusion of everything else, even nursing: she projected a rigidly hierarchical government for the school that would make it independent of the War Office and effectively subject to her.

Her lust for authority always overset her concern for her policies. A secretary prepared to press reforms, yet vest their authority and prestige in existing government officials, might have found the task harder and might have achieved less in the short run. But Miss Nightingale set her reforms apart from official power and kept them dependent upon her personal force — a force that was really factitious and which often collapsed, taking her reforms with it — as her pretensions were exposed.

Miss Nightingale projected the Royal Commission into the sanitary condition of the army both as a further exposure of Hall, Smith, Fitzgerald & Co., and as an engine for further work on the army. Panmure procrastinated for six months and finally issued the warrant in May 1857.[13] There was, after all, every likelihood that her health would fail in the meantime. Unfortunately for Panmure, the frail Miss Nightingale did not yield and instead forced his hand. She had, she claimed, at their meeting with the Queen at Balmoral in mid-1856, been ordered by him 'in principle' to prepare a confidential report on the sanitary condition of the army. Panmure again had procrastinated until February 1857 before confirming this order. Miss Nightingale meanwhile had already compiled much of her draft. He surrendered to the inevitable and formally gave Miss Nightingale what she wanted — undefined scope. She was invited to discuss not only 'the medical care and treatment of the sick and wounded' but 'the sanatory requirements of the Army generally'. 'In principle', the report was to be confidential, but Miss Nightingale let it be known through Sidney Herbert that she retained the right to publish it if the War Office tried to bury it. In the event the report was absorbed by the Royal Commission, but not before Miss Nightingale had it privately printed and distributed among influential people, including A.W. Kinglake, the historian of the war, who was then beginning his work.[14]

The *Notes On Matters Affecting the Health, Efficiency, And Hospital Administration of the British Army . . . presented by request to the Secretary of State for War* amount to about 230,000 words over 830 pages. The presentation is the granite index of a strong ambitious mind: certainty of opinion at every point; inexorable argument against opponents; digests; recapitulations; numbered brief recommendations artfully planted among the sections; spontaneous audacity in proposing nothing less than a thorough reconstitution of the army medical and purveying departments based on exact detail and elaborate statistical charts to buttress the arguments, all presented in the mimic format of a parliamentary blue book. Three things stand out. The chain of authority planned for the newly independent army medical department would lead ultimately to Miss Nightingale, not to the Commander in Chief. The new Director-General and his subordinates were to report to a 'board of inspection' which was to comprise her nominees. Second, Miss Nightingale's novelistic gifts show both in her flashes of rhetoric:

The observance of sanitary laws should be as much part of the future regime of India as the holding of Military position or as Civil government itself. It would be a noble beginning of the new order of things to use hygiene as the handmaid of civilization — [she was writing during the Mutiny] and in her invention of an exploded piegraph to reinforce visually her assertions about the relative causes of mortality at Scutari through time. Such was her art that her certainties served, apparently incidentally, to highlight the faults of the enemy:

> 'typhoid fever' is well known to be pre-eminently due to foul air, arising from overcrowding and want of drainage; and, till the sanitary works at Scutari were executed [i.e. by Nightingale and the Sanitary Commission], it appears, by Dr. Cumming's own showing [i.e. his report on the varying incidence of diseases] to have prevailed there.[15]

Sanitary reform was her talisman. Only by pressing it as a better preservative of life than clinical treatment could she maintain her standing and keep the doctors and officers at bay. The fall in the death rate after March 1855, following the improvements in drainage and sewage disposal at Scutari, does support her case. But there were other important contributory factors which she played down or ignored. The improvement in the weather after March and the mild second winter must have helped, together with the relative quiescence of the war and the consequent opportunity to improve supplies and shelter for the troops. Miss Nightingale's impressive-looking statistical tables and exploded piegraphs hide these components. None the less her argument was rendered the more persuasive because the doctors were such easy targets. Menzies did ignore the blocked drains at the Barrack Hospital and the overflowing privies at the General Hospital. His notion of sanitation consisted in whitewashing walls. Hall and the purveyors did nothing to expedite the delivery of limejuice while scurvy was rampant. Hall's innate stinginess, reinforced by regulations which he revered both as shield and Holy Writ, led him to delay consignments of medical supplies, even during cholera outbreaks, until each amounted to a full load. Dr Smith let his subordinates assume that only preserved vegetables were to be used at Scutari; yet Scutari was adjacent to a city of 600,000 people who lived on vegetables. Similarly, the purveyors supplied green unroasted coffee beans to troops camped in Turkey where good coffee was the national drink. The Navy Board, Miss Nightingale pointed out, supplied antiscorbutic and fresh vegetables without trouble. Indeed, she had secretly been in touch with the Board while writing this part of her report.[16] But in the Navy anti-scorbutics had been for three-quarters of a century part of the normal food issue, whereas in the army they were 'medical' and therefore to be had only by doctor's requisition. Despite her vehemence on this point, Miss Nightingale's own notions on prevention of scurvy were as limited as the doctors'. She had 600-800 Scutari patients on her extra-diet rolls during the winter of 1854-5: scurvy and allied disorders were widespread yet, according to her own figures, her only contribution was eight quarts of lemonade. Like the doctors she made her stand-bys beef-tea, barley-water and rice puddings. During the summer she had, by doctors' requisition from the official stores, 8,200 oranges and 4,000 lemons, 57 apples and six pounds of quinces, to be distributed among several thousand patients. Her recommended recipe for lemonade for military hospitals was five lemons to 12 pints of water. (Mrs Beeton's 'Nourishing Lemonade' in 1861 requires the juice of 4 lemons and the rinds of 2 to every 1½ pints of water. Modern authorities on diet suggest a daily intake of vitamin C roughly equal to one lemon or orange a day.)[17]

Once she had established the doctors' and purveyors' guilt, Miss Nightingale dismissed them. The fault lay in 'the system'. There was no proper chain of authority, no precise allocation of responsibility, no codes for purchase and distribution of supplies. She brilliantly projected a new system in which every man, from Director-General to hospital orderly would have his set tasks and defined accountability. Medical officers were to be empowered not only to advise, according to an official code, on the siting and sanitation of camps but also they were to insist, upon threat of an official inquiry if things went wrong, that the commanding officer implement their recommendations. Should the commanding officer refuse he was to be required to do so in writing to the War Office.[18] At one stroke a new scale of authority was being planned for the army. (The Horse Guards saw the threat and blocked this provision.) Stewards and purveyors were to be made independent of medical officers' requisitions and were to become responsible for obtaining and distributing all supplies according to prescribed lists, subject only to the orders of the responsible general officers. All failures in supply and distribution were to be reported in writing. Miss Nightingale adopted this procedure from the East India Company hospital system; probably she learnt about it from McNeill, who had been a Company surgeon. Every element of army hygiene, diet, shelter, ventilation, latrines, clothing, rest periods, provision of orderlies, was to be codified. Miss Nightingale, drawing upon excellent advice from her Crimea cronies, provided the codes.

Together the *Notes* constitute an astonishing example of her gift for imagining palpable needs and assembling workable remedies. She was creating a self-acting, self-regulating system, embodying individual will-power in action, designed to secure the maximum output of useful work for the total money and manpower expended. 'Minuting', the War Office's method of gathering opinions and sharing responsibilities for decisions — and of muffling and delaying action — was to stop. Decisions were to be taken quickly, by identifiable officers. 'Minuting', moreover, kept information and decisions inside the War Office: decision-taking by single officials would open the Office to Nightingale influence. The 'minuting' process, in her view, both increased and hid the waste of time, men and materials that accompanied the merely ornamental tokens of status and misdirection and misappropriation of public resources endemic in the closed administrative system.[19] At one blow Miss Nightingale was proposing the transformation of a traditional hierarchical, haphazard and irresponsible yet hidebound establishment into a modern bureaucracy. Private business was to become public service. Miss Nightingale's inclusion of 'efficiency' in the title of her *Notes* is one of the first usages of the word in its modern sense (it did not enter the official military vocabulary until 1864); her use of the word, coinciding with the early moves to reform the civil service, universities, and local government, is a portent of things to come.

Even medical treatments were to be standardised. Miss Nightingale pointed out that at the Crimea, as in every preceding campaign, each surgeon observed the traditional decentralised practice of keeping to his own regimental wards and never officially exchanging reports with his neighbours. No army medical man had the opportunity to specialise. Only a new army medical school could provide the uniform, particularised training that would produce, as the navy medical school at Haslar already did, soundly equipped surgeons trained by experts who were enabled to pursue research. This research necessarily had to be founded upon the reports of a new army medical statistical department, also devised in detail by Miss Nightingale, drawing upon advice from the great statistician, Dr William Farr. Moreover, she pre-empted the findings of the professors and statisticians by providing for a future Barracks Improvement Commission to implement their recommendations about the removal of deleterious influences such as bad ventilation and ill-managed camp canteens.[20]

Each recipient of the report received his particular instructions with it. Earl Grey, for example, was warned that the report was 'confidential' and really intended only for Lord Panmure. Miss Nightingale tactfully directed his attention to the digests by assuring him that he need not 'go through the details ... but it would be the greatest advantage to our cause if you would give the weight of your influence in the House of Lords to such parts as you approve'. The third Earl, a cantankerous, clever man, upset Miss Nightingale's expectations and rebelled: 'I disagree with the emphasis of your report – it was the leadership – not the system – Raglan as compared with Wellington.' Wellington, he argued, dismissed officers who failed in their duty, whereas Raglan neither knew that Hall and Filder had failed nor dismissed them when he was finally informed about them. 'Your standing commissions ... will only *lessen responsibility* of Commanding Officers and Medical Officers', Grey remarked. The Navy had already reformed its medical services without commissions. Grey's precipient truculence endangered Miss Nightingale's whole position. Without the commissions she would have no standing. She immediately sent a vague, emollient reply which Grey graciously accepted as a surrender to his opinions. He was 'glad you think there is no great difference of opinion between us'. Yet she furiously annotated his letter with reiteration of her views: 'only a skilled trained Medical Officer can deal with ... diet, clothing etc.; 'Medical Officers did nothing at Scutari.; 'Army and Navy not to be compared – navy not in barracks and constantly see their men – in relatively stable conditions – army medical officers always confronted with something new'; and then, verging upon a direct negation of Grey's argument, 'must create separate sanitary Division of Army'.[21] Grey is not recorded as referring to her views in the House of Lords. Miss Nightingale was later to try to use him for other objects, but she and Grey never became allies.

She similarly failed to snare A.W. Kinglake. He was willing to make eloquent obeisance in his laborious history to the Lady with the Lamp, but he was much too shrewd to break his links with the War Office and the official clubland world and become a propagandist for the crusading female and her nondescript, elderly, unworldly supporters. Miss Nightingale was astute about people and she summed up Kinglake after their first meeting. She had sought to 'educate' him but he proved non-committal. 'I have been much worried', she told McNeill,

> by making the acquaintance of Kinglake, the historian (to be) of the late war – He had no judicial mind – not much feeling – not much conscience – & takes a superficial view of the whole thing. But his history will be as clever as everything he writes, and every body will read it and be deceived – He repeated to me all the *fadaises* of the Staff; & he gives the whole fund of unexamined commonplaces

(... about the non-supply of clothing etc and the QMGs Dept.) as historical material.[22]

She sent him, indirectly through Mrs Monckton Milnes, a book containing juxtaposed extracts from McNeill's report and the Chelsea Board. Her *Notes* arrived as reinforcement.[23] But Miss Nightingale's estimate that he would not use the critical evidence is borne out by the *History*. It is the first model bland war history: everyone is valiant and no one is to blame, and results are less important than the action. 'He is a good Counsel', she remarked, '[but] he strikes me as a very bad historian.'[24]

After these heady secret dealings with the Queen, Panmure, Lord Murray and other notables, the public Royal Commission on the sanitary state of the army at the Crimea was an anti-climax for Miss Nightingale. Once launched on her secret *Notes*, she had dismissed the projected Royal Commission as a mere public performance. She had not backed Herbert in urging Panmure to proceed with it; indeed, among her intimates she had denigrated Herbert's efforts. Yet when Panmure finally announced it, she insisted upon drawing up, in concert with Sutherland and Dr Alexander, the subjects to be canvassed and the men to be questioned.[25] During the sittings of the Commission she tended to leave the day-to-day management to Sidney Herbert. She proved lax about priming witnesses before they appeared before the Commission and Herbert had to undertake the major part of telling them 'what you want to get out'.[26] Herbert also took the initiative in isolating Dr Andrew Smith on the Commission by altering Smith's draft for the inquiry, without informing him. Miss Nightingale's letters to McNeill and her memorandum of the 1860s (written after Herbert's death) about the Royal Commission, claim that she 'shaped it's daily questions' and imply that she did the work while Herbert played the dilettante figure-head.[27] Their surviving correspondence from this period suggests the opposite: behind Herbert's back she was envious and disparaging.

During the sittings of the Commission Miss Nightingale's concern was to ensure that her spokesmen, Rawlinson, Sutherland, Balfour, Storks, McNeill and Tulloch, were enabled yet again to publish the shortcomings of Hall and his friends and to designate the work in sanitary improvement necessary to prevent such knaves and fools perpetrating another catastrophe. Hall's appearance as a witness posed a dilemma for Miss Nightingale. She wanted to punish him, but she could not risk a further alienation of the army's counter forces in

Parliament and the War Office. His examination had therefore to be as subtle as it was inexorable. She deputed Sutherland to do the job, coached by her after she had checked her brief and copies of Hall's reports with McNeill:

> Sir John Hall is to be examined next week. I have been asked to ask you to give some hints as to his examination . . .
> My own belief is that Hall is a much cleverer fellow than they take him for − almost as clever as Airey [Quartermaster-general at Crimea − he had by agreeing with the implications in every hostile question dextrously evaded the Commission's questions and exonerated himself a few days earlier] . . . I recall to you the long series of proofs of his incredible apathy . . . his not obtaining − lime juice Fresh bread Quinine etc and not denouncing salt meat . . . this man is (morally) the worst of liars. We do not want to badger the old man in his examination, that will only harm us − but we want to take the best out of him for our case.

As Miss Nightingale feared, Hall did well at his examination. He easily answered Herbert's rather vague questions. Sutherland remained mute, while Smith performed brilliantly in feeding Hall obviously prepared questions which enabled him to develop the argument that the death rate at Scutari fell during and after March 1855 because the numbers of sick men admitted to the hospitals fell from 6,000 to 3,000 and further declined thereafter. Miss Nightingale was vexed with Sutherland. 'He lets very inferior men put him down, owing to his want of pith.' Hall, Airey and Smith, by contrast, had lots of pith and were nimble too. In fact, the fair-minded Sutherland agreed with Hall's explanation and privately told Miss Nightingale so. Hall's escape, she lamented to McNeill, 'upsets the conclusion I want to impress on Mr Herbert'.[28]

This setback persuaded her that she must, in addition to having her *Notes* incorporated into the Commission's report, rehearse her main findings in the Commission's printed evidence. Her decision embarrassed Herbert. It was *outré* for a female to appear as an expert witness before a public inquiry. Mrs Caroline Chisholm had done so in 1847; but she was a married woman, and her appearances had been before a select committee of the House of Lords. Moreover, the Commission was Herbert's show. Miss Nightingale was likely to swamp it. But her popularity was such that he could not prevent her appearing should she decide to do so. He realised also that she was vulnerable.

Smith and Hall had demonstrated that the reduced death rates at Scutari could be attributed to causes other than her ministrations. Smith was a cool man. If she tried to hector him she might divide the Commission and ruin its standing. Herbert tried to restrict her to presenting evidence only on hospital construction.

> But this [she complained to McNeill] leaves untouched the great matters which will affect (& have affected) the mortality of our sick more than any mere Architecture could do ... People Government and Sovereign think everything has been remedied — but nothing has — It would be treachery to the memory of my dead if I were to seem to give in to the popular error ... Please advise.[29]

She did not want advice. She wanted McNeill's acquiescence in her decision to give evidence, and possibly a letter from him to Herbert approving her plan, because on that same day she sent an almost identical letter to Herbert announcing her intention to canvass the whole issue of disease, mortality and medical organisation in the army. She had also decided that she would not appear in person, but tender evidence in writing — thousands of words from the *Notes*, tables, graphs — a procedure as outlandish as a female expert giving evidence in person. Herbert then tried to persuade her to make her evidence 'confidential' and to leave it out of his report. She reluctantly agreed at first, but it appeared none the less.[30]

This episode is a signal illustration of the contrariety in her nature between the craving to dominate unseen and the impulse to enjoy public recognition of that dominance. She began by flattering herself with outright refusals, then played hard to get and finally made herself available for capture.

Her life is crowded with such contrarieties. At Scutari she repeatedly evaded requests from Jerry Barrett, the painter, to sit for her portrait. He had travelled specially from England to accomplish the feat. 'I have determined in no way to <u>forward</u> the making a show of myself or of any ... thing connected with that work though I cannot always <u>prevent</u> them from being made a show of.' She never refused Barrett outright. She visited his studio and although she would not sit for him she took a continued interest in his picture of 'Florence Nightingale at Scutari' and frequently came to study its progress.[31] The painting is now in the National Portrait Gallery and is reproduced on the £10 note. She never refuted Parthe's story that she refused to sit for or to look at the bust by John Steell, presented to her by the non-commissioned officers of the army in 1862. Yet she permitted the distribution of replicas.[32] In 1868 she refused a request for a photograph from Dr William Rendle, her ally in attempting to reform workhouse infirmaries. 'I never had one done, except once by command. [The portrait of 1856, taken for Queen Victoria.] I have a superstition, as far as myself am concerned, against "images made with hands" − & would rather leave no memorial . . . either of name or anything else − but only of God, whose unworthy servant I am.' Cook lists five portrait photographs taken before this letter was written. In 1887 she refused her 'ever dearest "Little Sister"', nurse Pringle, a photograph of a portrait statuette. Next year she gave one of the statuettes to a Scandinavian admirer.[33] These coy fluctuations in her projection of her self sometimes plunged into flamboyant self-extinction. Quite apart from her anonymous, celebrated return from the Crimea as Miss Smith and her unheralded but again celebrated return to Lea Hurst, she twice announced her impending death. In November 1857 she placed among her papers an envelope addressed to Sidney Herbert, marked 'to be sent when I am dead'. The letter comprises four pages of mingled recrimination, hints at reconciliation and arch withdrawal:

> I hope you will not regret the manner of my death. I know that you will be kind enough to regret the fact of it. You have some-times said that you were sorry you had employed me. I assure you that it has kept me alive. I am sorry not to stay alive to do the 'Nurses' [Report on female nursing in army] . . . I must be willing to go now as I was to go to the East . . . Perhaps He wants a 'Sanitary Officer' now for my Crimeans in some other world where they are gone.

In February 1862 she prepared a similar letter, leaving directions about their future joint publications, for Dr Sutherland. The letters appear not to have been sent.[34] She survived on both occasions and there is no evidence to suggest that she had grounds for believing that she would die or commit suicide. Both letters appear to have half-stifled pleas for work and sympathy. Between 1864 and 1872 she separately told Mrs Bracebridge, Mary Jones, her High Church nursing disciple, and Dr Jowett of Balliol, that when she became infirm she wished to be taken to St Thomas's, left anonymously in a general ward 'and left there to die', thence to be buried anonymously. Each was 'not to breathe a word of this'. Apparently only Jowett was alarmed enough to try to dissuade her, or at least only his reply survives. He was down to earth. Her intention was 'eccentric'; besides 'it will kill you . . . and it will annoy your father'.[35] Jowett, like the rest of Miss Nightingale's friends, believed that she suffered from impaired health, the results of her privations at the Crimea. I shall return to this belief later.

Extinction of self also saved bother. Miss Nightingale regularly pleaded mingled modesty, pressure of business and ill health for refusing to allow her name to be used in connection with public committees and good causes. Moreover, as she explained to Richard Aspden, the secretary to the Manchester Clinical Hospital for Children which had elected her an honorary governor, she could not join organisations which she had not helped to create because there was always something wrong with them. In the Manchester case, she could not approve the rules by which they conducted their nursing.[36] Yet the self-hatred that issued from insecure narcissism ran very deep. Miss Nightingale, the stickler for accurate statistics, described herself in her return for the 1871 census as 'Imbecile & Blind'; and then boasted to Sutherland of having done so.[37] In 1872 she drafted a note to Aunt Mai remarking that she was glad she had never married and had children. Children ensured the continuance of self in the world, beyond the control of self and that was a prospect, in the light of Francis Galton's recent discoveries about heredity, 'immeasurably awful'.[38] 'Be of good cheer. I have overcome the world', she quoted St John of the Cross on a scrap of paper about 1873. 'Verily he has overcome all things in whom the pleasures of them excite no joy, & the bitterness of them no sadness.' That is 'indifference', she commented, 'not overcoming'.[39]

Sometimes Miss Nightingale thought herself to be the crucified Christ. At other times she thought herself to be an animate nothing, existing only in the will. But whether Christ recrucified or animate nothing, her will to work was continually thwarted by lazy, hostile men. Her struggle, she liked to tell others, was so much onerous because she was so womanly and diffident. She mused beguilingly to Jowett that she wished she 'had the combative faculty. It _is_ such a power to carry me [sic] through life.'[40]

The Herbert Commission's report fell flat. The press and the quarterlies were preoccupied with the Indian Mutiny, while Panmure, probably deliberately, tabled it in the House of Lords in February 1858 in the midst of the row over the Conspiracy to Murder Bill. The report was never debated in Parliament. The shaky ministries of the late 1850s did not dare upset the parliamentary colonels. The colonels' contributions to a short debate on a resolution moved by Viscount Ebrington, the sanitary reformer, deploring high mortality in the army, demonstrated the wrath that could descend from both sides of Parliament. The Commander in Chief, the Duke of Cambridge, received a special copy from Sidney Herbert. He very sensibly declined to give an opinion on it because it dealt with 'matters with which he is unacquainted'.[41]

Had the report been Miss Nightingale's rather than Sidney Herbert's, she would have busied herself promoting it. But she spent most of the autumn and winter of 1857 recruiting her health at Great Malvern. She left the task of arranging for favourable reviews in the quarterlies to Herbert and Edwin Chadwick, who had lately offered his services as sanitary ally to the great lady.[42] Late in December she casually told McNeill in a dictated letter − for she now declared herself too ill to write − that she 'had 10,000 copies printed − to circulate among medical and commanding officers'. In a draft in her own hand to McNeill, presumably made before the dictated note, the number was 2,000 and there was no suggestion that they had yet been printed. This idea she had presumably from Chadwick, who had used it to win acclaim for his Poor Law and Sanitary Reports. There is no evidence that she proceeded with the scheme. She was more concerned with having copies of her exploded piegraphs of army mortality framed, glazed and then sent to be hung at the Horse Guards, War Office and Army Medical Department. This gift was to be a 'flank march upon the enemy . . . "God's revenge upon Murder"'.[43] When Chadwick confessed in March 1858 that he had made little headway with publicising the report and getting a cheap edition onto railway stalls, Miss Nightingale complacently told Sidney Herbert that it did not 'really matter . . . Army matters are going on too well for that'.[44]

The commissions for army sanitary improvement, as provided for in Miss Nightingale's *Notes* and the report of the Royal Commission, were already at work. Panmure had finally conceded them official recognition in November 1857,

with such ample instructions for 'preparing draft Instructions & Regulations defining the duties etc etc etc etc and revising the Queens General Medical Officers, Barracks, Purveyor's and Hospital Regulations' − as you may guess, she crowed to McNeill, who had by now largely replaced her father as recipient of such confidences

> they were written by me — What a fool Panmure must be! Does he not see or does he not care where this will lead him? . . . All that is necessary now is to keep Mr Herbert up to the point . . . This new Sub-Committee [on Army Hospital organisation and management] entails upon me a labor I must gladly undertake.[45]

She had immediately repaired to Great Malvern, taking Aunt Mai with her.

Three days after Panmure's commission arrived, on 19 November 1857, Aunt Mai was compelled to finish a letter that her niece had begun but was unable to complete. The letter was to Lady McNeill. Aunt Mai had to

> say at her desire that her health is failing every week, and that she is compelled to give up any writing not absolutely necessary for business . . . She desires me to add . . . that it is of the utmost consequence to her, that no alarm concerning her health should be communicated to anyone. If it were to reach Mr Herbert he might from a desire to spare her, refrain from giving her the means of helping in the work, which would . . . fatal to [her] health, for which the only relief possible is advance in the work, to which she feels herself devoted.

The kindly, motherly Lady McNeill was expendable, unlike her husband. She was upset by the bad news and wrote to enquire more particularly about Miss Nightingale's illness. Aunt Mai replied that 'Dr [Walter] Johnson [the fashionable hydropathic practitioner] calls it "tension of the nerves" . . . Her head is as clear for work as ever . . . She is quite unable to do more than this, or you would hear from her . . . please ask Sir John to send copies of the Hospital Diets of Edinburgh Infirmary and tell him that she and Mr Herbert have fixed the Field Purveyorships.' (A second draft of this letter says that Herbert 'would not go far enough on the Purveyorships . . . and so the Report does not show this'.[46] This second version seems to be more correct. The recommendation was never pressed.)

It is universally accepted that Florence Nightingale endured a lifetime of debility and confinement to her bed after the Crimea. Sir George Pickering, in *Creative Malady*, argued that her illness, in common with that of other valetudinarian celebrities, gave her room to think and work. Sir George relied upon the evidence published by her biographers. Her unpublished papers suggest a more complicated story. Aunt Mai, the ill-used secretary, reported to Lady McNeill in January 1858 that Florence's health varied 'from week to week, with no real change or progress'. Yet she had 'very little treatment in the way of water cure, but the . . . comparative quiet makes it very suitable for her'. She remained in her room and saw no one 'except on business'. Aunt Mai thought that despite Florence's nervous tension, 'her head was never clearer or more able for business'. Miss Nightingale herself described her illness as 'nervous fever'.[47]

She was still hard at work on hospital matters in March 1859, when she wrote in her own hand to thank McNeill for data he had sent her. She invited him to visit her when next he was in London: there was 'much to talk about . . . Ministers are insecure.' (She was right. Lord Derby's second administration finally crashed in June 1859.) As an afterthought she invited Lady McNeill, too. But they had to come at a time of her choosing, when she was well enough to talk. She further stipulated that she was 'not able to see more than one person at a time, especially those who interest me so much' — to the end of her life she continued this practice of excluding witnesses — And she reinforced the prohibition by announcing that she was 'not able to sit up at all'. Nowhere in this letter does she say that she is ill.[48] Instinctively she had devised the perfect situation for compelling the attention of her chosen visitors and maximising the chances that the visitor would confide in her and undertake her behests. In mid-1861 she recruited as secretary her uncle Sam Smith, Aunt Mai's husband. (Aunt Mai had returned to her family in 1860, after two and a half years' absence, and thereafter Miss Nightingale refused to speak to her for almost 20 years.) He was directed to answer all letters from unimportant 'fools'. A few months later, in August 1861, she instructed him that she was too ill to see callers, 'especially Chadwick and the Herberts'. Uncle Sam was to give no one her address. In future he was to receive all her correspondence at his address, and bring it to her daily. She would leave the 'fools'' letters to him while, 'To anyone whom I want to see I can write myself.' Like others dismayed at her illness, impressed by her selflessness, and awed by her imperiousness, Uncle Sam acquiesced.[49]

Occasionally she diagnosed her indeterminate illness to suit her correspondent. In 1860 she drafted a note to Mrs Monckton Milnes telling her that a mutual friend had a 'weak heart and dropsy' and that he might 'die tomorrow — or live on for years to a painful death'. 'Alas', Miss Nightingale went on, 'it is [words deleted] in some respects the "prognosis" which has been made of me.' At other times she reported herself to be suffering from, according to Mrs Gaskell, 'over-pressure of the brain telling on the spine . . . necessitating rest' (1863); rheumatism of the spine and right elbow (1865); shortage of breath (1865) and 'spasms' of the lungs (1866), both on occasions when she had to visit her mother; chest 'attacks', which left her unable to speak, when Lizzie Herbert sought to call (1867); bereft of an 'ounce of strength' when she refused Chadwick's request to back him publicly in his parliamentary candidature (1868); 'feeling as if the top of my head was blown off' while excusing herself to Sutherland for being behindhand in correcting a draft (1869); 'too ill to move-probably' in 1870, when she put off a visitor, and instead travelled to the country on the day of the proposed visit; attacks of ague while discussing Indian ague with Sir Ranald Martin, 'completely knocked down with uncountable pulse and 90 hours of no sleep' again while she was visiting her mother, and forestalling another visitor (1879). In 1884, when apologising for being out when W.E. Gladstone called, she claimed to have a 'threatened return' of diabetes which she said she had first suffered in 1880. During the spring of 1888 she told Douglas Galton, her nephew and ally in sanitary reform, that she had had pleurisy for three months and been scarcely able to leave her bed, and was too ill to see him. Galton, as one of her team, had had his salary paid by the War Office. A dispute about this procedure had arisen in 1887 and Miss Nightingale had neglected to pull strings on Galton's behalf.[50] Miss Nightingale's 'Household Book' for 1888 shows that she ate heartily throughout that year. When she did suffer precise functional disorders, she did not broadcast the fact. In January 1877 she recorded with surprise that she had had 'diarrhoea all night'. (She seems to have come through the Crimea with no stomach disorders.) The diarrhoea attack did not prevent her from working all the next day. In 1873 she had the first intimations that her eyesight was impaired, but this disability did not seriously hinder her work until about 1884, when she was in her mid-60s; although her powers and interest in the world had begun to diminish about thirteen years earlier. In 1887, the jubilee, as she recalled, of Christ's first appearance to her and of her consecration to His work, she admitted to herself that 'old age had set in'.[51]

Before then her difficulty had been that she looked so well. During the mid-1860s she became plump and lost the wan spareness of her youth and Crimean years. Her journalist ally Harriet Martineau, herself an invalid who found that condition convenient, wrote silkily to Miss Nightingale in 1865 that an acquaintance had reported her to be looking very healthy: 'Julia has written that your face is deceptive, — that wld make uninformed people suppose you to be much less suffering than you are.' Miss Nightingale reassured her: 'I fail much. I never leave my bed, except to see my masters. My face is so swelled, especially when I make any such exertion, that I suppose this is what is meant by my "looking well".'[52]

Although she kept to her bed during interviews, she was always fully dressed and even into old age she sat upright unpropped by pillows.[53] Her indeterminate illnesses did not give her doctors much to work on. There is but one medical prescription among the Nightingale Papers: a general 'appetizing tonic' based on salicylic acid, phosphoric acid and sodium hypophosphate. She regularly purchased seltzer in 1877. Sir James Clark advised not to overstrain her brain in 1867 because that organ, if overworked, appropriated 'more than its own natural share of the nervous energy of the system', but nowhere in his diagnosis does he mention any general weakness or physical disability. Nonetheless, the family always reported her to be feeble, despite her looks, and her intimate, Dr Benjamin Jowett, when they took communion privately together, usually read her the lessons from the service for visitation of the sick.[54]

It remains indisputable that whenever Miss Nightingale announced herself to be ill she was busy. She told Rev. Mother Clare Moore in 1867 that she had been delayed in writing, because she had had a very bad 'attack on my Chest', which had prevented her from lying down 'for 17 nights'. Miss Nightingale added that she could 'scarcely . . . get on' with her work. This last was vexing because, 'We are having a very uphill fight about the workhouses.' Even when she complained of the rheumatism in the spine and elbow, and could not 'crook my finger and think to hold my pen', she did not stop writing 'for a single day'.[55] On official visits outside her house she travelled with great fuss in an ornate invalid carriage. When she went to Lea Hurst or Embley she took a special carriage on the train. Yet surreptitiously she walked in Hyde Park and there are two episodes which suggest that her weakness was feigned. Her niece, Rosalind Nash, recalled visiting her at South Street in the 1880s. Miss Nash encountered two of the junior servants racing each other down the stairs to the basement. One fell. 'I hurried upstairs to report, feeling very anxious . . . I opened the door, and there was Aunt Florence standing near me. I had always seen her half lying down ... I was struck with wonder.' On another occasion, probably also in the 1880s, Miss Nash and her brother met their aunt in the garden,

> We should have kept out of the way ... because of her health ... I saw the reason, for she flushed at seeing us and for once looked slightly disturbed ... She had been sailing along down the little glade ... and I saw then how beautifully she walked.[56]

She had conscripted her very body in her cause. Despite her misuse of her flesh and bone she lived for ninety years. Like many great figures in history she possessed a frame that matched her will.

Disabled or not, her work in the later 1850s and through the 1860s was unremitting. In most of her campaigns Miss Nightingale was in the right. The War Office perpetrated its blunders blatantly and uncaringly, without regard to her advice. Panmure and his officials drew great applause for their decision to build a new military hospital worthy of the men of the Crimea. They proceeded to buy a site on marshy ground near a sewage outfall, at a grossly inflated price of £30,000. Then they built a hospital costing £300,000, about twenty times the amount then customarily spent upon such a project. Much of the money went on the facade and even more on the special foundations required for the unsuitable ground. The interior was skimped. Miss Nightingale criticised the nine bed wards as being too small for 'discipline', and she was the more offended because the authorities had ignored her suggestion that the hospital be designed on the pavilion system, to provide maximum ventilation and light to reduce infection. Each ward opened off a long central corridor and the beds were ranged along the dim, unventilated blank walls.[57]

Sidney Herbert played a double game about the hospital. He had helped press for it and ensure that money was lavished on it. Once the scheme went wrong he sheered off and became a mild critic. Miss Nightingale meanwhile, having diagnosed the shortcomings, found herself blocked from effecting changes. Herbert, without telling her, finally secured from Palmerston in January 1857 an agreement to refer the plans to his Barracks and Hospital Improvement Committee.[58] She used the Committee to force through a redesign of the water closets, which had been provided without ventilation in the original plans, and a few other improvements. But it was Herbert who enlisted Douglas Galton, the future great engineer, to improve radically the

Netley ventilation system, and then Herbert boasted of it to Miss Nightingale.[59] But the damage was done. Netley Hospital never worked efficiently. Every winter the water froze in the washrooms along the corridor. Indian patients caught pneumonia. The floors, against her advice, were made of wood rather than encaustic tile, and were always damp.[60] Herbert's real interest in keeping Miss Nightingale at bay, apart from their rivalry for reputation as reformers, was to ensure that one of Mary Stanley's ladies at the Crimea, Mrs Shaw Stewart, a widow with impeccable social connections and High Church allegiance, should be appointed matron. She was a mettlesome woman, experienced in nursing and controlling staff, and she had clashed with Miss Nightingale at the Crimea. Mrs Shaw Stewart and Herbert together had stipulated, illegally, that the female nurses at Netley must all be Church of England by persuasion.[61]

After Herbert's death in 1861 Miss Nightingale found herself able to take a closer interest in Netley. Although she disliked Jane Shaw Stewart she consistently backed the matron in her endless rows with the army authorities. In a typical brush Miss Nightingale fought to get the matron the right to possess keys to the linen cupboards, hitherto held only by the purveyor.[62] When in the mid-1860s Mrs Shaw Stewart was finally driven out and the hospital reverted to male nursing management it fell into a dreadful state. There were no fixed times for dressing or feeding patients, bed sores became widespread and 'the medical cadets tried all sorts of "fancies" on [their patients] and no one interfered'.[63] A new matron, Mrs Deeble, and six nurses, all from St Thomas's Hospital, were appointed with Miss Nightingale's connivance, against the will of the Netley medical authorities. Mrs Deeble, trained in a hard school, soon put matters to rights. The timetable became effective and the bed sores and much else were reported in writing to the senior medical officer. She rebuked cadets in front of patients. Miss Nightingale rejoiced: 'They have caught a Tartar in her – Mrs S. Stewart was a dove!'[64]

The establishment of the hospital at Netley upset Miss Nightingale's plan for a large army medical school. She had wanted the new hospital to be built at Aldershot 'where the troops will be'. Ideally, it should have been added to the Woolwich hospital but this institution, so far as Miss Nightingale and Sidney Herbert were concerned, was a lost cause because it was controlled by Dr Andrew Smith. Netley's small wards and distance from London seemed likely to keep the numbers low. But delay could kill the project, so she settled for the inauguration of the medical school at Fort Pitt at Chatham and acquiesced in the decision that the school would move to Netley when the hospital there was sufficiently developed to receive it.[65]

Miss Nightingale and Herbert had succeeded in nominating old Crimean friends, Longmore, Martin, Parkes and Aitken, to the professorships. But the War Office contrived to appoint the safe Dr Gibson as Director-General. Throughout his regime he managed to hinder the researches of his colleagues and upset the female nursing staff. The school was never a success. The low status of surgeons in the army continued to deter good applicants. The teaching seems to have been mediocre. The senate of the school, dominated by Gibson and the War Office, regularly forestalled attempts to make hygiene a compulsory subject. Even Miss Nightingale's admirers among the staff were embarrassed by her attempts to institute a 'system of marks to be assessed on each day's work', a procedure she devised to rid the school of indolent 'Irishmen who can pass examinations'.[66] Its best teaching standards were probably attained during the early 1870s when, against Miss Nightingale's wishes, naval medical teachers and surgeons were introduced into the school. Its best practical results were probably achieved in India, where the army surgeons could apply the sanitary measures they had been taught. Miss Nightingale had insisted from the outset upon courses in hygiene but equally Parkes, Martin and their colleagues, devoted practical sanitarians all, would have emphasised such teaching without her dictation. After her influence waned in the later 1860s, contemporaneously with advances in antiseptic surgery and other clinical procedures, the Tory governments of 1867 and 1874-80 set about dismantling the Netley medical school and the succeeding Liberal government completed the destruction by enabling intending army surgeons to enrol at university medical schools. Edward Cardwell, as War Secretary, had already ended the old invidious regimental medical system in 1870 and had made all medical officers staff officers. The Netley school eventually moved to London and became an affiliate of the University of London medical schools. Miss Nightingale fought every move, striving to retain her grip on appointments and curricula, but from the later 1860s she lost every battle.[67] But she and Sidney Herbert had raised army medicine nearer to the level of navy medicine and without their lobbying it would have dragged on in its old routines a great deal longer.

Miss Nightingale's attempts to capture the whole army medical department through her projected supreme 'board of inspection' had equally mixed results. The War Office successfully fended off the board, which threatened their autonomy. They were unable to prevent

Sidney Herbert gaining a royal warrant to improve the pay and promotion opportunities of medical officers, but they managed to exclude guards' regiments' medical officers from it and thereby destroyed its effectiveness. The warrant failed Herbert's and Nightingale's hopes that it would raise medical officers' standing with their brother officers and thereby attract better men to the service. Medical officers of appropriate rank were still blocked from presiding at a board or in the mess. The warrant was finally withdrawn, under Horse Guards' pressure, in 1864.[68] Cardwell's reforms of 1870, which ended the regimental medical officer system, proved equally ineffective in raising the medical officers' standing.[69] Devious and authoritarian though her methods were, Miss Nightingale's priorities were right. But the inward-looking upper-class army headed by the stupid Duke of Cambridge would not learn. In every campaign during her lifetime, except the China War of 1857-8 when Crimean memories made the army careful in sanitary matters, disease continued to kill more men than battle.

Miss Nightingale's two main successes were associated with improvements that had been proceeding since the 1830s, in the collection of army health statistics, which T.G. Balfour had already organised, and in the improvement of barracks and camp accommodation. In both endeavours she drew on expert advice: from William Farr for epidemiological statistics and Douglas Galton for barracks construction. The War Office saw no threat in strengthening the statistical office of the army and Balfour, aided by Farr, went on to produce admirable sets of figures. Miss Nightingale's view of statistics was a simple one which she shared with her reforming contemporaries. Exact enumeration was the basis for the indication of exact social laws, from which the moral consequences of various forms of action could be predicted. Statistics were the unequivocal indicators of weaknesses and strengths in a system and the inescapable tests of the responsible human agents. Statisticians were the testers and moral guides.[70]

Barracks improvement really got under way in mid-1855 when Lord Shaftesbury took it up and induced Palmerston to provide some money for it. He, like Miss Nightingale, who came to the question in 1856, saw the problem chiefly as one of bad ventilation and filth which in turn produced physical and moral debility in the troops.[71] The Barracks Improvement Commission, comprising Herbert, Sutherland and Galton, worked extremely hard, visiting barracks all over England and recommending changes. At Wellington Barracks, for example, they urgently suggested ten additional baths, to cost £1,263; at St George's Barracks, additional latrines, baths and improved ventilation, at £5,786. G.C. Lewis, the Chancellor of the Exchequer, vetoed their recommendations. 'NCOs and Privates', he declared, did not 'understand the use of water closets.'[72] There were grounds for his opinion. At the Crimea the new WCs had been regularly blocked with old boots and food scraps. Miss Nightingale tried to evade this Treasury ruling, to Sidney Herbert's amazement, by launching a building programme and presenting the Treasury and War Office with a *fait accompli* when the bills came in. Apparently Herbert succeeded in warning her off.[73] But improvements did go forward. By 1862 the barracks at Chelsea, Gravesend, Colchester, York, Fleetwood, Pembroke, Malta and Gibraltar had variously received better ventilation, cookhouses and recreational dayrooms for the soldiers. Expenditure rose from £233,000 in 1854 to over £756,000 in 1859. By 1864 every barracks in England had 'ample water', one washbasin for every ten men and a bath for every 100. Unfortunately, there were still no regulations to compel the troops to wash themselves or their clothes.[74]

The Barracks Improvement Commission succeeded partly because it escaped Treasury and War Office control. It was chartered, like the Sanitary Commission and McNeill-Tulloch Commission at the Crimea, to institute improvements on the spot. This potentially enormously powerful breach in Treasury suzerainty had been conceived, not by Miss Nightingale or Sidney Herbert, but by Lord Shaftesbury, who had been appalled by the reports of mismanagement at the Crimea and had persuaded his step father-in-law, Palmerston the new Prime Minister, and the new War Secretary, Panmure, probably without any of them realising the constitutional implications, to send improvement commissioners with executive powers.[75] Shaftesbury also took a keen interest in the barracks question and travelled on tours of inspection, followed by Edwin Chadwick, in 1855. But possibly only Miss Nightingale glimpsed the opportunities that such commissions opened to outsider-reformers.

The improvements began to save life almost immediately. The death rate of the army at home fell from 17 per 1,000 in 1855 (double the rate of male civilians in comparable age-groups) to 9.95 per 1,000 in 1860 and to 8.86, or slightly above the comparable civilian average, in 1865.[76]

The Nightingale-Sutherland-Herbert barracks and hospital improvement programme rested upon the fixed idea that overcrowding and dirt were the prime and only generators of disease. Miss Nightingale had held this belief since at least her Harley Street days, when probably she had acquired it from Chadwick and other sanitarians writing in the 1840s. Subsequent speculations about the mechanics of the miasmic theory, whether the inhalation of putrescent substances oxidised and corrupted the bloodstream, or whether the exhalations of such substances or affected persons introduced poisons into neighbouring bodies, never interested her. Her objects were political, not scientific. Such speculations, especially theories about specific causative agents of specific diseases, and germ theory emerging in the 1860s, she detested because she perceived them as barriers to action, devices to enable medical practitioners to dabble uncontrolled whilst practical sanitarians were shackled.

Epidemiologists who questioned these assertions were attacked with lofty severity. In 1858 Dr E. Headlam Greenhow inferred from the history of measles epidemics in the Faroe Islands that there was an 'incubative' stage in disease 'carried by contagion'. He also argued that scarlet fever was a 'contagious' disease, that is, it developed from a specific illness-inducing agent transmitted from one infected person to another. Miss Nightingale, writing anonymously, rejected his theories.

> This is not sanitary doctrine and would be sustained . . . by no careful observer . . . It never appears to occur to the advocates of specific 'contagions' that there must have a <u>first</u> case in the world, which could not have received its 'infection' or 'contagion' from any other case; and hence, according to Dr Greenhow's doctrine, the Supreme Being must have directly infected it.

She went on to affirm that it was better to work on the proven rule that 'disease results from the infringement of known and unknown laws . . . The cure for "infection", if there be "infection", is cleanliness and fresh air'. Miss Nightingale, self-proclaimed as a passionate statistician, did not attempt to meet Greenhow's figures. His so-called evidence was 'utterly futile . . . All such alleged facts require to be tried by the ordinary rules of evidence, and when so tried, they fail.'[77] As we now know, Greenhow was right in his brilliant surmises. Miss Nightingale's scorn was the more virulent because Greenhow, recently appointed to the first lectureship in public health in the kingdom, at St Thomas's Hospital, was a dangerous rival. His paper was published as an official report to the Board of Health. He was also the ally of an even more threatening figure, Dr John Simon, then just beginning his great career as the proponent of scientific epidemiology and public health under the wing of central government.

The statistician, G.P. Neison, also challenged the 'sanitary-amateurs' by demonstrating, rather dubiously, that 'overcrowded' areas did not show significantly higher rates for consumption than uncrowded areas. His measures were crude, and his explanation, 'want of exercise', was even less commonsensical than the Nightingale-Sutherland argument that consumption resulted from 'shortage of good air' caused by overcrowding. The reply to Neison, published in the *Westminster Review* is signed, against the journal's custom, S(idney) H(erbert). But it reads as if it was drafted, at least, by Miss Nightingale. Typically, Neison's statistics pass unremarked. Instead the author simply reiterates that it is 'obvious . . . that the habitual admission of vitiated air will injure the lungs and produce pulmonary disease, just as the admission into the stomach of poisoned food will destroy that organ'.[78]

Apart from Herbert, Miss Nightingale marshalled other friends to write 'independent' condemnations of Greenhow's and Neison's papers. She tactfully indicated the lines of each reply and supplied its substance, her unpublished report on the army medical service in the Crimea. 'It is strictly private and confidential', she insinuated when sending a copy to Chadwick. 'I thought however I was in duty bound to send a copy to you who have always been our leader.' He duly seconded the Nightingale-Sutherland line at the Glasgow meeting of the National Association for the Promotion of Social Science in 1860. She often used Chadwick to bell cats, as he sought to use her reputation and money in his attempts to enter parliament. But she regarded him as a lightweight who was 'not scientific'; he was among those forbidden to visit her.[79] He in turn frequently defaulted on his promises as publicity agent: she equally refused to support his campaigns publicly. They were wary rivals, allied by necessity in promoting their separate careers as sanitary reformers.

Miss Nightingale continued throughout her life to support defenders of the miasmic theory. Diehards such as Douglas Galton in the 1870s, (he quietly changed his mind in the mid-1880s) Sir J. Clarke Jervoise in the 1880s and Dr Elizabeth Blackwell in the 1890s were inspired by her example when disputing specific germ disease theory.[80] Each advance in germ theory diminished the sanitary reformers' opportunities to advocate work that won public esteem. Miss Nightingale liked to say that 'facts are everything — doctrines are nothing'[81] but the fight during the 1860s about the classification of disease data shows how doctrines can create facts. Dr Farr and Miss

Nightingale fought to retain generalised 'zymotic' categorisations — engendered from outside from dirt and other avoidable conditions — which implied a rebuke to government and a need for preventive action. Dr Simon and the medical profession, including Dr Balfour who proved traitor to the Nightingale group on this issue, pressed for a less politically charged, more precise 'gridiron' classification listing the disease, the parts affected in every case, and as many special pathological features as could be conveniently included. Simon won.[82]

Quarantine also posed threats to Miss Nightingale's usefulness and she fought it equally vehemently and unavailingly. Despite increasing evidence to the contrary, especially in relation to smallpox in Britain and cholera in India, she never departed from the assertion that 'Quarantine is a complete failure.' Quite apart from its restrictions on individual freedom and international trade, quarantine implied official endorsement for contagionist theory and, as the Ottoman Empire demonstrated, an excuse for authority to evade its sanitary duties.[83] Depending upon her correspondent, she could even make contagion theory and quarantine anti-Christian. She informed Jowett that whenever the facts were established 'in Science . . . those facts will show a "moral" — the best "moral" . . . [showing] best the perfect God, leading men to perfection. "Contagion" would then shew God a Devil.' When smallpox broke out in Oxford in 1871 she instructed Jowett to ensure that the college rooms were 'thoroughly aired'; this would obviate the need to send the undergraduates away.[84]

The Herbert-Nightingale work for army sanitary reform had become firmly established by the time of Herbert's failure in health in late 1860 and ensuing death in August 1861. Their partnership, thanks to Miss Nightingale's and her biographers' celebration of it, is one of the most famous in British history. The surviving evidence suggests a more precarious alliance. Until the Crimean episode, Miss Nightingale had been closer to Mrs Herbert than to her husband. In 1849, two years after their first meeting in Rome, Florence called her 'the Spirit of Love'.[85] Miss Nightingale found Lizzie Herbert a useful mouthpiece during the Harley Street escapade, but their intimacy turned cold when Lizzie succumbed to Mary Stanley and abetted the Anglo-Catholic party at the Crimea. Thereafter Florence's career demanded that she cultivate Sidney Herbert rather than his wife. He was a genuine reformer imbued with a mixture of *noblesse oblige* due to family piety and Peelite impatience with muddle. Doubtless he would have moved independently to improve the army medical service and camp accommodation after the Crimean débâcle but he proved dilatory even under Miss Nightingale's goading and rivalry and his efforts would have been limited and weakly pursued. Above all, Miss Nightingale established for him what had to be done. He needed her to lend momentum to his cause but in acceding to the alliance he found himself gundog to an inexorable and untiring huntress.

Herbert had been unwell since at least January 1858 when he complained to Miss Nightingale that he suffered 'neuralgic headache and tic in the temple and jaw'. He was inhaling and, as he remarked, making himself sick with, 'Christchurch Remedy' – a mixture of chloroform and camphor, topped off with numerous glasses of brandy. She apparently countered by claiming to suffer the same affliction. Herbert's ailments left Miss Nightingale unmoved.[86] Behind his back she waged a quiet battle for the total allegiance of their shared factotums. 'Sidney Herbert is very forgetful', she warned young Captain Galton in 1860. He had failed to move on the 'Cape Hospital Huts (which you are to design) ... No one appreciates as I do Mr Herbert's great qualities. But no one feels more the defect in him of all administrative capacity in details.'[87]

The worse his illness became, the more exigent she became. She needed him to reform the War Office before he became incapable. Her view of 'reform' meant removing the Permanent Under-Secretary, Sir Benjamin Hawes, and other obstructionists and replacing them with men 'of business from outside'. She did not complain about their competence: simply they were in the way of her ambition to plant her nominees in the Office, to abolish 'minuting' and to make all officials directly responsible to the Secretary for War, who would report to her. In place of 'minuting', all important documents bearing upon soldiers' health were upon completion of drafting or receipt to be sent to her for perusal. Dr Sutherland was, of course, already in the Office, but effectively he was seconded to her service and he spent most of his time working at her home. Similarly, Captain Galton called with papers and to receive instructions almost every morning. Sir Edward Lugard, Military Under-Secretary, was also a Nightingale devotee. Some of the old guard were now in their sixties and probably they were tired, although Miss Nightingale never remarked on it. The Peninsula War veteran, Sir John Burgoyne, Inspector-General of Fortifications, was to be edged out in favour of Galton, who was to take 'Buildings' (including barracks etc.), while Major Jervois, another rising young engineer, was to have 'fortifications' which was unimportant in her scheme. The reactionary Commander in Chief, the Duke of Cambridge, was beyond her reach but she intended to neutralise him by replacing his private secretary, W.F. Forster, with a more amenable go-between.[88]

Apart from dilatory Herbert, the man who stood between her and this audacious coup was Sir Benjamin Hawes. Miss Nightingale's biographers have uniformly accepted her characterisation of him as devious, procrastinating and self-serving. The little evidence we have suggests that Hawes deserves better. At the time of the Crimean hospital crisis he was imaginative and innovative. He instigated I.K. Brunel, his brother-in-law and dearest friend, to design and superintend the construction of the hospital at Renkioi, much the best hospital in the East. The hospital was designed in the pavilion style linked by covered walkways. The 22 wards were prefabricated, with special provision for ventilation, ducted heating and plumbing. It is little celebrated in the literature but, more than the cumbersome and inefficient Lariboisière in Paris, it is the first modern hospital and yet another proof of Brunel's manifold genius. Renkioi's lack of fame partly results from Miss Nightingale's silence about it, yet pavilion hospitals with protected ways and sound plumbing became her trademark as the authority on hospital design.[89]

Hawes was equally creative in working to reform the Army Medical Board and army medical education. Himself a political radical, he was fully aware of the inefficiency of the Horse Guards. He wanted to free the Board and Medical School both from the grip of Miss Nightingale and the old Crimean gang, and to ensure that it functioned at the highest standards of civilian practice. To this end he proposed that H.W. Acland, who already possessed a great reputation and was newly appointed Regius Professor of Medicine at Oxford, join with an unnamed leading London specialist to review the proposals for the army medical school, and that a civilian medical man of the first rank should be invited to join the Board. The threat of such unmanageable expertise was too much for Miss Nightingale and Sidney Herbert, who fended it off by asserting that Hawes's proposals were meant only to delay the project. Possibly, but they would also have improved it by bringing army medicine nearer to the best practice.[90]

Hawes's third and greatest offence was his resistance to Miss Nightingale's takeover of part of his department and the wrecking of his authority. Her scheme that every senior official in the division handling matters that affected health, clothing, contracts and buildings should by-pass their permanent head and report directly to the minister, could and did lead to chaos, when such a system effectively came in after Hawes' death in 1862 and prevailed until Cardwell reorganised the office in 1870.[91] Only a full-scale study of the War Office will reveal the truth about Hawes but such little evidence as we currently have suggests that he is a maligned man. Perhaps Herbert recognised Hawes' virtues, despite Miss Nightingale's nagging. He temporised with her but never removed Hawes.

When in December 1860 a leading British authority on diabetes, Dr Henry Bence Jones, advised Herbert to retire from public life, Miss Nightingale worked hard to reverse the verdict. She argued with Herbert but initially failed to persuade him. He had decided to put his young family first. Florence then approached Lizzie Herbert, but failed with her too. However, within a fortnight Miss Nightingale had induced Herbert to retain the War Office, while moving to the House of Lords. 'The doctors don't give him a year unless he retires from the House of Commons', she confided to Harriet Martineau, who wrote for the *Daily News*. Although Herbert was 'no statesman' and had 'no organizing capacity', he did possess 'great persuasiveness', and 'he alone could carry the Estimates we wanted ... [and] the reorganization of the War Office'. 'I feel it so important just now that "D. News" should help him through [Martineau had lately attacked Herbert in the *Daily News* for a minor scandal concerning army promotions] ... We must get Hawes out & Herbert is not the man to turn him out but no other Secretary of State would turn him out either.' Miss Martineau duly wrote to order.[92]

But it was too late. Herbert had received a fresh medical ultimatum and decided to retire. In desperation Miss Nightingale besought Bence Jones to change his prognosis. The letter is a remarkable example of ruthless wheedling:

> I have seen both Mr Herbert and Mrs Herbert ... since I saw you
> I know him so very well that I can see that the strong impression, (somewhat falsely derived from your words) is upon his mind *viz.* that he is the subject of hopeless disease, that, ... he cannot expect to live a year – that he ought to have devoted this year to retirement and his children – altho' he has yielded to our prayers that he would retain office ...
> I am sure that we must all of us bless you for having the means of prolonging his life by <u>pulling</u> him out of the Ho: of Commons & that we do not wish one word unsaid which you did say.
> But, if you would just say to him now what you did to me *viz.*

that you have known worse cases recover, that, because a man is told to prop up his house he need not think it <u>must</u> tumble down. I am sure that you would not make him more careless, but that you would give him more vitality.

Indeed his wife asked me to ask you to do so. [This might be true, in a literal sense. But there are indications that Lizzie would have preferred him to have retired altogether.]

For the sake of sparing your time, I have written. But, if you liked to call here, I would give you the circumstances.

Common sense tells me never to interfere between a Physician & his Patient.

So that I hope and trust you will not think this is interfering

And above all, that, whatever you may think it right to say to Mr Herbert, you will not let him know that I have written to you . . . He is so very peculiar in temperament that I think scarcely any man knows him.[93]

During the following month Herbert became unable to walk upstairs without distress and his condition continued to deteriorate through the spring, although he kept on working and attending the House of Lords. Apparently he was living on brandy. On 7 June, after discussing ventilation and sanitary commission matters, he told Miss Nightingale that he intended to resign the War Office and leave for Spa to recoup his health. She was furious: 'You have left no impress of yourself on the War Office. You have not even coloured it . . . No man in my day has thrown away so noble a game as Sidney Herbert with all the winning cards in his hands.'[94]

Upon his death eight weeks later she produced at least five heavily corrected drafts of an anonymous obituary, each emphasising his sainthood and her discipleship and the necessity to continue his work. For the first time she projected Herbert as 'her dear master'. Each draft covers about 16 pages: in each about 11 pages deal solely with Miss Nightingale's labours for the army. He, she said, was an 'ideal' man, but she alone knew 'how to <u>do</u> things'. Miss Nightingale also secretly supplied the funeral sermons to be preached at the official service.[95]

With Herbert gone, she set out to recruit W.E. Gladstone. His efforts to reduce Herbert's service estimates and his opposition to barracks and hospital improvement made Gladstone an unpromising quarry, but he was a Peelite, a High Churchman and former personal friend of the Herberts, and he was obviously the coming man. She sent Gladstone her draft obituary and begged him to take up the great work.

But prudent Gladstone replied that he accepted Lizzie Herbert's view that Sidney's work was done. Miss Nightingale was irate, but canny enough not to attack Gladstone direct:

> She has made a natural blunder between administrative reforms and organization − a blunder which he never made − He did improve the War Office administratively at every step. He did not re-organize it. And alas! he knew it . . .
> Deep disappointment with himself, especially as regards his not having reorganized the War Office according to his plan . . . hastened, I am certain, my dear Master's end . . .
>   You will not let a word of this go beyond yourself to any human being . . . My dead master would at this moment approve of what I am doing in appealing to you . . . His was the purest ambition I have ever known.

Gladstone returned a sober, detailed description of the 'beautiful' funeral. Miss Nightingale had declared herself too ill to attend and had 'never even thought' of going to view the body. The pith of his letter is a consummate piece of Gladstonian filigreed evasion:

> I read last night with profound interest your important paper [Miss Nightingale's draft panegyric]. I see at once that the matter is too high for me to handle. Like you I know that too much would distress him, too little would not. I am in truth ignorant of military administration . . . It is your knowledge and authority more than that of any living creature that can do him justice, at the proper time, whenever that may be.

As for the War Office, Gladstone professed himself 'reluctant to touch that subject . . . for fear I should spoil it'. But meanwhile, as insurance, he 'ventured' to keep a copy of her paper. Miss Nightingale confided to McNeill that she had written another letter to Gladstone (which I could not trace) 'asking him whether I should ask him to help in it for S. Herbert's sake. The reply was truly Gladstonian − cautious, cold, complimentary, yet eloquent − but evidently intending to do nothing.' Undeterred, she sent Gladstone her memorandum on Sidney Herbert and War Office reform 'to be dealt with at your own discretion . . . I understand that it is at your request I am sending you this. My only stipulation is that, if you think it necessary to mention my name in connection with the paper, you will say that it was drawn up at your request, not volunteered by me.' Gladstone appears never to have used her paper. In 1863 and 1864 she again attempted unsuccessfully to enlist him, but finally in 1869 after he backed a nurse training scheme in Ireland without consulting her she dismissed him as 'the most unsanitary brute that ever was'.[96]

After her first rebuff from Gladstone Miss Nightingale began to broadcast Sidney Herbert's famous last words: 'Poor Florence — our unfinished work'. The provenance of these, like many famous last words, is doubtful. Herbert's physician, Dr Williams, reported the death-bed in detail to Miss Nightingale. He mentioned Herbert's taking leave of his family but he did not transmit, as he surely would have done had he heard it, any final message for her. Lady Catherine Dunmore, Herbert's sister, also recounted the death-bed tableau to Miss Nightingale. She said that Williams arrived 'too late to hear His Expressions of perfect Happiness, his Gratitude to God . . . his Blessings to his Wife & Children & to all of us', She, too, does not report a last message for Miss Nightingale. The first record of these words, in a variant of the usual version which came from Miss Nightingale, occurs in a conciliatory reply from Lizzie Herbert dated 12 August 1861, ten days after the death: 'I send you some of his last words — those to you were "Poor Florence! Poor Florence! Our joint work unfinished!"' The phraseology of both versions is implausible, although the first reflects Florence's curt style and the second Lizzie's gushing wordiness. Implausible or not, Miss Nightingale immediately inflated the purport of the phrase and circulated it. 'His last words, several times repeated were: "Poor Florence — & our work unfinished"' was the version she confided to McNeill.

Simultaneously, and instinctively, she appropriated Herbert's reputation and denigrated his work by interpreting the death-bed scene.

His wife & his sisters interpret his death-bed in their own way. And great pains have been taken to represent it as a 'glorified death'. I understood him as no one else did. I loved him & served him as no one else — I have letters from him, as long as he could hold a pen at all, up to the last fortnight. [The last letter I have found is dated 7 June — his announcement of his retirement — for which Florence castigated him by return, nine weeks before his death. There is no reason why he should have written after that — and she would have kept the letter had he done so.] And his death, had it been as they represent, would have been purely selfish, going to heaven himself & leaving 'us in the storm'. But it was not. He died with manly cheerfulness, because he felt he had no more work in him — but with a deep regret for failure.

She sent Douglas Galton yet another version of the last words (this time 'said ... twice') coupled with an admonition to hold tight at the War Office, keep an eye on Herbert's successor and bring her as many of Herbert's recent War Office papers as he could lay hands on. 'This is the last opportunity I shall ever have of carrying out my poor Master's wishes.'[97]

When preparing her memoir Lady Herbert had asked Miss Nightingale's permission to read his letters to her. The request put Miss Nightingale in a rage. In the midst of a rambling, incoherent 24 page letter to McNeill she sought to justify her refusal to herself:

I have hundreds of Sidney Herbert's letters — I cannot give them to Lady Herbert or refuse them to her —

Up to this time I could not burn them because they have stood in good stead about some things at the War Office.

His letters will prove ... his failure ... they will prove (to use his own words) that 'all that' he 'had done' he 'had coined out of "my brain"'. [I have found no letter which says this] ... I will never be the one to tell to his wife or his fellow-Ministers what he did not tell himself.

Miss Nightingale intended to refuse Lizzie's request 'by hiding ... away'. Lizzie asked again in 1890 when the family was gathering materials for the projected biography. Florence's reply is quintessential Nightingale: insidiously unctuous, effortlessly evasive, thoroughly egotistical and iron-hard, glossing a lifetime of deceit and cherished enmities:

Dearest, Indeed that loss, unspeakable, irreparable, is always before me ... Would that I could help you in giving you materials for the proposed 'Life' as you ask — But alas! I cannot. I am altogether unable, I am sorry to say, to do what you wish & what I should wish so much.

I have no letters from him that I could lend you. His letters while

I was in the Crimean War, were not on very important business, &
not such as one cared to preserve. [Many, probably all, of these
letters are among the Nightingale Papers in the British Library.]

Afterwards, there were the five years, all but a week from August
7 1856 ... to August 2 1861 ... the day that took him home to
minister to still greater works for his, for our Heavenly Father —
you know — who better? — how it was — letters do not pass between
those who see each other day after day ... during the whole period
there were no letters or none kept and not a line of record or of
copy have I ...

How sorry I am to have to say this to you you will know ...

After this, perhaps you will hardly wish to see me, as you kindly
offer. My illness is so much increased that I am not equal to the
work constantly increasing upon me. And I hardly see anyone not
closely connected with that present work.

I hope you are pretty well ...

ever your old friend

F.N.[98]

Miss Nightingale paid a small penalty for withholding the letters.
Stanmore's biography of Herbert is a rare instance of a contemporary
work which treated Miss Nightingale as a little lower than the angels,
and indeed found her 'jealous', intolerant and 'censorious'.

Nonetheless, by the time of Herbert's death her aggression and his
careful work had ensured that in the short run at least, War Office
business was conducted less haphazardly and that greater attention
would be paid to the well-being of the common soldiers. Between
Herbert's resignation and Edward Cardwell's advent at the War Office
in 1868, the Duke of Cambridge and the Horse Guards were to undo
many of the administrative reforms, but the improvement in army
sanitary arrangements was a more permanent gain. Thousands of men
in the British army at home and abroad lived healthier, longer lives
in better conditions because she had acted the bully for them.

Notes

1. F.N. to [Sidney Herbert?] draft, n.d. [June 1856?], BL Add.Mss 43401,
ff.201-4; F.N. to McNeill, 1 Mar. 1857, GLRO HI/ST/SU/75.

2. 'Return Relating to the late Army in the East', *Parliamentary Papers*, 1857,
vol.IX, pp.1-4; R. Thompson Jopling, 'On the Mortality among Officers of the
British Army in the East', *Report of British Association for the Advancement of
Science, 1856*, p.144; Thomas Longmore, *The Sanitary Contrasts of the British*

and French Armies during the Crimean War (London, 1883), pp.5-14; J.S. Curtiss, *The Russian Army under Nicholas I, 1825-1855* Durham, NY, 1965), pp.249, 359, has a critical discussion of the various estimates for the Russian losses. The Russians did not collect figures on disease in their army until 1859.

3. Sir Edward Cook, *The Life of Florence Nightingale* (2 vols., London 1913), vol. I, p.318.

4. Report of the Board of General Offices appointed to inquire into . . . the reports of Sir John McNeill and Colonel Tulloch . . .' *PP*, 1856, vol. XXI; War Office minute on McNeill and Tulloch Report, n.d. [Oct. 1856], PRO WO33/3A; Florence MacAlister, *Memoir of the right hon. Sir John McNeill* (London, 1910), p.404.

5. F. N. to McNeill, 4 Sept 1856; F.N. to Lady McNeill, 7 Oct. 1856, GLRO HI/ST/SU65-70.

6. F.N. to Lord Murray, 24 Sept. 1856 (draft), BL Add.Mss 43401, f.252.

7. F.N. to Peter Pincoffs, 'Private & Confidential', 21 Oct. 1856, BL Add. Mss 45796, ff.92-3; Peter Pincoffs, *Experiences of a Civilian in Eastern Military Hospitals* (London, 1857).

8. Hall 'Observations . . . on the Medical Department of the Army' Oct. 1856, PRO WO33/38 *The Panmure Papers*, ed. George Douglas, and George Dalhousie Ramsay (2 vols., London, 1908), vol. II, pp.305-6, 321.

9. Cook, *Nightingale*, vol. I, pp.356-7.

10. Sidney Herbert to F.N., 16 Jan. 1856, BL Add.Mss 43394, f.3; Lefroy to F.N., 28 Aug. 1856, in Cook, *Nightingale*, vol. I, pp.322-3.

11. Cook, *Nightingale*, vol. I, p.329-31.

12. Cook, *Nightingale*, vol. I, p.330.

13. F.N. to Sidney Herbert, 6 Jan. 1857, BL Add.Mss 43394, ff.1-2.

14. Cook, *Nightingale*, vol. I, pp.335, 442-5; F.N. to McNeill, 16 Nov. 1857, GLRO HI/ST/SU94; F.N. to Monckton Milnes, 3 May 1857, Houghton Mss, Trinity College, Cambridge 3793(2).

15. Florence Nightingale, *Notes on Matters affecting the Health, Efficiency, And Hospital Administration of the British Army, founded chiefly on the experience of the late war* 'Presented by request to the Secretary of State for War' (London, 1858), pp.566, XXVI.

16. F.N. to Sidney Herbert, 20 May 1857, BL Add.Mss 43394, ff.45-6. Miss Nightingale shared with contemporaries and with later historians a belief that the navy was much healthier than the army. It might have been so, but convincing evidence is lacking. The navy's procedure of paying off seamen after each tour of duty and then recommissioning only the able-bodied greatly enhances the sickness and mortality figures. Cf. Sutherland to Edwin Chadwick, 15 Oct. 1883, Chadwick Papers, University College, London, CP1920.

17. F.N., *Notes*, pp.XXII, XXXV, 156, 205, 323, LIV.

18. F.N., *Notes* pp.350-65, Appendix 7, pp.XXXV-IX.

19. F.N. to Sidney Herbert, 24 Mar. 1859, BL Add.Mss 45768, ff.88-9.

20. F.N., *Notes*, pp.188-90, 287-301.

21. F.N. to Lord Grey, June-July 1857, BL Add.Mss 45796, ff.205-30.

22. F.N. to McNeill, 3 May 1857, GLRO HI/ST/SU79.

23. F.N. to Mrs Milnes, 3 May 1857, BL Add.Mss 45796, f.190.

24. F.N. to McNeill, 3 May 1857, GLRO HI/ST/SU/79.

25. F.N. to McNeill, 1 Mar. 1857; 3 May 1857, GLRO HI/ST/SU/75, 79.

26. Sidney Herbert to F.N., n.d. [23 May 1857?], BL Add.Mss 43394, ff.47-8.

27. Sidney Herbert to F.N., 26 Apr. 1857; F.N. Memorandum on Royal Commission, n.d. [1861?]; BL Add.Mss 43394 f.29; 45823, f.1.

28. F.N. to McNeill, 12 June 1857; 27 June 1857, GLRO HI/ST/SU/85, 86; 'Report of the Commissioners appointed to inquire into the . . . Sanitary

condition of the army . . .'. *PP* 1857-58, vol. XVIII Qs.5343-73; F.N. to McNeill, 25 June 1857; Sutherland to F.N., 7 Sept. 1857, BL Add.Mss 45768, ff.55-6; 45751, f.45.

29. F.N. to McNeill, 7 July 1857, GLRO HI/ST/SU/87.

30. F.N. to Sidney Herbert, 7 July 1857, 21 July 1857; Sidney Herbert to F.N., 20 July 1857, BL Add.Mss 43394 ff.95-8, 112, 116.

31. F.N. to Jerry Barrett, 18 July 1856, GLRO HI/ST/SU/193; Henry Newman, 'Letters from Scutari, 1856', in *Friends' Quarterly Examiner*, Oct. 1910, pp.550-2. (Newman accompanied Barrett to the Crimea.)

32. Parthe Verney to McNeill, 3 Apr. [1862?] GLRO HI/ST/SU/112; F.N. to Benjamin Jowett n.d. [mid-Sept. 1865?] Jowett Papers, vol. I, Balliol College, Oxford.

33. F.N. to [William Rendle?], 1 Dec. 1868; F.N. to 'ever dearest "Little Sister"' (Miss Pringle), 21 Oct. 1887, GLRO HI/ST/NCI/68/4, 87/47; Ulricke M. [Lienicke?] to F.N., 27 Oct. 1888, BL Add.Mss 45809, ff.10-11.

34. F.N. to Sidney Herbert, 26 Nov. 1857, F.N. to Sutherland, 2 Feb. 1862, BL Add.Mss 43394, ff.190-4, 45751, f.205.

35. F.N. to Mrs Bracebridge, Jan. 1864, BL Add.Mss 43397, f.195; F.N. to 'very dearest friend' (Mary Jones), 12 Sept. 1869, GLRO HI/ST/NCI/69/2; F.N. to Jowett, 22 Jan. [1872?] Jowett Papers, vol. IV, Balliol College, Oxford.

36. F.N. to Richard Aspden, 8 July 1867, GLRO HI/ST/U26/67.

37. F.N. to Sutherland, 31 Mar. 1871, BL Add.Mss 45755, f.198.

38. F.N. to Aunt Mai Smith, 30 Aug. 1872, BL Add.Mss 45793, f.222.

39. F.N. Note, n.d. [1873?], BL Add.Mss 45841, f.84.

40. F.N. to Jowett, n.d. [late July 1865?] BL Add.Mss 45783, f.41.

41. *Parl. Debs.* 3/vol.CL cols. 474-95; F.N. to Monckton Milnes, 25 Feb. 1857, Houghton Mss, supp. 3543, Trinity College, Cambridge; Sidney Herbert to F.N., 26 July 1859, BL Add.Mss 43395, f.192.

42. Chadwick to F.N., 31 July 1857, F.N. to Chadwick, 11 Feb. 1858; Chackwick to F.N., 16 Feb. 1858, BL Add.Mss 45770 ff.5-15.

43. F.N. to McNeill, 27 Dec. [1857?], GLRO HI/ST/SU/100; F.N. to McNeill 27 Dec. [1857?] (draft), BL Add.Mss 45768 f.72. The phrase comes probably from John Reynolds, *The Triumph of God's revenge against the crying and execrable Sinne of Murther* (1621).

44. F.N. to Sidney Herbert, 12 Mar. 1858, BL Add.Mss 43395, f.5.

45. F.N. to McNeill, 16 Nov. 1857, GLRO HI/ST/SU/94.

46. Mary Smith (Aunt Mai) to Lady McNeill, 19 Nov. 1857, 2 Dec. [1857?] BL Add.Mss 45768, f.252, 254. Another draft is at GLRO HI/ST/SU/96-8.

47. Aunt Mai to Lady McNeill, 29 Jan. 1858 F.N. to McNeill, 10 Oct. 1857, GLRO HI/ST/SU/101, 93.

48. F.N. to McNeill, 19 Mar. 1859, GLRO HI/ST/SU/110.

49. F.N. to Uncle Sam, 28 June 1861; and [Aug. 1861?], BL Add.Mss 45792, ff.197, 229.

50. F.N. to Mrs Milnes, 18 Aug. [1860?], Houghton Mss, Trinity College Cambridge, Supp. 354(2), Mrs Gaskell to C.E. Norton, 13 Jan. 1863, in J.A.V. Chapple and Arthur Pollard (eds.), *The Letters of Mrs Gaskell* (Manchester, 1966), p.707; F.N. to Rev. Mother Clare, 28 Feb. 1865, BL Add.Mss 45789, ff.43-4; F.N. to Lizzie Herbert, 19 July 1865 BL Add.Mss 43396, f.193; F.N. to Mary Jones, 23 Sept. 1866, GLRO HI/ST/NCI/66/16; F.N. to Lizzie Herbert, 21 Feb. 1867, BL Add.Mss 43396, f.206; F.N. to Chadwick 7 Nov. 1868, Chadwick Papers, University College London, CP1490; F.N. to Sutherland, n.d. [early Jan. 1869?] BL Add.Mss 45753, f.165; F.N. to Sutherland, n.d. [July 1870?], BL Add.Mss 45753, f.239; F.N. to Martin, 23 July 1874, BL Add.Mss 45803, f.233; F.N. to Miss Mackenzie, 11 Sept. 1879, GLRO HI/ST/79/4; F.N. to Gladstone, 4 Dec. 1884, BL Add.Mss 44488, f.202; F.N. to Galton, 5 May,

19 June 1888, BL Add.Mss 45766, ff.60-1, 93.

51. F.N. 'Household Book' 1888, BL Add.Mss 45849; F.N., Diary, 9 Jan. 1877, BL Add.Mss 45847, ff.48-9; F.N. to [Sutherland?] 22 July 1873, BL Add. Mss 45803, f.86; F.N. to Gladstone, 3 Dec. 1884, BL Add.Mss 44488, f.196; F.N 'Note , 6 Aug. 1887, BL Add.Mss 52427, f.4.

52. Harriet Martineau to F.N., 23 Jan. 1865, GLRO HI/ST/VI/65; F.N. to Martineau, 12 Feb. 1865, BL Add.Mss 45788, f.283.

53. Mary Scharlieb, *Reminiscences* (London, 1924), p.46.

54. Dr C.B. Williams, prescription, 24 July 1870, BL Add.Mss 45802, f.164; F.N Diary 1877, BL Add.Mss 45847, f.55; Clark to F.N., 31 Mar. 1867, BL Add.Mss 45772, f.199; F.N., Diary, 3 Feb. 1877, BL Add.Mss 45847, f.51.

55. F.N. to Rev. Mother Clare, 1 Mar. [1867?]; and 28 Feb. 1865 BL Add. Mss 45789, ff.51, 43.

56. Rosalind Nash, 'I Knew A Man', typescript, GLRO HI/ST/NC12/14, pp.5-6.

57. F.N. – signed by Herbert, Sutherland et. al., 'Objections to Netley, 12 Mar. 1858, PRO WO 33/6A.

58. Herbert to F.N., 2 Jan. 1857, BL Add.Mss 43394, f.224.

59. F.N. to Sutherland, n.d. [June-July 1857?], BL Add.Mss 45751, ff.30-3; Herbert to F.N., 12 Feb. 1859, BL Add.Mss 43395, f.144; [FN?] anonymous leader on Netley Hospital in the *Builder*, 24 July 1858, p.493.

60. F.N. Memorandum of interview with Mrs Deeble, matron at Netley, [24 Feb. 1870?], BL Add.Mss 45754, f.89.

61. F.N. to Sutherland, n.d. [16 July 1861?] BL Add.Mss 45751, f.195.

62. F.N. to Sutherland, n.d. [July 1861?] BL Add.Mss 45751, f.198; F.N. to Galton, 17 Jan. 1865, BL Add.Mss 45763, f.12.

63. Sir Edward Lugard, Draft report to War Office on Netley Hospital, 26 May 1868, BL Add.Mss 45774, f.101.

64. F.N. to Sutherland, n.d. [10 Dec. 1869?], BL Add.Mss 45754, ff.35, 89.

65 F.N. *Notes*, p.11; F.N. to Martineau, 23 Jan. [1859?], BL Add.Mss 45788, f.21.

66. E.A. Parkes to F.N., 17 Jan. 1861, BL Add.Mss 45773, f.25; F.N. to Galton. 7 Apr., 3 Nov. 1864, BL Add.Mss 45762, ff.92, 237.

67. F.N. to Acland, 31 Mar., 8 Apr., 17 Apr., 12 July 1876, 29 Jan. 1881, Acland Papers, Bodleian Library, Oxford, d.70, ff.70-87.

68. Herbert, 'Regulations for Medical Organization of War Office', 9 July 1858. PRO WO33/6A; F.N. to McNeill, 24 Mar. 1859, GLRO HI/ST/SU/III; F.N. to Clark, 7 Oct. 1863, 7 Apr., 8 Apr., 11 Apr., 5 June 1864. BL Add.Mss 45772 ff.174-90; F.N. to Galton, 29 Nov. 1864, BL Add.Mss 45762 ff.64-6; 22 June 1866, BL Add.Mss 45763, f.192-4.

69. G.J.H. Evatt, *Army Medical Organization* (London, 1878), p.28; J.M. Grant, Memorandum ... on Hospitals, Dec. 1878, PRO WO33/33; Anon., Report on Shortage of Recruits to Army Medical Department, 1879, PRO WO33/32.

70. F.N. Notes for 'Suggestions', n.d. [late 1850?] BL Add.Mss 45842, f.51; John M. Eyler, *Victorian Social Medicine* (Baltimore, 1979), esp. Chapters 2 and 7.

71. Shaftesbury, Diary, 2 June 1855, Broadlands Mss, National Register of Archives, SHA/PD/7.

72. Report of Barracks ... Commission, 15 Oct. 1858, pp.1, 22, PRO 33/6A.

73. Herbert to F.N., 20 Aug. 1857, BL Add.Mss 43394, f.143.

74. Alan Ramsay Skelley, *The Victorian Army At Home* (London, 1977), p.36; War Office memo. 'Condition of the Soldier', n.d. [1862?] Broadlands Mss, National Register of Archives, ND/B/21/5; Sutherland to Chadwick, 15 Aug. [1864?] Chadwick Papers, University College, London, CP1920; *PP*, 1857-58,

vol. XXXVII, p.1. The expenditures given here are conservative. Higher totals are printed in *PP*, 1857, vol. IX, p.167 and *PP*, 1860, vol. XLI, p.95. Presumably, they vary according to the time of year at which they are calculated, amongst other factors.

75. Shaftesbury, Diary, 15 Feb. 1855. Broadlands Mss. PRO, SHA/PD/6.

76. *PP* 1857-58, vol. XVIII, p.527; *PP* 1862, vol. XXXIII, pp.5-6, 33; *PP* 1867, vol. XLIII, pp.5, 24-5.

77. E. Headlam Greenhow, *Builder*, 5, 30 Oct., 20, Nov. 1858; (F.N.) *Builder*, 6 Nov. 1858; F.N. to Chadwick, 11 Aug. 1858, Chadwick to F.N., 21 Aug. 1858, BL Add.Mss 45770, ff.32, 43.

78. F.G.P. Neison, 'On Phthisis in the Army', *Report of British Association for the Advancement of Science 1858*, pp.189-92; (SH) 'The Sanitary Condition Of The Army', *Westminster Review*, vol. 51, 1859, pp.668.

79. F.N. to Chadwick, 7 Oct. 1858, BL Add.Mss 45770, f.35; Chadwick to F.N., 27 Sept. 1862 BL Add.Mss 45771, ff.62-4; F.N. to Balfour, 28 Sept. 1858, BL Add.Mss 50134, ff.47-50.

80. J. Clarke Jervoise, *"Infection"*, 2nd edn (London, 1882); Elizabeth Blackwell, *Why Hygienic Congresses Fail* (London, 1892).

81. F.N. to Walker, 10 Apr. 1866, GLRO HI/ST/NCI/66/4.

82. Farr to F.N., 23, 25 Apr. 1860, BL Add.Mss 43399, ff.109-12.

83. F.N. to R.J. Ellis, draft, n.d. [Aug. 1867?] BL Add.Mss 45782, f.100.

84. F.N. to Jowett, [draft] n.d. [1866-67?], BL Add.Mss 45783, f.142; and 3 Oct. 1871, BL Add.Mss 45784, f.1.

85. F.N. to 'Dearest' (Lizzie Herbert) 4 Sept. 1849, BL Add.Mss 43396, f.5.

86. Herbert to F.N., 2 Jan. 1858, BL Add.Mss 43394, ff.227-8.

87. F.N. to Galton, 24 Apr. 1860, BL Add.Mss 45759, ff.36-8.

88. F.N. to Galton, 1 Sept. 1860, 8 June 1861 *'Burn This'*, BL Add.Mss 45759, ff.51-3, 223.

89. L.T.C. Rolt *Isambard Kingdom Brunel* (London, 1970), pp.292-8. Brunel is masked as Bonnel in George Douglas and George D. Ramsay (eds.), *Panmure Papers*, (2 vols., London, 1908), vol. II, pp.401, 405.

90. Lord Stanmore, *Sidney Herbert*, (2 vols., London, 1906), vol. II, 153-61.

91. F.N. to McNeill, 24 Mar. 1859, BL Add.Mss 45768, f.88-90; F.N. to de Grey, 16 May 1862, BL Add.Mss 43546, f.19. Edward M. Spiers, *The Army and Society 1815-1914* (London, 1980), pp.157-200.

92. Herbert was probably suffering from renal disease as well as diabetes. Tests of his urine disclosed very high and increasing proportions of albumen, which baffled his doctors. P.E. de Strzelecki to McNeill, 5 Nov. 1861, BL Add. Mss 45768, f.161; F.N. to Lizzie Herbert, 5 Dec. 1860, BL Add.Mss 43396, ff.89-95; F.N. to Martineau, 4 Jan. 1861, BL Add.Mss 45788, ff.103-10.

93. F.N. to [Dr. C.B. Williams?] [draft?] 7 Jan. 1861, GLRO HI/ST/NCI/61/1.

94. Herbert to F.N. 7 June 1861; F.N. to Herbert, n.d. [9 June 1861?] BL Add.Mss 43395, ff.303-9.

95. F.N. drafts of obituary, BL Add.Mss 45818, [Aug. 1861?] ff.8-210; Rev. R.S.C. Chermside to F.N., BL Add.Mss 45797, f.254.

96. F.N. to Gladstone, 8, 9 Aug., 25 Nov. 1861; Gladstone to F.N., 10 Aug. 1861, BL Add.Mss 44397, ff.28-50, 188-9; F.N. to McNeill, 21 Aug. 1861, BL Add.Mss 45907, f.24; F.N. to Sutherland, n.d. [March 1869?], BL Add.Mss 43573, f.202.

97. C.B. Williams to F.N., 2 Aug. [1861?], BL Add.Mss 45797, ff.246-7; Dunmore to F.N., n.d. [4 Aug. 1861?] BL Add.Mss 43396, f.147; Lizzie Herbert to F.N., 12 Aug. 1861, BL Add.Mss 43396, f.153; F.N. to McNeill, 21 Aug. 1861,

BL Add.Mss 45907, ff.22-3. F.N. to Galton, 16 Aug. 1861, BL Add.Mss 45759, ff.255-7.

98. F.N. to McNeill, 21 Aug. 1861, ff.28-29; F.N. to Lizzie Herbert, 24 Feb. 1890, BL Add.Mss 43396, ff.226-9.

4 INDIA

Miss Nightingale took up India when her leverage on army medical services and barracks slackened during the early 1860s. With Sidney Herbert's death she lost her *point d'appui* on the War Office and government. The War Office regained the initiative and army sanitary improvement settled into a slow bureaucratic routine. She yielded readily enough, behind a barrage of complaining letters. The battle for power always engaged her more than the business that ensued in its aftermath.

She had discovered India during the Mutiny in 1857. In the midst of her post-Crimean enterprises, she had half-heartedly asked McNeill to 'advise' her whether to go to India to nurse the British soldiers. Apparently he rejected the idea and she acquiesced.[1] She had noted also the need for sanitary reform in India but it was Sutherland who formulated the justification for an Indian sanitary crusade. In September 1857, on the occasion of her nephew leaving with other unseasoned troops for India, he remarked that there would be much sickness among them. 'The whole sanitary work in India will require reconsideration in the altered state of matters.' Native soldiers could no longer be trusted; henceforth British troops would have to hold the country, and that could be effected only if their sickness and mortality rates were reduced:

> It would be a beautiful thing to do it, and I am certain it could be done, and India kept in hand . . . by the Anglo Saxon race.
>
> It would be a greater thing to do than it was to conquer Hindoostan.[2]

Miss Nightingale adopted the project in the autumn of 1858 after her *Notes on the Army* . . . were finished. In August she began pressing the argument on Edwin Chadwick, hinting that he propagate it in the quarterlies. This was cool, because Chadwick, who probably had picked up the notion from Sutherland and Farr, had already sketched it for her only a month before. Chadwick had given the Indian scheme his distinctive emphasis: he urged sanitary reform as the cheapest way of maintaining a white Indian army. He probably supplied Dr Andrew Wynter with the impressive-looking figures used to back the idea in his anonymous article in the *Quarterly Review* for January 1859.[3] Wynter asserted that about 100,000 British soldiers had died of disease in India between 1815 and 1855. At an estimate of £100 per man for training and experience, their untimely and unnecessary deaths, measured by rates of about 76 per 1,000 in 1836 declining to 41 per 1,000 in 1855 among an average strength of 25,000 men, represented a loss of ten million pounds to the British empire. If the 1855 rate persisted among the 95,000 men stationed in India since the Mutiny the ultimate monetary cost would be prohibitive. There is reason to believe that the figures were overstated, but the argument remains powerful.[4]

Miss Nightingale's Indian campaign followed the lines of infiltration of the War Office. During the spring of 1859 she secured a Royal Sanitary Commission for India. Lord Stanley, the Tory Secretary for India, temporised for eight months, but gave way when it appeared that his government was doomed: a Nightingale commission would be an irritating legacy to his Liberal successor. His permanent officials at the India Office were opposed to her meddling and their fears were justified by the membership of the Commission: Herbert as chairman, Sutherland, Sir R. Martin, Farr, Alexander, and two inescapable gestures to the Indian Council, Sir Proby Cautley and Sir R. Vivian. Fortunately her uncle Sam was friendly with the latter: 'Vivian must be soaped', she told him, 'so as not to let him think we undervalue his opinion.' Chadwick had sought nomination but Miss Nightingale and Stanley ignored him.[5] The composition of the Commission reflected her isolation from men possessing recent Indian experience; Martin, Cautley and Vivian were big names and great men, but they were nearing the ends of their careers – her reputation as Crimean heroine cut no ice with younger Indian bureaucrats and soldiers.

The work of the Commission fell to Sutherland and Farr and it soon turned out to be frustrating. The officials at the India Office prevaricated for six months over a request for mortality and sickness figures. Even after Farr secured an order from the Secretary for India, Sir Charles Wood, the Office stalled. Stalling was easy because there were no reliable health statistics for civilians and natives in India. There had been no effective censuses, there was no regular registration of deaths, estimates on the incidence of disease among natives were made randomly from records of admissions to native hospitals. The situation was ready-made for Miss Nightingale to create her own data. In consultation with Sutherland, Farr and McNeill, she devised an extensive questionnaire and sent it to 200 British stations in India.[6]

The questionnaire is a remarkable example of Miss Nightingale's pertinacity, practicality and sense of the actual, honed by Sutherland's grasp of medical possibilities and Farr's mastery of vital statistics. The ruling assumption is that ill-health is caused by bad environmental factors which can be identified and remedied. There are fourteen sections, covering 'topography', 'climate', 'sanitary condition of station', 'health of the troops', 'intemperance', 'diet', 'dress, accoutrements, and duties', 'instruction and recreation', 'military prisons', 'field service', 'statistics of sickness and mortality', 'hospitals', 'burial of the dead', and instructions for a general report from each Presidency. The questions are precise and searching: for example, number four among the fourteen relating to topography asks,

> At what distance from the station is the nearest water, whether sea, river, lake, marsh, nullah, or canal? Is the vicinity liable to overflow of water? if so, at what season, and how long does the overflow last? Is there any broken ground, or are there any ravines or water pits near the station, and what is their effect on health?

Amongst the 23 questions about the sanitary conditions of the station the respondent was required to supply sketches of the ground-plan of the camp, the barracks, kitchens, urinals, drainage system, and to state the distance from the barracks at which animals were slaughtered, the regulations governing the practice and how the offal was disposed of, and if 'nuisance is experienced . . . how you propose to prevent it'.[7] Nothing attests so vividly to Miss Nightingale's gift of accendency as her presumption that every dutiful Indian medical officer and military engineer would labour to answer the questionnaire in full. She seems not to have understood that an honest respondent might endanger his career. The miracle is that there are so many detailed, critical replies. No modern army would permit it.

The evidence must have fulfilled her expectations. Nearly 1,000 pages of small type, it amounts to a massive, intricately informed phantasmagoria of poor water supplies, damp badly-sited camps, ill-built, hot and grubby barracks adjoining filthy native bazaars, endemic fever and (amongst British troops) venereal disease, a total want of field sanitary regulations, culminating in omnipresent, stolidly accepted death. Only drunkenness, which the doctors reported as rare, did not meet the stereotype of the pre-Nightingale army. She had provided an outlet for dozens of technicians and junior officers, many of them Scots, whose aspirations and expertise had been slighted by their superiors. 'The medical officer has no power in these matters' (camp-sites etc.), reported army surgeon Cox from Muttra on the Jumna river south of Delhi, 'and he would lay himself open to rebuke if he interfered'. Assistant-Surgeon Howell of the Madras Engineers, reporting from Cuddapah, complained that his superiors consistently camped their men in paddy-fields, ignoring the rising ground on either side, which left the camp in up to six inches of water after rain. Dr Joseph Ewart, of the Mewar Bheel Corps at Kherwarrah, recounted similar stupidities and asked that sanitary officers be given 'executive and responsible functions' to be exercised independently of their immediate commanding officers. Dr Duncan Macpherson, Inspector-General of hospitals for the Madras Army, rehearsed, perhaps unconsciously, to Miss Nightingale's commissioners the lesson she had sought to teach:

> in England, the last place where sanitary considerations obtained a hearing was in those influential quarters where rests the highest military authority. The terrible ordeal of the Crimea came and laid bare to the world the defects of our system . . . it is for us to profit by this great example, and to hasten to amend what is faulty in our system here.[8]

The embattled subordinate improvers had found a champion in Miss Nightingale and she found in them a network — though many soon defected — of irregulars who would abet her in her skirmishes with the India Office and Presidency governments.

Early in 1862 Miss Nightingale took to bed for four months — she was 'much worse' she told McNeill in the course of a business letter and unable to come to felicitate his daughter on the birth of her child — while she arranged the evidence, prepared coloured graphs displaying the gross extent of preventable mortality, digests and recapitulations of the evidence and statistics, together with a reprinted volume of 'Observations' on the *Report*, reiterating its main findings. The Treasury and State Paper Office baulked for six months at the cost of the Blue Book but Miss Nightingale finally overrode them, and the *Report* appeared in mid-1863. She herself paid for the figures and wordcut illustrations. She sent special copies of the 'Observations' to the Queen and other notables and ensured that prominent members of both houses of parliament asked for the *Report* and 'Observations' in their respective libraries. She also arranged for favourable reviews in the daily press and quarterlies.[9] Beyond this she produced a brilliant précis of the 'Observations' entitled *How People May Live and not Die in India*, for presentation to the Edinburgh congress of the National Association for the Promotion of Social Science. Prince Alfred attended the session and the gathering concluded with cheers for Miss Nightingale. On every front the result was a triumph for her pertinacity. Two powerful Indian proconsuls, Sir John Lawrence and Sir Bartle Frere, were confirmed as disciples.[10] Temporarily at least she had outflanked the India Office.

Miss Nightingale and Sutherland proposed in the *Report* to establish for India a system of sanitary reconstruction, modelled on their Army Sanitary Commission, designed to maintain their authority distinct of the India Office. There were to be three new bodies, ranked vertically. At the base there was to be a 'public works executive' in each of the three presidencies, composed of sanitarians and engineers. They were to oversee small local improvements and to execute the larger schemes approved by their respective presidency sanitary commissions. These last were to comprise leading sanitarians, senior medical officers and government officials. Their role was vaguely described as 'consultative and advisory'. Above them there was to be a 'home commission' composed, although Miss Nightingale did not say so, of her cabinet drawn from the War Office. 'The function', she equivocated, 'could of course be consultative only.'[11] Her practice soon proved that she expected all Indian sanitary projects to be referred home. Moreover the 'public works executive' was to implement instantly, without awaiting local permission, such improvements as the home commission might direct.

This audacious mechanism impelled Miss Nightingale into endless intrigue. Almost two years before the Royal Commission even reported, she had tried to send 'Instructions' about Indian barracks improvements and soldiers' day-rooms through Earl de Grey during his brief stay as Indian Under-Secretary in 1861. He quietly held up despatch of the 'Instructions' while in office and then evaded her demand that he commend them to his successor. His Indian Office officials meanwhile adapted the 'Instructions' to fit the little money available and sent them to India as their own invention. Miss Nightingale was furious. Moreover, the India Office had acted without informing the War Office, thereby declaring their refusal to be directed by Miss Nightingale through her War Office agents. The India officials also moved to ensure that papers were retained in their office and not circulated to the War Office, thereby blocking her sources of information. The India men had effectively negated her bid for control.[12] The three-tiered sanitary commission was not finally instituted until September 1863 and even then it remained inactive.

Lord Stanley, her chosen replacement for Herbert as her agent, was little help. He was both in Opposition and lacking in Herbert's graces. Jowett, when advising her about possible recruits, had characterised him as 'a cold ill mannered Radical Aristocrat rather [?] cut off from the religious world & equally from the jolly world, but still a man with higher aims than any other politician.'[13] He proved a languid go-between. He 'does nothing for us', Miss Nightingale complained to Harriet Martineau in July 1863. 'I have to do it all . . . a poor invalid woman'.[14] Stanley had once at her behest persuaded the Secretary for India, Sir Charles Wood, to forbid alterations to the Bombay Hospital until the plans had been referred home. This small intervention taught Stanley a lesson. Miss Nightingale moved to have the alterations redesigned by the fashionable, expensive Matthew Digby Wyatt. Stanley struggled to hold her to their initial understanding that the plans were to be studied by the War Office architects. The project apparently was stalemated. The hospital was not rebuilt until much later and there is no evidence that Wyatt was ever called in.[15] After this episode Stanley evaded her demands with vague but coy conspiratorial notes. He made no commitments although at important dinner-tables he readily boasted of his acquaintance with her.

Her drive to get things done, her secrecy and her craving for recognition and proprietorship made her a shifty ally. Even the faithful Sutherland was quietly denigrated. In October 1863, for instance, she privately hinted to Galton that he should correct the implications of an India Office minute she had seen on a document he had spirited out for her. The minute noted that Miss Nightingale's summary of some report from Ceylon was 'merely a résumé' of fuller notes compiled by Dr Sutherland. This 'curious minute', she protested, 'put [her] into a very false position'.

All the <u>original</u> Ceylon documents are in my hands – in my house at this moment – were all <u>abstracted by</u> me It was only in my house that Dr Sutherland could, or did, consult them – He made his 'Notes' from the <u>original</u> documents . . . I mine. I saw his 'Notes' – he mine – as we always do – But I did not look at his 'Notes' even – while writing mine. I had not got them.

This is not very clear. Her explanation becomes more confused as it proceeds:

> I had rather my handwriting (or name) had not appeared at all in this matter . . . I have given Dr Sutherland the whole credit, if that be an object, of the India Commission, and have got him £1500 [through Stanley] for it . . .

She faced a future of resentful toil at the periphery, of being less and less in the know, of wielding less and less power: 'But I have had a great deal more to do with the original documents than he has . . . also why do we only see this minute of 10/7 on Oct 28?'[16] Galton, too, had his future to look to, and he had no right to show her documents.

Suddenly, before the year was done, Miss Nightingale came in from the cold. The surprise nomination of Sir John Lawrence as Governor-General was announced at the end of November and she pounced immediately. His appointment gave her 'a most unexpected hold on India', she exulted to McNeill '. . . few have had such extraordinary chances as I have had – twice – a Secretary of State and a Governor-General delivered, as it were, into my hand'. The great-hearted saviour of Delhi during the Mutiny would 'play . . . [the] noble . . . game . . . as Sidney Herbert . . . had not played it'.[17] After Lawrence's death in 1879 she was to tell Gladstone that:

> Sir John Lawrence came to me in those last hurried days [he sailed for India within ten days of his appointment] we sketched out the whole plan of Sanitary proceedings not only for the Army but for the native populations for all India, which he carried out . . . thank God for it.

They met at her house on 4 December. The meeting had been arranged by Stanley. Their talk was about sanitary reform for India:

> I have had the great joy of being in constant communication with Sir John Lawrence – she told Farr on 10 December – and of receiving his commands to do what I had almost lost all hope of being allowed to do – viz. of sending out full statements and schemes of what we want the Presidency Commissions to do. I should be glad to submit to you copies of papers of mine which he desired me to write . . . They are, of course, confidential . . . with Sir John Lawrence's commands we feel ourselves empowered to begin the Home Commission . . .[18]

Biographers have accepted Miss Nightingale's fiction and presented her and Lawrence as united in their pursuit of the grail of salubrious India. There is no evidence that Lawrence acceded to any of her overtures. His responses which survive suggest that he was non-committal and that his subsequent actions in India were consistent with his knowledge of what was possible rather than with Miss Nightingale's dream of making India a clean, sober Arcady. He remarked of her terrible descriptions of native towns in the *Report* that though their state was generally bad much had been done to improve them. Moreover, 'the cost of improvements ... is great, and the great bulk of the people are very poor'. Miss Nightingale asserted that 'opinion' was unanimous that spirits should be banned from Army canteens and grog-shops in the bazaars. Lawrence was 'inclined to think it would not answer absolutely to prohibit the sale in canteens'. After all, canteens helped finance the army. Six months later he bravely reduced the rum issue to one dram per day. This hardly fulfilled Miss Nightingale's boast that 'he ... carried out everything we suggested'.[19]

Lawrence used Miss Nightingale's reputation and the expertise of her team when it suited him. He adopted her — or Galton's — plans for stone or brick two-storied, white-washed barracks. He envisaged rehousing the 25,000 white troops who had arrived since the Mutiny and were still crowded into existing dilapidated barracks and temporary cantonments. But Lawrence was a careful spender and in no hurry, especially as he encountered opposition on every front. In India his permanent officials were bent upon reducing taxation and expenditure and had moved decisively to that end just before his arrival. At home the Horse Guards, the India Office and War Office, locked in inter-departmental warfare, were united in wanting to retain a cheap army and doubly united in keeping out Miss Nightingale.[20] In India Lawrence named men to Miss Nightingale's projected Presidency Sanitary Commissions, but then delayed the announcement of rules upon which they could proceed. This allowed local medical men, suspicious of the new commissioners, to develop the habit of refusing to supply information, in which they were backed by suspicious army officers who regarded the new Commissions as threats to their independence. The senior civil officials did not like the Commission either. As John Strachey loftily informed Miss Nightingale, after telling her that the 'draft' rules followed her suggestions, 'no measures involving an immediate large expenditure could have any chance of being adopted'.[21]

In the event the few army building programmes begun during

Lawrence's regime were restricted to some urgent works in Calcutta and to his beloved hill-stations, especially Simla. He disagreed fundamentally with the Nightingale team on the strategy for holding India, a disagreement that had been manifest since at least 1861. Lawrence believed that the Indian plains could never become healthy and habitable for white troops and that the alternative was to establish permanent settler-garrison forces on the climatically more equable, and therefore salubrious, hills. Miss Nightingale, Farr and Co. argued that the key to India lay in the plains which carried the communications, rivers, railways and roads, and which contained the great towns, the breeding grounds of sedition. The white army must be stationed near these strategic points and therefore the plains must be rendered wholesome. Lawrence never wavered in his preference: he directed such little money as he had to the hill-stations. Miss Nightingale never admitted to herself that she was dealing with a strategic, sanitary heretic.[22]

Her moral improvement plans for the soldiers were part of her design to make the plains habitable. They hinged on the barracks building programme, and failed. Her 'dayrooms', on the Crimea model, to encourage troops to pass their free time reading, letter writing and playing innocent games, were to be housed in the ground floor space of the new barracks. Very few seem to have been built. There were also to be 'workshops' for hobbies, and garden plots allocated to the men. These foundered on the niggardliness of the Indian Government and War Office. The army would not supply tools or instructors, the gardens required water which was scarce and expensive. Moreover, with reveille at four each morning, the men preferred an afternoon siesta to toiling in stifling sheds or sun-baked gardens: such work was native work, anyway. Miss Nightingale, who never understood that India was very hot, ascribed the failure to want of leadership from officers; and, indeed, no general order was ever issued to compel men to work in the sheds or gardens. Everywhere beset by procrastinators, she longed for the power to work miracles of obliteration: as Christ would have done 'if Christ had had to work through Pilate!'[23]

Her tie to Lawrence was strained further by the counter attack by senior Indian medical officers upon the statistics in the *Report*, published in August 1864. The doctors' ignorance and former neglect now served them. Miss Nightingale and Farr had indeed made statistics without straw. It emerged that the Nightingale figure silently omitted two Presidencies, Madras and Bengal, because estimates were unavailable, yet the *Report* by implication covered all India. There were no figures for 1857 and the year following because statistical work ceased during the Mutiny. This too was glossed in the *Report*. It emerged that the Nightingale team had estimated the recent sickness and death rates by calculating from the numbers of troops sent out to India, without allowing that these numbers were inflated by the move to build a post-Mutiny white army. The doctors asserted that the 71 per 1000 death rate of 1836 was exaggerated and unprovable and that the assumption that the 41 per 1000 rate had continued undiminished since 1855 was false; as was the average over the period of 69 per 1000. They declared that the death rate had been dramatically reduced from about 1859, and quoted their figure for 1863, 20 per 1000, without adding that it had been an extraordinarily fever-free year. None the less, the doctors' figures for the post-Mutiny period were probably closer to the real order of magnitude than those publicised by the Nightingale team. Her angry claim that the army had cut the Indian mortality and sickness rates by a new, secretive policy of invaliding home much larger members of troops at earlier stages of their illness was an admission, although she made it look like a rebuttal.[24]

'We have been replying with all our might', Miss Nightingale told Harriet Martineau, when seeking her journalistic support, 'The opponents are always stronger than the supporters of good.'[25] Miss Nightingale fought, as she had done when her tuberculosis statistics were impugned, passionately on every front. She sent Lord Stanley to Sir Charles Wood to persuade him to withhold two of the Indian critiques, by Messrs Norman and Baker, from the House of Commons. Wood, who neither cared much about Indian death rates nor liked parliamentary rows, readily complied. Miss Nightingale rejoiced to Farr that craven Wood had 'wisely held his tongue'.[26] She also quickly revised and reprinted her pamphlet on *How People May Live ... in India*, incorporating into it a letter from Sir Hugh Rose, the Commander-in-Chief in India, praising the *Report*. Rose had written his letter to the Horse Guards, in reply to one from the War Office drawing his attention to the *Report*. It is very probable that Galton sent this uncharacteristic War Office memorandum to Rose, at Miss Nightingale's instigation. Galton then spirited Rose's reply to Miss Nightingale. She incorporated his letter, before asking Galton's permission. She went further, somehow:

The letter has been quoted in the 'Times'. By the way I did not send it to the Times. I sent the 'Abstract' and 'Suggestions' to Mr Delane [the Editor] through Count Strzelecki, & told them of the existence of Sir Hugh Rose's letter and got those articles written. But I did not give them Sir H. Rose. Probably they came to you for it.

Why did she tell Galton he had given it, if he had given it? Galton's short, cool reply ignored the point.[27]

The *Report*'s most dangerous critic was Dr A.C. Leith, chairman of the Bombay Sanitary Commission. He was a capable man who resented the carping tone of the *Report*, and who had independently kept figures on army health (which he must have withheld from the Royal Commission). Like his colleagues he argued that the *Report* overstated recent mortality and illness rates. His estimate for the recent army mortality rate for Bombay was 12/1000. Miss Nightingale apparently heard about Leith's threatened reply from a newly returned Indian official. She secretly obtained a copy from J.J. Frederick, an official at the War Office and secretary to the Army Sanitary Commission, who had illicitly borrowed it from Sir Proby Cautley — Miss Nightingale cultivated Frederick with gifts of game and subscriptions to his favourite charities. In India news of Leith's criticisms had appeared in the Bombay press. She moved first to capture Leith by sending him a sweet letter, accompanied by 'valuable books' and 'suggestions'. Among the latter was an invitation to send his findings to her Indian Barracks Committee rather than to the India Office. Leith professed himself flattered by her interest, but he stolidly evaded capture and even fought back, remarking that, 'It is easy to point out what is required but there are many delays . . . as everything . . . has to be submitted for approval to those without local knowledge.' Stanley was alarmed: Leith was a person of consequence who could not be brushed aside. Stanley proposed that he be openly 'answered', courteously and cautiously and not be made 'an enemy'. Miss Nightingale ignored this unsubtle suggestion and — without telling Stanley that she had already tried to silence Leith — advised Stanley to prompt Sir Charles Wood 'privately' to invite Miss Nightingale to inform him about the errors in Leith's report. She supplied a draft. Stanley dodged: it would be wrong to 'put my name to a letter I have not written'. He suggested that she write. She refused. Finally, they agreed that Sutherland should write to Wood. Stanley and Miss Nightingale might then write to support him. In the event Miss Nightingale prevailed upon Stanley to write; Wood agreed to refer Leith's report to the Indian Barracks and Hospital Improvement Commission.[28] Miss Nightingale then mobilised Farr to devise answers to Leith's 'statistical objections' and urged Galton, a member of the Barracks Commission, to have the report referred to Sutherland, in accordance with 'Lord Stanley's desire'. Their replies were to be officially printed. She would send copies to influential people, beginning with Lawrence. Miss Nightingale also set out to split the Bombay Commission and isolate Leith by warning their secretary, Surgeon J.P. Walker, 'strictly in confidence', that Wood was on her side. She undertook that the draft replies would be circulated among the full membership of the Barracks Commission; but after they were completed on 5 December 1864, she insisted that they go into type on that very day. Stanley, as chairman, did not even see the draft until three weeks later.[29]

Cautious Sir Charles Wood learned from this episode. He directed that all correspondence between India and the Barracks and Hospital Improvements Commission should go through him. Stanley and Miss Nightingale then promptly agreed that she would have to work through the Governor-General, who was not a 'sanitary commission'. After delicately hinting that Wood was likely to approve, she asked Lawrence,

> Would you not think it well that papers which involve sanitary principles of permanent importance ... all the papers from the Bengal Sanitary Commission ... should be sent home officially through Sir Charles Wood to the Barracks and Hospital Improvement Commission?

Wood meant well, she allowed, but he was 'very ignorant of sanitary matters' and it 'does not do to depend upon the life of one person'. After delaying his reply for six months Lawrence declared himself honoured by her faith in his capacity and promised to help where he thought her plans were 'plausible'. But as for addressing sanitary reports to her through the India Office, 'you will think me timid – but ... only the Secretary of State for India can do that'. Miss Nightingale savagely marked this part of his letter.[30] 'Our difficulties', he informed her in another evasive letter, 'are ... very much beyond your conception.' The British, he explained, were 'birds of passage' and did not look to a long-term future. The natives were apathetic, and even opposed to sanitary changes. The European townspeople were united to blocking increased taxation to pay for new water and drainage schemes.[31] Moreover they could always drum up support back home. From this time onward, India was beset by cyclones, drought, famine and commercial collapse and Lawrence dismantled his sanitary commissions and virtually ceased to communicate with Miss Nightingale.

The unhappy Leith row continued throughout 1865. Farr was persuaded by Leith's calculations; so too was Stanley. Miss Nightingale urged Farr to alter his report: 'otherwise people will miss the point. e.g. they think _we_ told the lie'.[32] But it seems that Farr quietly stuck to his figures. Poor Galton was in trouble after it emerged that Miss Nightingale had seen Leith's report before Wood had released it, (thanks to Frederick, of course), Galton found her unsympathetic and resistant to accepting some blame: 'All I regret is my excessive discretion (which indeed is my besetting sin).' She accused him of siding with the forces of unsanitary, complacant truth: 'it would be far better if the temporary 12 per 1000 had remained at 69 per 1000, if people are to be deluded by it into the belief that any material improvements . . . have been made'. She then proposed that the team attack another damaging report, by Colonel Norman, but this time they all seem to have backed off.[33] The Leith and Norman episodes suggest that the men on the spot were achieving a much greater saving of life, with only limited resources, than Miss Nightingale and the writers who have followed her, have allowed.

In December 1865 Miss Nightingale heard that Lord de Grey, an upright Christian reforming aristocrat, was likely to succeed the ailing Wood as Secretary of State for India. She immediately cast her nets. She had, she told de Grey,

> been busy with Sir John Lawrence . . . He was most strongly of the opinion that your 'home' Commission should begin operations at once – in sending our plans of Barracks & Hosps, with complete 'instructions' – this was his own word . . . I urged repeatedly that it would be much less offensive (to India authorities) if this were done by the home Commission under a direct instruction from the Secretary of State for India. And he answered repeatedly – Just the reverse – you have lost time – you should volunteer all this . . .

There is no evidence for this version, and much evidence to indicate that it could not have happened. As usual Miss Nightingale began with a reverie of desire and ended with a dramatic imperative. The letter continues for twenty pages. Miss Nightingale, once more faced with dislodgement from business, was desperate to hang on. Manipulation was her very being. She apologised by implication for the rambling, repetitive missive and explained that a short plea 'cannot go down on its knees – And that is . . . my position (morally) at this moment to you'. De Grey rebuffed her.[34] Six months later she finally lost Stanley.

He came into office in July 1866. He had been ready to tinker while in Opposition but now he tartly informed her that he had no time to help in sanitary matters and, besides, he could 'not interfere in a colleague's department'.[35] They never collaborated again.

The colleague at the India Office was stern Lord Cranborne, later Lord Salisbury. He was an intelligent reactionary, outside Miss Nightingale's ambience of Whiggish, reforming aristocrats. She did not know how to collar him and drafted several approaches, varying from fully 'flattering' to fully businesslike. Finally she must have sent a business letter, because he curtly replied that he had no time to attend to her proposals. Miss Nightingale tried again in the following year: 'weak as I am I should be glad to have the opportunity of discussing the subject [cholera in India] with you when you could conveniently do so'. Cranborne never came. Meanwhile he quietly countermanded a despatch from his predecessor, de Grey, permitting a start on minor sanitary works — 'finance must come first'. Miss Nightingale blamed Galton and Sutherland. Their laziness in 'Indian sanitary matters [had] lost my locus standi with Cranborne — bequeathed by Stanley'.[36] Here, as she often did when defeated, Miss Nightingale constructed a world in which she was both heroine and victim, betrayed by her acolytes. It seems to be that in these situations her lies, as told to acolytes and prospective supporters, lose their ordinary connotation as being intended to deceive and instead become the materials for a fantasy which was real enough to her as she wrote. And so it might have seemed to Galton and Sutherland, who accepted her reproaches and continued loyal to her.

Even at this desolate stage in her career Miss Nightingale exemplified for many Britons the spirit of reform: of preservation and improvement of human life as a means to national strength and therefore true economy under God's laws of incorporation of the British and Indian masses into British middle-class norms of cleanliness and sobriety as a way to national perfectibility under Providence. As had happened before with Sidney Herbert, Sutherland and Jowett, like-minded spirits consecrated themselves to her unexpectedly at critical points in her pilgrimage. Sir Bartle Frere, the former Governor of Bombay, returned to England in the early summer of 1867 and joined the Council of India. He was a kindred visionary to Miss Nightingale. He too was a spender. In Bombay he had defied the financial control of the central government and built lavishly, employing expensive home architects and setting his crest on his public buildings. He had also upset local British dignitaries and their wives by entertaining native gentlemen and their ladies at Government House. Miss Nightingale obtained from Galton Frere's London address and advice on how to approach him. After Frere's visit to South Street she indulged herself in a small but characteristic piece of superfluous deceit. The great man came, she boasted to Galton, of all people, 'by his own appointment'. The meeting was a success. 'I think perhaps we start at a fresh advantage now.' Frere's faith, she discovered, was 'save . . . lives, cost what it will, then we can work'.[37]

Bartle Frere became her spy in the India Office. He provided her with copies of Cranborne's minutes to despatches. His 'rummaging through . . . papers' supplied Miss Nightingale with proof that the Indian government was building hospitals with ventilation systems which ignored her Barracks and Hospital Commission's prescriptions. She and her commission, working by English precedent, were keen on fully opened windows allowing air to sweep along the corridors. The Indian hospital builders, mindful of the heat, designed verandah-shaded windows which could be closed during the sweltering afternoons and through dust storms. Frere, who had in effect been sacked by Lawrence, turned Miss Nightingale against him. Lawrence, he alleged, did nothing but commission reports. The Governor-General was niggardly with money, even in cases of obvious need. He was afraid of offending the home government.[38] A romantic egotist, Frere was determined to fulfil the destiny that had been thwarted in India. 'He offered', Miss Nightingale confided to Sutherland, 'almost with tears in his eyes, to be "our aide de camp".' Together, they decided to press the new Secretary of State, Sir Stafford Northcote, a pressible man, they believed, to create a public health department in the India Office, headed by Frere and comprising Sutherland, Galton and Farr.[39]

This project revived Miss Nightingale's hopes of by-passing the Indian Government and India Office by having Indian sanitary matters directly referred home, to her. She intended the department to rule on the 'doors and windows' question, thereby correcting error and avenging the slight she had suffered from Indian army engineers and doctors. Above all, the department would enable her to see papers and know what was going forward. Frere's hopes paralleled hers. He envisaged the department as a mechanism for enabling Presidency governments to ignore the Indian central government. The department would approve, in the name of the India Office, local budgets for 'public' improvements.[40]

Northcote was to be edged into granting 'confidential' permission to Frere to send on papers to Sutherland and Galton in the War Office, and thence to Miss Nightingale. But Sutherland, Miss Nightingale scoffed, turned 'etiquette-ish' about the scheme. He was worried about losing his job. Enmity between the War and India Offices made his position awkward and he was already suspect from his association with the bothersome lady. He sought a 'formal' agreement between Northcote and his War Office chiefs. This did not suit Miss Nightingale.[41] An open agreement would alert the senior officials of both camps: each group would work to evade the agreement while both would collaborate to ensure that she saw only trivia, and those belatedly. Besides, she enjoyed espionage. She instigated moves, through Galton at the War Office, to get at documents even before Northcote was approached. Galton offered to the India Office on behalf of a 'sub-committee' of the War Office (presumably himself and Sutherland) to exchange information as a prelude to renewing co-operation. Miss Nightingale then wrote to Northcote commending this enlightened magnanimity and suggesting that the India Office reciprocate. Her proposal offended the tradition of departmental insularity. She never understood that rationality was not enough and was surprised when Northcote, whom she deemed weak, hedged on agreeing and fled on holiday.[42] It is a measure of his weakness that he did not refuse outright. Meanwhile Frere and Galton, aided by the prevailing inefficiencies of their respective offices, had already begun to abstract and exchange papers, which duly came to South Street.[43]

Northcote gave way within the month. On 20 August 1867 he accepted the Nightingale-Frere department within the India Office and undertook to instruct local Indian sanitary bodies to defer to it. Having won the victory Miss Nightingale despised the vanquished: 'He is very well intentioned – but he has not the elements of Sanitary', she recorded for herself, forgetting the noun; and indeed, 'Sanitary' for her was a means to power rather than a science. She thought he would carry out his undertakings because he was too soft to break them. He obeyed her summons to visit her. 'He kept his eyes shut all the time – and I kept my eyes wide open', she recorded after the interview. Ruthlessly, she seized her chance to pursue a larger dream:

Then I began about Nurses [for army, European civilian and native hospitals]. He said he was pestered by private persons with their philanthropic schemes about India (like Miss Carpenter, he said). [I wonder if he did. I shall return to Miss Carpenter later.] I said – I'm not a philanthropic person. It's they who are pestering me.[44]

After years of evasion and rebuffs from Sir Charles Wood, Lord de Grey and Lord Cranborne, she now had half under her thumb at least, a Secretary for India, a potentate who could deliver up to her not only the army, but India. The great plan she had shared with Sutherland since the Mutiny, and which had since lain quiescent, of regenerating native India and thereby justifying British suzerainty to God and man, now sprang to life. Having gained her public health department and received no outright rejection of her nurses, she informed Galton that our 'work will really be introducing the elements of civilization into India'.[45] Miss Nightingale had emerged as an imperialist.

Miss Nightingale rejected the philanthropist tag because she presented herself as being inside government, as an engine propelling 'national' efficiency, in contrast to outsiders who self-indulgently and ineffectually busied themselves with uplifting individuals or special groups among the poor. Her family standing, wealth, tenacity and good luck had enabled her to worm further into government than other improvers, especially female ones, but she was more like other philanthropists of her time than she cared to admit. They vied for the same fiefdoms and pursued indistinguishable strategies. While Stafford Northcote was merely 'pestered' by them, her rivals threatened her very purpose in living – by threatening her unique eminence as a reformer. Among these rivals Mary Carpenter and the National Association for the Promotion of Social Science are worth discussing because they impinged upon Miss Nightingale's career, they illuminate certain of her ambitions and they are interesting in their own right. Miss Carpenter, moreover, has been the beneficiary of almost as much ill-founded hagiography as Miss Nightingale.

In mid-1867 Miss Carpenter had emerged as Miss Nightingale's main competitor for India. Like Miss Nightingale, she had first had her hopes raised by Lawrence's appointment, then had been rebuffed by Wood, tried de Grey and Cranborne and failed, and then had tackled Northcote, whom she found, she informed Miss Nightingale possessively, 'very amenable indeed'.[46] Like Miss Nightingale again, her ambition was to use government to implement, that is, build and pay for, her chosen innovations – the emancipation of Indian women, the introduction of children's reformatories and a strict regime in Indian gaols, and sanitary reform. They began to circle one another in April 1867. Miss Carpenter opened by seeking Miss Nightingale's acquiescence in her projected visit to India. Miss Nightingale turned to Jowett, who knew everybody, for his usual shrewd malicious appraisal of the interloper.

He pronounced her 'worthy — but a terrible bore'.[47] Prospectively, she was a formidable competitor. She was thirteen years older than Florence Nightingale and had already become famous as an anti-slavery advocate and Ragged Schools manager almost a decade before Miss Nightingale went to the Harley Street Institution. Miss Nightingale found herself 'terribly busy' and postponed Miss Carpenter's intended visit until it became impossible for the lady to come: 'It is very good of you', Miss Nightingale purred, 'to think of me during your short & busy stay in London.' When she finally permitted a meeting, she refused to be impressed. She noted after the visit; 'Well — Miss Carpenter came here ... on very serious business. She began by telling me what every one knows but which seemed to have struck her as something new — the awful state of the Indian women ... She wants to put me into communications with divers people at Madras and Bombay.'[48]

Like Miss Nightingale herself, Josephine Butler, the campaigner against the Contagious Diseases Acts, Lord Shaftesbury and other Victorian reformers, Mary Carpenter was given to dedicating herself in God's name to her successive causes, and to recounting that determination on paper. Lawrence's preferment, as it did with Miss Nightingale, alerted her to new opportunities. She recorded on 12 January 1864:

> my solemn resolve that henceforth I devote my heart and soul and strength to the elevation of the women of India ... I shall obey the remarkable call which has been given me so unexpectedly ... Without any ... apparent change of plan, I shall watch openings ... and later — A grand and new life appears opening upon me, Heavenly Father, by tokens drawn from the marvellous workings of Thy providence.[49]

She had lit upon India after venturing successively on Home Visiting, Ragged Schools, children's reformatories and convict reform projects. In each she had made the rules, done the managing and taken the credit, but rarely actually worked in the enterprise. She was domineering, sentimental and cruel, suspicious of fellow reformers and intolerant and inept in handling her subordinates and her charges. Each venture increased her power and reputation, but there is no evidence to show that the subjects of her endeavours were made happy or better.[50]

Again like Miss Nightingale she had a father who had educated her, whom she publicly esteemed but privately despised. He had been a

Unitarian clergyman. He was 'lost at sea' in 1840 (when Mary was 33), while on a Mediterranean tour recovering from a nervous breakdown. She disliked her mother and sister and was 'not lonely' when they died. They envied, she said, her 'secret consciousness of having performed . . . any service . . . better than others would have done'.[51] As a child she had insisted on running her own Sunday School. Before she was twenty she knew that God had chosen her for 'distinguished' work. Her earthly reward was public 'affection and gratitude'. She never married. In serving her heavenly father she made reparation, she believed, to the earthly father whom she could not love, indeed to her unloved self, for, as she often recalled her mother telling her, she was very like her father in mind and body. The parallel with Miss Nightingale extends even further. Miss Carpenter adopted a little girl, whom she apparently left, as did Miss Nightingale, to be raised by others: 'a little girl of *my own*! . . . Ready to my hand and nicely trained, without the trouble of marrying etc., etc.,'.[52] Rarely can two egotisms have been so mirrored. Florence Nightingale's and Mary Carpenter's restless possessiveness, their attitude to their respective fathers, their craving for fame through self-sacrifice, illuminate the motivations of other Victorian females who adopted bizarre, unpopular causes – Ellice Hopkins, the social purity campaigner, for instance, or her crony, Sarah Robinson, 'the soldier's friend', or another Unitarian campaigner, Octavia Hill. Social isolates from childhood, their work is characterised by voyeuristic condescension, complacent parsimony and an unwavering resolve to use the state to underwrite their pursuits and coerce the subjects of their careers. The stock explanation for the involvement of spinsters in Victorian social reform, the 'superfluous women' argument, is inadequate to explain the sheer drive and flair of these crusaders who remained unmarried apparently by choice.

When Miss Nightingale refused to treat, Miss Carpenter countered by appealing to the National Association for the Promotion of Social Science, where Miss Nightingale had earlier made her triumphant plea for India. The NAPSS had been created in 1856 by a vigorous, newly graduated briefless barrister, George Woodyatt Hastings, the son of a founder of the British Medical Association. Hastings used the prestige of old Lord Brougham, the first president of NAPSS, to bring about a coalition of old Benthamites, social statisticians like Farr and William Newmarch, sanitary reformers like John Simon and Lord Shaftesbury, law and education reformers such as Brougham, James Kay-Shuttleworth and M.D. Hill, earnest paternalist aristocrats like Lord Ebrington and Stanley, representatives of the Unitarian and Quaker reforming cousinhoods, Howitts, Taylors and Sturges, and social work careerists like Mary Carpenter and her juvenile reformatory and convict discipline rivals. Hastings succeeded in recruiting almost every great name in the reform calendar, including Miss Nightingale.

The NAPSS provided a platform for amateurs working from outside Parliament, or at least the Cabinet and the bureaucracy, to forward their particular objects. The celebrated annual meetings, held at a succession of provincial cities, provided opportunities for public oratory and displays of concentrated reforming strength. The sub-committees and deputations enabled individuals to press their particular aims and arrange cabals. Rivalries between crotcheteers were particularly sharp on the timing, size and presentation of deputations to important people. The published reports of special committees and the *Transactions* were intended to sway governments and municipal corporations through reproduction in the daily press. The NAPSS was open to ladies, even to their speaking publicly at the congresses. Women could not serve on the Council, but at the 1858 meeting they comprised one-third of the 1500 participants. The journal was printed, at higher than ruling rates, by Emily Faithful at the Victoria Press.[53] The NAPSS's model was the British Association for the Advancement of Science. 'Social Science' for the members of NAPSS neither carried its contemporary Comtist meaning of progressive sociology nor its modern connotation of controlled social inquiry into social and class structures. NAPSS members already knew the answers: their problem was to rouse 'public opinion' and make government act. Hastings paid lip-service to prevailing orthodoxy in the first issue of the journal:

> Advancing knowledge has proved an inseparable connexion between the various branches of physical science, and disclosed to us, as Newton foreshadowed ... a unity throughout creation, a vast expansion of purpose, based on a few simple laws ... as promulgated by ... the ... Divine Legislator.

But he immediately qualified this profession by remarking that the NAPSS's strength was 'the practical knowledge and actual experience of social reformers'. Indeed, Hastings off-handedly foisted 'social science' on the Association -- in the midst of arguing against the intention of some of the founding fathers to have 'law' in the name of the proposed journal: 'People so hate the name of *law* ... whereas under general social science a good deal of law & legislation might be worked in & made popular.' Ambitious Hasting's chief concern was that the infant Association should be 'National'.[54] And so it became: within ten years NAPSS had 1600 members, almost double the enrolment of the British Association.[55]

The reformers' practical knowledge found expression through the five original departments: Law Amendment, Education, Punishment and Reformation, Public Health, Social and Political Economy. The members' object was not to change the world but to manage it. They intended, now that Old Corruption and Chartism were defeated, to produce rationales for middle-class control over the urban masses who were now beyond village tutelage, whose ignorance, turbulence, criminality and poverty were faults or misfortunes within themselves, not their society. The NAPSS had considerable influence on protective legislation for the middle classes during the 1860s and 1870s: reforms in the law of bankruptcy and other areas of commercial law including patents; married women's property; the Endowed Schools Act; reform of the law of evidence and innovations in prison discipline; the Public Health Act of 1875 and compulsory notification of infectious diseases; and the great report on strikes in 1860 which crystallised a view of trade union activity which has endured to the present. The NAPSS also led in creating international associations in statistics, weights and measures and, especially, international law. This remarkable organisation is now largely forgotten, partly because it petered out in the mid-1880s as its founding generation dropped away and their particular line of indirect state interventionism became unpopular among the harshly polarised advocates of anti-statism and socialism, and partly because Hastings, the very embodiment of the NAPSS, was disgraced in 1892 when he was sentenced to five years imprisonment for fraud.[56]

From the outset Miss Nightingale deemed the NAPSS a rival for public interest. She lent her name to the Association, Hastings's assemblage of big names did not permit her to do otherwise, but privately she disparaged it: 'If the whole of the 1st vol. of the Transactions had been burnt, the world would have been none the worse', she confided to Chadwick, another old hand threatened by the new organisation.[57] None the less, she offered to present a paper at the next congress in Liverpool. She had the paper on 'The Sanitary Conditions of Hospitals' read, but she did not appear despite allowing rumours to circulate that she would; her paper duly appeared in the second volume of the *Transactions*. Her contributing lent *éclat* to the journal but she spoiled the effect and upset Hastings by issuing the article as a separate pamphlet before the *Transactions* appeared, and then again as a book, padded with material from the Army Sanitary Commission.[58] Her paper, which developed into *Notes on Hospitals* in its third edition of 1863, remains a brilliant polemic. She vividly rehearsed the evils of overcrowding, bad ventilation and lighting as correlatives to yet another denunciation of the belief that 'hospital diseases' were spread by contagion. Her argument now looks bizarrely simplistic, but set in its context of seedy, grubby hospital buildings, doctors and patients, it becomes apt and beneficial. Miss Nightingale used the NAPSS as a rostrum on three more occasions. The committee was glad to have her name, but after her brush with Hastings over her premature pamphlet both sides kept their distance.

Her feud with Mary Carpenter over India continued through the 1860s. In 1867 Miss Nightingale used her kinsman and acolyte, Henry Bonham Carter, to dissuade Miss Carpenter from delivering an Indian paper, probably on female education and its promise for sanitary reform, at the forthcoming NAPSS congress in Belfast. The letter, signed by Bonham Carter, warned 'that no good is to be done in the way proposed' because it would 'induce misdirected efforts which might embarrass your present negotiations or relations (whatever they may be called) with government'. Bonham Carter offered to draft, 'for Miss Carpenter' to read at Belfast, an alternative document stating general principles but rejecting immediate action. She delicately riposted by addressing herself directly to Miss Nightingale: 'your letter ... is really right', and noting her particular obligation to Miss Nightingale for enclosing a copy of Miss Carpenter's original letter declaring her intention to speak at Belfast — signals sent and received. Miss Carpenter then feinted beautifully. She claimed to have lost her voice and therefore could not 'undertake to read any papers aloud at the meeting'. Indeed, she hinted that her illness would prevent her from attending. A week later in Belfast, doubtless to Miss Nightingale's vexed surprise, Miss Carpenter delivered two papers on India, the first concerned with prison discipline, the second, given 'extemporaneously' to ringing applause and the encomium of her chairman, the influential Lord Dufferin (of the War Office, formerly of the India Office, and future Governor-General of India), on Miss Nightingale's forbidden subject, 'Female Education'.[59] Miss Nightingale had met her match.

Their next and last confrontation occurred two years later, in September 1869, when Miss Carpenter sought to enlist Miss Nightingale's support for her Indian Association for the Promotion of Social Science, a body she had created among British civil officials, Bombay Parsees and a few Hindu gentlemen. Miss Carpenter had plunged into India with almost as little knowledge and understanding as Miss Nightingale. Her experience on her first and second journey had disabused her of the notion that simple proselytism among deferential natives would lead to the introduction of cleaner, classified prisons and female education among Hindus. The government would not provide money for the first and Hindu fathers, husbands and mothers, resisted the second. Such female schools as existed dated from long before her visit and indeed were upset by her interference. Apparently only one of the schools she launched survived: she had nominated herself Lady Superintendent of the Bombay Normal School but typically had immediately left the running and teaching of the school to subordinates — who in this case turned out to be effective. Miss Carpenter found native gentlemen to be complaisant but unreliable. She moved in 1869 to circumvent them by proposing a separate women's section of the Indian NAPSS. It would also circumvent British officials like Sir Alexander Grant, the Director of Public Instruction in Bombay, who blocked her requests for money after discovering that her schools were to inculcate Christianity. A ladies' section, Miss Carpenter confided, would engender '*sympathy* . . . without any *possibility* $\frac{Private}{\text{of suspicion}}$ on the part of the *natives* . . . or of the *government* of absurd fanaticism'. Miss Nightingale was invited to endorse, but not annex, the proposal: 'of course I do not suppose that you can take any part, but it will be a . . . benefit if you will write me a few lines of sympathy which I may read to the ladies'. Miss Nightingale pleaded ill-health and inability to hold a pen. Miss Carpenter begged. Miss Nightingale provided 'something'. Miss Carpenter returned 'many thanks for your loving note'.[60] There is no evidence that she used it. She would have had small opportunity to do so: agreeable Indian gentlemen such as Keshub Chunder Sen, now revered as fathers of the Indian freedom movement, proved wholly unenlightened when it came to allowing their own womenfolk to join Miss Carpenter.

Miss Nightingale found Miss Carpenter's interventions singularly disturbing because they emulated at every point her own discovery that India provided a multifarious, unspoiled field for a woman of business. (At first sight, it is strange that they did not try Ireland which was closer and obviously in need of improvement, but both ladies, like most of their colleagues, avoided Ireland. There, government was already in the field, the proud Anglo-Irish gentry appeared hostile and the common Irish were uncouth, resistant to advice and ultimately hardly worth preserving. As Miss Nightingale once remarked, Hindus were gentlemen, compared with the Irish.) Lawrence, partly because of the army sanitary improvements already achieved and largely because he was parsimonious, had disappointed Miss Nightingale's ambitions but she had early realised that she could by-pass him and his officials by tackling sanitary, civil and economic problems among the native population. Prison reform, nursing, village institutions, irrigation and canal building, and control of cholera had all been added to her agenda before Miss Carpenter took to India.

In each case Miss Nightingale herself was belatedly adopting initiatives already taken by dedicated medical men and engineers in India. The earliest evidence of Miss Nightingale's interest in prisons comes from mid-1864, when she began to demand of Lawrence's private secretary Dr Charles Hathaway — significantly, she did not raise the issue with Lawrence — that the Indian government produce accurate prison death rates. Hathaway had earlier been the Inspector of Prisons. Her demand was an implied rebuke.[61] The Inspector-General of Prisons in Bengal had already calculated death rates of about nine per cent of inmates per year, compared with a one per cent rate in British gaols.[62] Indian prisons were dilapidated, overcrowded, ill-ventilated, undrained, filthy and supplied with poor food. The inmates, unsegregated by age or crime, had, according to Sutherland, 'low resisting power ... they do not stand penal work as our men do'.[63] Local reformers and English activists such as Miss Carpenter were bent upon building panopticons and children's reformatories (there were only 400 child prisoners in all India in 1868) and introducing new graduated dietaries and punishments. Lawrence vetoed their plans. Privately he agreed that there were 'no good jails here', but warned that the reformers' ambitions would 'cost millions'. He added resignedly that prisoners were 'at least as well off as the rest of the people'.[64]

Miss Nightingale was interested in building new gaols to preserve life, not in new regimes of discipline for prisoners whose average expectation of life wearing 60 pound punishment chains was 15 days.[65] She went further than other reformers, too, in campaigning for redesigned lunatic asylums, which she was told were worse than the gaols. She wanted Lawrence to ask her Sanitary Commission to draw up schedules for cell sizes, latrines, bedding, airing and exercise. She was indifferent to the actual shape of prisons, but settled for the Pentonville model because it promised that surveillance and discipline would entail regular cleansing, meals and exercise. After Lawrence failed to seek her Sanitary Commission's advice she sent detailed plans and schedules anyway. She also intended to 'bring in the India Office somehow . . . they hold the purse strings'. They had lain low during the eighteen months that the prison issue had been canvassed in England. Miss Nightingale professed to be surprised when shortly after this letter *The Times* began to print the horrible details of Indian prison life and to advocate reforms. She told Galton that she had not furnished *The Times* with the information, 'however it makes our path much easier'.[66] She prodded Stanley into speaking to Sir Charles Wood, the Secretary of State, and supplied him with information for Wood's instruction. But Stanley was lukewarm — 'our suggested reforms are very costly' — and Wood did nothing. Stafford Northcote again proved more pliable. A NAPSS deputation waited on him and he told Lawrence to start on new gaols, on the basis of NAPSS assertions that they could be erected for £4. 10s 0d a cell. No building ensued. As General Strachey, Inspector-General of Irrigation and a senior member of the Governor-General's Council, remarked:

> When I think of all that has to be done in India for the honest part of the community, how roads and railways and canals have to be made . . . and 10,000 works of improvement to be carried out, it seems to be monstrous that we should have to discuss these schemes, which I can only characterise as . . . petty sentimentality.[67]

But clearly a clean-up did occur. Possibly fortuitously, cholera virtually disappeared from the prison compounds. At Bhagulpore prison in Bengal the annual death rate fell from an average of 16 per 100 inmates over the period 1844-65 to 1.9 per 100 in 1866 to 0.4 per 100 in 1869. The Madras gaol reported an improvement from 12.6 per 100 in 1865 to 5.3 per 100 in 1867 and 1.7 per 100 in 1871. Apart from the cheaply installed but apparently efficient new water storages in the gaols, and hence isolation from cholera (with luck), the British foreshortened the problem by unobtrusively halving the admissions.[68] Miss Nightingale's influence was indirect, but by lending her reputation to local reformers such as Doctors Mouat and Walker, who were trying to enforce cleansing schedules, she helped them to persist and gain a little from complacent, penny-pinching officials. This battle won, Miss Nightingale showed no interest in Indian prisons after the 1860s. Her interference had been well justified: she had helped break the terrible sequence which had made imprisonment in India a near certain death sentence.

Miss Nightingale's brief involvement with female nursing in India also arose from reaction to local initiatives. Early in 1864, in the first flush of his governor-generalship, Lawrence had permitted Dr Walker to proceed with his ambition to create a trained female nursing service in Bengal. Walker had decided upon his plan before he 'officially' informed Miss Nightingale of the project in November 1864. Apparently he intended to recruit Eurasian Christian women – Hindu and Moslem women were unavailable – and instal them in regimental hospitals to be trained effectively by the medical officers. Soldiers' widows, European and Eurasian, were already employed, untrained. This chain of authority broke Miss Nightingale's cardinal rule about the independence of the matron.[69] She also saw it as a challenge to her eminence as the authority on nursing. She made a take-over bid for the project by printing and circulating her own more elaborate scheme. She let it be known that Lawrence had asked her to despatch 66 head nurses and 112 assistants for regimental hospitals. There is no such request from Lawrence among the Nightingale Papers. There is not even a letter 'sanctioning', as Miss Nightingale oddly put it, such a plan. She also envisaged creating training schools in civilian general hospitals. 'There is a private and most pressing invitation to me to go out. If the Doctors would give me six months there, I would go', she confided to McNeill in the reasonable expectation that the story would spread, as it did. In all the Nightingale Papers, which preserve so much trivia, no such important invitation exists. Miss Nightingale admitted the fantasy of her plan in a concluding sentence in the letter to McNeill: her scheme was impossible because no trained nurses were available in England, but it served its purpose in smothering Walker's more feasible project.[70]

Eighteen months later her interest revived when Mary Carpenter threatened to move in on the nursing question:

Be assured that I never think you neglectful for not answering letters, [Miss Carpenter proffered] I am well aware that you have long turned your attention to India, & doubtless your efforts have produced valuable fruit. But I have seen no effort to train nurses, & there is a universal want of . . . decent nurses in the hospitals etc. [Then Miss Carpenter, fresh back from India, turned the screw] I believe that little is done in India by correspondence.

She added that she had secured Frere's support.[71] Miss Nightingale now moved to stop the intrusion. She obtained somehow the minutes of the governor-general's council on the nursing proposal and littered them with savage marginalia. She mobilised McNeill against the plan, warning him that she had 'always been against' placing nurses in regimental hospitals — a reversion to her old Crimean battles but a false affirmation in its present context. She even wrote to Lawrence. After three drafts, each declining in vehemence, she finally begged him to delay his decision and seek her help. Her plea must have crossed with the news that Lawrence had indeed vetoed the grandiose — though less grandiose than Miss Nightingale's own proposed contingent of 178 — scheme devised locally by Major G.B. Malleson and espoused by Miss Carpenter.[72] Miss Nightingale now countered with a reduced plan for a core contingent of four lady-superintendents to travel from England under contract from the India Office to recruit and train local women, an idea she had earlier totally opposed. She had lately despatched a similar core group to Sydney to begin training locals there. Again she remarked that she 'fain would' go to India to establish the system herself, 'then we should not have to worry', but this time she did not claim to have been invited. Again the Indian government vetoed this plan.[73] They were preoccupied with famine and flood and falling revenues. Miss Nightingale gave up. In her hard-headed way she recognised that so long as the government and the army could use slave labour and the chain of command remained unbroken, nothing could be done: 'Englishmen command Hindoo males and Eurasian subordinates — who give orders to the poor coolies — who do the actual nursing.'[74] Thereafter attempts by well-meaning governor's ladies, Christian missions and presidency governments foundered under lack of money and avoidance by Englishwomen 'who lose all desire to exert themselves', Eurasians who were too proud and 'native women' who were 'too ignorant'. When Miss Nightingale was last consulted about the problem, in 1889, matters had not changed.[75] Only with the coming of women doctors and a sufficient number of lady-superintendents for independent mission hospitals in the 1890s did effective nursing training and management really begin.

Miss Nightingale alwáys preferred the larger arena of public preventive sanitation. The indications for action were straightforward because the laws of health and cleanliness were simple and proven. The monetary outlay was relatively small and it was more than repaid by the strengthened national efficiency which resulted. Even in crude terms of lives preserved for money spent, her priorities, as against expenditure upon large hospitals and a highly skilled medical service, both in her own age and during the century since, were the right ones.

Ineluctably and not unwillingly, her concerns with barrack building, public sanitation and protection from cholera led her into Indian social and economic questions about which she knew little. Her ignorance never hindered her from making pronouncements, yet her common sense generally saved her from the callous inanities promulgated by better informed but more owlish authorities.

Miss Nightingale's opinions about cholera varied through time, but she passionately held to whatever notion happened to occupy her mind and always tried to forbid the propagation of rival theories, even if they were theories she had lately espoused. In 1854, she had drawn upon her transitory − or mythical − experience at the Middlesex Hospital to inform Mrs Gaskell that cholera was not contagious, that is, in her view, transmitted from victim to victim by contact. Miss Nightingale 'never had a touch even of diarrhoea'. By 1861 she had come to believe that sufferers caught cholera by drinking dirty water; she tried to stop the professors at the Army Medical School acknowledging any other hypothesis.[76] Cholera was endemic in India, she told the NAPSS Congress in 1863, because the army stations and bazaars lacked clean water and 'when men drink water, they drink cholera in it'.[77] But she soon perceived that this doctrine narrowed her field of operations by diverting attention from overcrowding, lime-washing of barracks, street cleansing and removal of sewage. In mid-1864 she warned Dr Hathaway that 'Dr. Budd's paper (the classic demonstration that cholera is a water-borne infection) is of no practical value ... It is purely theoretical.'[78] Many eminent medical men shared her reaction to Budd's work, but her peculiarly exposed position as a non-medical, unbeneficed sanitary advocate made her edgily strident in her dogmatic confusion − especially when authority ignored her. During an epidemic at Mean Meer (now Lahore) in 1863 the government had withdrawn all troops to barracks and thereby created great overcrowding: but they ignored the Indian Sanitary Commission's rules about isolating cases within the compounds; privies stayed foul and water supplies remained unimproved. Miss Nightingale was further put out because the report had been secretly supplied to her and she could not attack the government without exposing Walker, her go-between.[79]

India is the home of cholera and epidemics flared regularly at pilgrimages, fairs and festivals and accompanied the famines that recurred every three or four years during the last third of the century. Cholera death rates are only available after 1881 and they represent gross under-registration but still they record that between 1881-1900 6-8 per cent of all registered deaths were cholera cases representing nearly one million victims.[80] Government, faced with the impossible task of providing safe water supplies, resorted to quarantine: when cholera appeared soldiers were confined to barracks, afflicted villages and towns were isolated, pilgrimages forbidden, festivals terminated. Miss Nightingale dismissed these improvisations — although they indisputably saved thousands of lives — because they treated natives 'like infants', instead of employing them as adults 'to clean up and exercise responsibility', and because, she alleged, quarantine was unscientific.[81] By October 1865, after another bad outbreak in India, she reverted to the old miasma theory. Herding people together under quarantine only fortified the 'cholera influence'. Thus strengthened, it 'may extend hundreds of miles atmospherically from the Centre . . . The moral is: that, unless you improve the sanitary condition of the Civil populations, you cannot insure immunity for the Soldiers.'[82]

To this end she composed a new set of rules to be issued by the Indian Sanitary Commission in 1866. Ventilation, strict allowances of cubic feet of air per man in barracks, drainage, water supply, were all prescribed but the new emphasis was on strict and immediate removal of ordure. She pressed Galton to ensure that the War Office and India Office endorsed the new regulations, so that Indian officials would be less free to ignore them. After all, she prompted Galton, 'you have the first authority in Europe as to preventive action (about Cholera) in Dr Sutherland. After him and Grainger (who is dead) [Dr R.D. Grainger wrote a valuable report on cholera in 1850] I don't think you have any better authority than I.' She was, she boasted to Galton, 'not modest'. She relished knowing she was right and delighted in the espionage required to help her prevail. Two days later she returned 'with the greatest reluctance', some Indian papers Galton had purloined from the War Office for her, and signed herself 'Betsy Prig'.[83]

Her new rules were largely ignored. At home, after the epidemic of 1866 even Dr Farr defected to the water-borne camp, admitting to her belatedly — he had sought to hide his disloyalty — that 'the case against the water was very strong'. In India even stalwart allies like Dr T.G. Hewlett, the Health Officer for Bombay, settled for quarantine.[84] Miss Nightingale then set about outflanking them. At home she sounded influential people including Frere, de Grey and Napier of Magdala, the Indian military hero, on a proposal to establish a separate Indian Sanitary Service, independent of the medical officers and subject to her India Office Sanitary Committee. The fact that the medical profession had plumped for a specific water-borne causative agent for cholera proved that they had lapsed into 'contagionism' and thereby demonstrated that they were 'declining in ... accurate observation and deficient in theory ... The present decline in India dates from ... when a mere theory of a Bristol contagionist [Budd] was printed in an Indian government report & was accepted as a truth.'[85] In India she stirred a leading − and now lonely − believer in the miasma theory, Dr Cunningham, to write a report condemning the specific agent, water-borne theories and reliance on quarantine, and restating the case for thorough-going reconstruction and cleansing. The India Office, despite her efforts, buried the report.[86] Thereafter she, Galton and Sutherland, echoed unhelpfully by Chadwick, continued to preach the miasmatic doctrine. They reinforced the conservatism of like-minded medical men in India and the United States and at home.[87] But official opinion ignored them. Quarantine met the limits of what was possible; yet Miss Nightingale was never content with the possible when others defined it.

It is hard to be infallible, even when one is on the sidelines. Miss Nightingale's pronouncements upon Indian canals, irrigation and drainage always sounded authoritative but they slewed with each blunder and according to the allegiance of the particular high underling she was trying to catch. Her problem was to find work for her London sanitary committee and to give directions on matters highly disputed among medical men and engineers. In 1865 she commissioned the great analyst, Dr Robert Angus Smith, to produce a simple set of procedures for 'finding out how much dirt there was in water'. Smith proved characteristically cautious, changeable and slow in writing his recommendations. He rewrote the paper, she said, six times in five months and then destroyed it in order to begin anew. But Miss Nightingale trapped him by obtaining a draft and secretly setting it in type at her expense. Her object was to compel the Indian sanitarians to get on with their work *her* way, not necessarily the best way. Her timing was unfortunate. Smith was apparently groping his way towards a qualitative analysis rather than a straightforward quantity count, with the object of establishing differentials between kinds of 'dirt' according to their varying contents of disease-inducing agents. Advanced doctors in India were doing the same and they rejected Smith's report as old-fashioned. The War Office and India Office, too, had reservations about the report, which promised only expensive trouble. Miss Nightingale moved quietly to order the printing of up to 2,000 copies, at government expense. Without waiting for India Office approval she despatched copies of the proofs to Dr Walker in Calcutta. India Office approval was irrelevant because, she informed Walker, the report had been 'written at your instigation'. She reassured him that the Office liked the report, but would take 'two years' to get around to sending it to India. Meanwhile she had already sent 100 copies 'privately'. Her machinations appear to have been in vain. The India Office never ordered that Smith's procedures be followed and local officers seem not to have adopted them.[88] By backing the local officers' assertions of independence of higher Indian authority she had necessarily but inadvertently increased their independence of her commands. Despite her protestation that Smith's report represented 'the last and most perfect knowledge on this subject', the report was not even Dr Smith's 'last word'. I could not discover what Smith thought about Miss Nightingale's perfidy, but his dealings with her ceased soon afterwards.

Miss Nightingale was equally expeditious with drainage problems. Rawlinson, her engineering coadjutor from Crimean days, warned her that India was geographically various and everywhere poor. He plumped for a series of pilot schemes, employing diverse sizes of pipes and systems. This did not suit Miss Nightingale. Too much was left to local decision and no role remained for the home sanitary committee. Rawlinson, she said, was unhelpfully pessimistic, too.[89] The India Office ignored her overtures for instructions to her committee to provide drainage rules. She sent them none the less. Her rules betray a complete want of understanding. Pessimists alleged the 'impossibility of water drainage in a country with dry seasons', but this was 'no problem'. Water to flush the pipes had simply to be pumped from the rivers. Malta and Gibraltar were 'drier' than India (as indeed they are in terms of annual rainfall, compared with say, Calcutta) but their towns and British stations had no difficulties. As for the system, 'earthenware or iron pipes are now so universally introduced . . . that it is only necessary to name them'. With sublime aristocratic disdain she ignored costs and difficulties in survey, land tenures and taxation, water flow, plumbing skills, in a sub-continent short of trained men and notorious for jobbery and extravagance. The sewage could readily be used in 'sewage irrigation, as in England' — where it had largely failed — or be emptied into the rivers and sea by gravity flow. Miss Nightingale's severely logical, sanitary mind lapsed into ambiguity: 'A few thousand gallons . . . per day are nothing in India. If the latrines were discharged after sunset, there would hardly be the vestige of the water next morning'. She issued these dicta ten years after the outcry about sewage pollution of the Thames and midst growing criticism of the fouling of British bays and estuaries. 'Native habits', she admitted, were dirty, but piecemeal expedients devised by local incompetents would only pander to them. After all, she continued, she knew orientals and their practices, having been in the Crimea. Only an 'entire scheme' designed by her and her advisers could serve India.[90]

No one took any notice. Miss Nightingale retreated to offering advice about water filters and building brick tops to wells to prevent permeation. Meanwhile the men on the spot extended their dry earth closet systems, the only kind possible within the available money and water supplies, and pressed on with concrete open canal drains.[91] Miss Nightingale's last powerful comrade in India, Lord Napier, Governor of Madras, yet another duty-ridden, simplistic proconsul attracted to the national heroine, defied the central government and his advisors by ordering the building of a sewage farm and an underground sewage, drainage system. (Like others among her proconsul friends he faithfully obeyed her injunctions to burn her letters, and wrote regularly about their conspiracy to better India in a coyly flirtatious style whenever his wife was away in the hills.) The sewage farm proved inefficient and the six-inch pipes in the underground system, recommended by Miss Nightingale upon 'the best advice', could not cope in the wet season and blocked during the dry.[92] Cawnpore's sewers, built (it was believed) according to the specifications of Miss Nightingale's committee (there is evidence that Chadwick had a hand in it), proved disastrous. However, Bombay's cleansing system of deep open drains, devised against Nightingale-Rawlinson principles, also worked badly. The ratepayers and government were never prepared to pay for any sufficient system.[93] But Miss Nightingale never recognised this obstacle. In 1871, when she began to lose interest in the subject, she was still accusing local planners of inability to 'see the consequences of a fact and realize them in practice'.[94] Like the local doctors, the local engineers never took Miss Nightingale and her sanitary committee seriously, and she hated them for it.

By extension from her interest in drainage, Miss Nightingale took the side of the canal-irrigation interest in the controversy with the railway promoters. Fundamentally the conflict divided two kinds of imperialist: the canal builders saw themselves justifying British dominance in India by controlling the great rivers, expanding irrigation and thereby enabling the natives to work the land for the more effectual production of food and cash crops. River and canal transport was cheap and within the range of the natives. Men like Richard Temple, the great civil servant, and Arthur Cotton, the canal builder, were possessed by a vision of managing great waters and feeding the millions. Returns on government capital investment would be low but they would be certain. But above that stretched the prospect of using the state to achieve a design that would gloriously loft the British Empire above its pagan Roman predecessor by, as one engineer privately exulted, realising 'the gift of Providence in a well supplied river, turned to its proper account'.[95]

Railway men also protested the grandeur of their aims but their plans were more prosaic. They boasted 'Private Enterprise' but they required government support for construction loans raised among British capitalists and government guarantees on passenger traffic and freight rates. They argued that in times of famine they could bring food quicker. More attractively, at least to the War Office and sections of the India Office, they asserted that their trains could convey troops faster and in larger numbers than the river boats. They were, as Miss Nightingale put it, the 'merchants' of imperialism; her canal people were, like the Romans, the 'civilizers'. Behind the scenes and unbeknownst to her, the canal promoters were as hungry for government guarantees as their railway rivals.[96]

Railway advocates alleged that canals bred fever. Doubtless they were right. But Miss Nightingale's home sanitary commission and the presidency commissions were never empowered to investigate the charge. She was undeterred. The natives, she instructed Lawrence, must be directed to plough in the irrigation water and not let it stagnate. Rice farmers would have to change their ways. Napier warned her that there was small scope in India for innovation in agriculture: 'The more you see of the country the more you are struck with the practical simplicity and appropriateness of the native methods.'[97] But non-interference as a principle of administration was alien to Miss Nightingale.

She finally lost her irrigation friends when she circulated the proofs of a pamphlet on the subject in 1874. They could offer only embarrassed criticisms. Contrary to Miss Nightingale's assertion, no navigation or irrigation system made a profit. Her declaration that navigation and irrigation were simultaneously practicable throughout the year on every system was untrue of all except the lower Ganges. She had had the current Viceroy, Lord Northbrook, in view when preparing her text. Its errors gave Northbrook the opportunity to fob her off completely. Miss Nightingale's last resort was to charge Lord Salisbury, now returned to the India Office, with producing shoddy figures on canal and irrigation finances. The returns were poorly kept and possibly the losses were smaller than the railway lobby, especially, alleged but they remained losses to the general revenue rather than profits. Salisbury was a railways man. When he told Miss Nightingale that he did not know the precise figures and had no intention of collecting them she was baffled: 'And they call me a "dangerous man"!!!'[98]

From this point Miss Nightingale and other 'civilizing' imperialists began to devise ways of supporting irrigation in India that by-passed the authorities. They placed their hopes in the ryots, the agricultural peasants. The famines and disturbances of the mid-1870s had revealed the ryots as unwilling to take government water because they could not pay for it and because irrigation transactions further subjected them to the extortions of petty officials and zemindars. Miss Nightingale proposed that the government, through a co-operative land bank, lend money to the ryots, at seven per cent interest, to enable them to pay off their creditors, buy their land, and purchase government water. Thereby they would find self-respect, feed themselves and become forever faithful to their British emancipators. Their villages would become stable, efficient units. To this end she became a keen advocate of strengthened village councils and through this allegiance she moved, as did many other 'civilizers', into supporting the nascent Indian National Congress and towards a form — in the far future — of Indian Home Rule within the Empire. In pursuit of this ideal in 1882 she secretly advised the Queen not to accept a petition from the 'European ladies of Calcutta' against the Ilbert Bill, a measure (which failed), designed to enable Indian magistrates and sessions judges in country districts to try European settlers. Again the British and Indian governments moved slowly and reluctantly, and the proposed land bank remained a dream. As G.H.R. Hart, an official in the India Office, remarked, it would demean government to sponsor a '*mont de piété*', and the ryots would never repay their loans from a land bank.[99]

The village development scheme needed honest intermediaries. Miss Nightingale and Arthur Cotton developed an idea that she had discussed with Frere in the 1860s: there were to be two new ranks of officials. First, a corps of capable, respectable, properly paid natives had to be trained in India to oversee local agricultural practices and village accounting; there were too few Europeans to do the job. To this end, agricultural and 'public works' colleges had to be established in India and several were opened in the later 1870s. Second, a corps of British district officers had to be created to direct the native officials and keep them honest. Jowett — whose two brothers had died young in India —

backed the scheme and carried the statutes that enabled Oxford University to lead in establishing in the early 1880s agricultural education courses for candidates for the Indian Civil and later the Colonial Service. Half of the early, disappointingly few, probationers were Balliol men.[100] It was the small, unheralded beginning of a great force for good during the next seventy years.

These new cadres could have become Miss Nightingale's missionaries, but by the 1880s she was too old and out of touch to use them. By 1881 she was getting tired, Sutherland's hearing had failed and Galton had been promoted out of her reach. Her old Crimea allies were now feeble and in isolated retirement. The Liberal government led by Gladstone, the man she could not catch, first ignored her Army and Indian Sanitary Commissions and then in 1881 began to dismantle them. She drummed up sufficient support to save them but neither the War Office nor the India Office referred matters to them and they ceased to work. The Tory government finally abolished them in 1889.[101]

In India tens of thousands continued to die each year from malnutrition, typhoid fever and cholera, but thousands more lived because Miss Nightingale coached successive Secretaries of State, Viceroys and local medical men in what had to be done and how it could be done. She was never alone in seeing the problems nor in devising solutions but she used her reputation in Britain and India to make expenditure on such projects seem necessary and right. The public debt almost doubled from £90 millions in 1860 to £160 millions in 1880, while the land revenue rose by only a sixth, from £18.7 million to £22 million.[102]

Yet she never grasped the complexities of Indian geography, caste, poverty and social inertia. She dimly recognised them as prodigious obstacles but in her determination 'to do' she readily pretended that they did not exist. Only in 1898, midst a lucid interval during her encroaching senility, did she have a revelation of the problem that was India. Prince Aga Khan visited her. He talked much, she noted afterwards, of 'spirituality'. He asked doubtfully 'do you think that Sanitation can make much difference in life?' 'To him', Miss Nightingale added, 'sanitation is unreal and superstitious . . . I never understood before how really impossible it is for an Eastern to care for material causes.'[103] And then, quite out of character, she did not condemn him.

Notes

1. F.N. to McNeill, 15 July 1857, BL Add.Mss 45768, f.60.
2. Sutherland to F.N. 'Friday' [11 Sept. 1857?] BL Add.Mss 45751, f.49.
3. F.N. to Chadwick, 11 Aug. 1858; Chadwick to F.N., 12 July 1858, BL Add. Mss 45770, f.23, 18.
4. (Andrew Wynter), 'Lodging, food, and dress of Soldiers', *Quarterly Review*, Jan. 1859; Chadwick to F.N., 8 Oct. 1858 BL Add.Mss 45770, f.58.
5. F.N. to McNeill, (copy) 9 May 1859, BL Add.Mss 45768, f.98; Chadwick to Stanley, (copy) 23 May [1859?] Chadwick Papers, University College, London, CP1871; W.C.B. Eatwell to Farr, 9 Sept. 1859, Farr Collection, British Library of Political and Economic Science, London, vol. I, ff.36-42; Farr to F.N., 4 Dec. 1860, BL Add.Mss 43398, f.255.
6. Farr to Sutherland, [June 1859?], 30 Oct. 1859, BL Add.Mss 45751, ff.136-7, 140-1; F.N., Five Drafts of Questionnaire n.d. [late 1859?] BL Add. Mss 45824, ff.1-30.
7. 'East India (Sanitary State of the Army). Report . . .' *PP*, 1863, vol. XIX, pt. II, p.4; pt. III, p.20.
8. 'Report', *PP*, 1863, vol. XIX, pt. II, pp.311, 214-5, 519, 295, 654.
9. F.N. to McNeill, (copy) 15 Apr. 1862, BL Add.Mss 45768, f.170; Farr to F.N., n.d. [16 Sept. 1861?], F.N. to Farr, 17 Sept. 1861, BL Add.Mss 43399, ff.44-7; F.N. to Galton, 15 Aug. 1863, BL Add.Mss 45761, f.69;
10. Sir Edward Cook, *The Life of Florence Nightingale*, (2 vols., London, 1913), vol. II, pp.26, 158.
11. 'Report', *PP*, 1863, vol. XIX, pp.159-60.
12. F.N. to Galton 'Burn', 2 Nov. 1863, BL Add.Mss 45761 f.190.
13. Jowett to F.N., n.d. [late 1861?] Jowett Papers, Balliol College, Oxford, vol. I.
14. F.N. to Martineau, 19 May, 8 July, 22 July 1863, BL Add.Mss 45788, ff.186-91.
15. Stanley to F.N., 30 Apr. 1863, BL Add.Mss 45781, f.79.
16. F.N. to Galton, 28 Oct. 1863, BL Add.Mss 45761, ff.187-8.
17. F.N. to McNeill, 17 May 1864, GLRO HI/ST/SU/152.
18. Cook, *Nightingale*, vol. II, pp.45, 50; F.N. to Gladstone, 6 July 1879, BL Add.Mss 44460, f.234.
19. Lawrence − notes on galleys of F.N.'s Report on barracks [Dec. 1863?] BL Add.Mss 45829, ff.103-6; Lawrence 'General Order', 21 June 1864, BL Add. Mss 45798, f.239; F.N. to McNeill, 17 May 1864, GLRO HI/ST/SU/152.
20. F.N. to Galton, 21, 26 Dec. 1863, BL Add.Mss 45761, f.245, 264; Lawrence to Wood (copy), 1 July 1865, Mss EUR F90/30, India Office Library; F.N. to Stanley, [22 Apr. 1863?] BL Add.Mss 45781, f.5; F.N. to Lord Mayo, 23 Mar. 1870, BL Add.Mss 45754, ff.124-6; Sutherland to Chadwick, 5 Feb. 1870, Chadwick Papers, University College, London, CP 1920.
21. Strachey to F.N., 21 Sept. 1864, BL Add.Mss 45798, f.264.
22. Farr to F.N., 22 Apr. 1861, BL Add.Mss 43399, f.20; F.N. 'How People May Live and not Die in India' *Transactions of the National Association for the Promotion of Social Science*, 1863, pp.501-2; Hyde Clark, 'On The English Settlement Of The Hill Regions Of India', *Journal of the Society of Arts*, 21 May 1858.
23. F.N. to Charles Hathaway (copy) 'Private', 27 June 1864, BL Add.Mss 45782, f.156.
24. F.N. to Hathaway, 18 Apr. 1864, n.d. [mid-June 1864?] BL Add.Mss 45782, ff.152, 156; John M. Eyler, *Victorian Social Medicine* (Baltimore, 1979), p.175; Dr McClelland to Sir Charles Trevelyan, 13 Jan. 1864, BL Add.Mss 45798, ff.214-5.

25. F.N. to Martineau, 20 Feb. 1865, BL Add.Mss 45788, f.288.

26. Stanley to F.N., 25 Oct. 1864, 2 Nov. 1864; India Office to Stanley, 4 Nov. 1864, BL Add.Mss 45781, ff.144-7; F.N. to Farr, 5 Aug. 1864, BL Add. Mss 43399, f.204.

27. Cook, *Nightingale*, vol. II, pp.52-3; F.N. to Galton, 'Private', 19 Sept. 1864; Galton to F.N., 21 Sept. 1864, BL Add.Mss 45762, ff.208-14; *The Times*, 23 Aug. 1864.

28. J.J. Frederick to F.N., [Marked 3 Oct. 1865-recte 4?] BL Add.Mss 43397, ff.23-4; F.N. to Galton, 10 Nov. 1864, BL Add.Mss 45762, ff.243-4; A.H. Leith to F.N., 27 Sept. 1864, BL Add.Mss 45798, f.267. Stanley to F.N., 25 Oct. 1864, 26 Dec. 1864, BL Add.Mss 45781, ff.144, 149.

29. F.N. to Galton, 10 Nov. 1864, 5 Dec. 1864, BL Add.Mss 45762, f.243-4, 279; F.N. to Walker, '(strictly in confidence)', 19 Dec. 1864, BL Add.Mss 45781, f.258; Stanley to F.N., 26 Dec. 1864, BL Add.Mss 45781, f.150.

30. Stanley to F.N., 12 Jan. 1865; 20 Feb. 1865, BL Add.Mss 45781, ff.153, 157; F.N. to Galton, 26 Jan. 1865, BL Add.Mss 45763, ff.15-17; F.N. to Lawrence, 'Private', 26 Dec. 1864; Lawrence to F.N., 6 July 1865, BL Add.Mss 45777, ff.58-63.

31. Lawrence to F.N., 7 Apr. 1865, BL Add.Mss 45777, ff.64-5.

32. Farr to F.N., 28 Mar. 1865, 8 May 1865; F.N. to Farr, 10 May 1865, BL Add.Mss 43400, ff.24, 42-4; Stanley to F.N., 21 Oct. 1865, 25 Oct. 1865, BL Add.Mss 45781, f.177-8.

33. F.N. to Galton, 26 Jan. 1865, BL Add.Mss 45763, f.17.

34. F.N. to de Grey, 11 Dec. 1865, BL Add.Mss 43546, ff.88-94; F.N. to Galton, 'Private', 6 Jan. 1866, BL Add.Mss 45763, ff.123-4.

35. Stanley to F.N., 4 July 1866, BL Add.Mss 45781, f.195.

36. F.N. to Cranborne, drafts [July 1866?], Cranborne to F.N., 17 July 1866, F.N. to Cranborne, draft, [Feb. 1867?], BL Add.Mss 45779, ff.1-7, 198; F.N. to Galton, 28 May 1867, BL Add.Mss 45764, ff.70-1; 24 July 1867, BL Add.Mss 45752, f.198.

37. F.N. to Galton, 10 June, 16 June [1867?], BL Add.Mss 45764, ff.75-6.

38. F.N. to Sir Bartle Frere [10 May 1867?], BL Add.Mss 45780, f.2; F.N. to Sutherland, reporting conversation with Frere, [14 June 1867?] BL Add.Mss 45752, ff.179-80.

39. F.N. to Sutherland, 22 July 1867, BL Add.Mss 45752, f.188; Reginald Bosworth Smith, *Life of Lord Lawrence*, 6th edn. revised, (2 vols., London, 1885), vol. II, pp.316-20.

40. F.N. to Stanley, (draft) [10-11 July 1867?] BL Add.Mss 45781, ff.198-9; F.N. to Galton, 24 June 1867, BL Add.Mss 45764, ff.82-6.

41. F.N. to Galton, 24 June 1867, BL Add.Mss 45764, f.84.

42. F.N. to Galton, (draft) [16 July 1867?] BL Add.Mss 45764, f.88; F.N. to Sir Stafford Northcote (draft 3) 25 July 1867, Northcote to F.N. 30 July 1867, BL Add.Mss 45779, ff.93-101.

43. Frere to F.N., 27 July 1867, BL Add.Mss 45780, ff.13-17; John Martineau, *Life and Correspondence of Sir Bartle Frere* (2 vols., London 1895), vol. II, p.39.

44. F.N. Memorandum of interview with Northcote, 20 Aug. 1867, BL Add. Mss 45752, ff.216-19.

45. F.N. to Galton, 20 Aug. 1867, BL Add.Mss 45764, f.107.

46. Mary Carpenter to F.N., 7 June 1867, BL Add.Mss 45752, f.177.

47. Jowett to F.N., 22 Apr. [1867?], Jowett Papers, Balliol College, Oxford, vol. II.

48. F.N. to Carpenter, 21 Aug. 1867, Carpenter Collection, Bristol Archives Office, 12693/24; F.N. Memorandum of conversation, 7 June 1867, BL Add.Mss 45752, f.175.

49. J. Estlin Carpenter, *The Life And Work of Mary Carpenter* (London,

1879), pp.298-310.

50. Her biographers have glossed the sadism, deceit and self-righteousness revealed in her journal of her management of the Red Lodge, her female reformatory. On 15 April 1857 she noted that Crawford, Petty and Burke had all been in 'solitude for a week ... The ... house has been going on very promisingly'. In mid-June of that year she had put 'a strong case of hysteria ... feigning' in the cells. The case was later found unconscious and then to be dying. Miss Carpenter ordered it to be placed in an unused bedroom, out the way of 'common use', otherwise there 'might be a painful association'. The child died on 17 June. 'There was no sigh, no struggle! ... Never before did I desire to remember death rather than life.' Miss Carpenter preached a death sermon to the girls: 'said I had forbidden her the garden to save her health'. The body was laid out by five senior – i.e. about 14-year-old – girls and all the inmates were conducted in to see it. 'I preached that evening on the parable of the virgins ... It seemed to me that I had never loved my children so tenderly or they me'; but so as not to spend 'an unnecessary penny' Miss Carpenter denied their request for black ribbons and instead 'brought out my old crepe'. The coffin was left for three days in the main Oak Room of Red Lodge. Miss Carpenter preached again as the coffin was removed on Saturday 20 June. The girls erupted into a 'violent burst of sorrow' but, privately, Miss Carpenter recorded 'Solemn but not unhappy thoughts, She had not left Red Lodge to sin.' The next day Miss Carpenter went to London to attend to 'a call ... which I felt it right to attend to'. The trustees of Red Lodge were apparently never summoned to discuss the death.

Before Miss Carpenter's departure on the Sunday 21 April, another girl had been found to be dying. Miss Carpenter wrote her 'a long farewell'. The funeral was rushed and private. The girls were forbidden to see the body and were refused permission to attend the funeral. Again, there was no inquiry into the death. Miss Carpenter's absence was, she reflected, 'probably [erased] best for all ... when the last pains [?] of mortality and the last rites were passing. After her return, we (MC and her sister [?], who had buried the child) wept together at what had passed.' Carpenter Collection, Bristol Archives Office, 12693/1, Apr., June 1857.

51. Ruby J. Saywell, *Mary Carpenter Of Bristol* (Bristol, 1964), p.4; Carpenter, *Life And Work*, p.385.

52. Carpenter, *Life And Work*, p.252.

53. G.W. Hastings to Lord Brougham, 18 Sept. 1864, Brougham Papers, University College, London, BP 13032.

54. *Transactions of the National Association for the Promotion of Social Science*, vol. I, 1857, pp.XXVI, XXI; Hastings to Brougham, 5 Nov. 1857, Brougham Papers, University College, London, BP 13109.

55. Leone Levi, 'On the Progress of Learned Societies ...' *Report of British Association ... 1868*, pp.171-2.

56. G. Shaw-Lefevre. 'Presidential Address', *Transactions of National Association for ... Social Science, 1884*; B. Rodgers, 'The Social Science Association, 1857-1886', *Manchester School*, vol. XX, 1952, pp.283-310; Philip Abrams, *The Origins Of British Sociology: 1834-1914* (Chicago, 1968), pp.44-52.

57. F.N. to Chadwick, 11 Oct. 1858, BL Add.Mss 45770, f.60.

58. Farr to F.N., 16 Oct. 1858, BL Add.Mss 43398, f.83; Hastings to F.N., 29 Oct. 1858, BL Add.Mss 45797, ff.27-9.

59. Henry Bonham Carter to Carpenter, draft n.d. [15 Sept. 1867?], Carpenter to F.N., 17 Sept. 1867, BL Add.Mss 45789 ff.122-4; *Transactions, the National Association for ... Social Science, 1867*, pp.239-45, 405-18.

60. Carpenter to F.N. 15 Sept. 1869, 24 Sept. 1869, 27 Sept. 1869, BL Add. Mss 45789, ff.152-5.

61. F.N. 'Note on Irish Disestablishment' [late 1869?] BL Add.Mss 45754,

f.59; F.N. to Charles Hathaway, 18 June 1864, BL Add.Mss 45782, f.154; Richard Temple, *Men And Events of My Time In India* (London, 1882), pp.75-6.

62. Dharmapāla Mahājana, *The Administration of Sir John Lawrence in India, 1864-1869* (Simla, 1952), pp.103-4.

63. Sutherland to Chadwick, 21 Apr. 1883, Chadwick Papers, University College, London, CP 1920.

64. C.E. Gover, 'Memorandum on Juvenile Reformatories in Madras Presidency', 29 Jan. 1868, Chadwick Papers, University College, London, CP 87; Lawrence to Wood, 16 May 1865; Lawrence to Northcote, 21 Mar. 1868, Mss EUR. India Office Library, F90/30, f.63; F90/31/f.113; Mahājana, *Lawrence*, p.104.

65. Judge Gopal Rao Pauvery [?] to Carpenter, 14 Feb. 1876, Carpenter Collection, Bristol Archives Office. 12693/25.

66. F.N. to Hathaway, (copy) 18 June 1864, BL Add.Mss 45782, f.154; F.N. to Galton, 3 Oct 1864, 20 Oct. 1864 BL Add.Mss 45762, ff.224-5, 235; F.N. to Walker, 18 Dec. 1865, GLRO HI/ST/NCI/65/27.

67. Stanley to F.N., 22 Apr. 1865, 15 May 1865, BL Add.Mss 45781, ff.163-4, Northcote to Lawrence, 9 June 1867, Mss EUR, India Office Library, F90/31 f.98; Mahājana, *Lawrence*, p.104.

68. Dr F.J. Mouat to Chadwick, 10 Feb. 1873; Sutherland to Chadwick, 13 Feb. 1873, Chadwick Papers, University College, London CP. 1451, 1920.

69. Dr J. Pattison Walker to F.N., 21 Nov. 1864, BL Add.Mss 45781, f.251.

70. F.N. McNeill, 7 Feb. 1865, GLRO HI/ST/SU/156.

71. Carpenter to F.N. 2 June 1867, 7 June 1867, BL Add.Mss 45789, ff.104, 108.

72. Minutes of Governor-General's Council of India, 10 June 1867, BL Add. Mss 45782, f.246; F.N. to McNeill (copy) 21 Sept. 1867, BL Add.Mss 45768, f.216; F.N. to Lawrence (draft) n.d. [26 Sept. 1867?] BL Add.Mss 45777 ff.148-56.

73. F.N. to R.S. Ellis (draft) Aug. 1867, BL Add.Mss 45785, ff.93-6; F.N. to McNeill, 10 Sept. 1867, GLRO HI/ST/SU/157; Ellis to F.N. 26 Jan. 1868, BL Add.Mss 45782, ff.105-8; D.G. Bowd, *Lucy Osburn* (Windsor, NSW), 1968.

74. F.N. to Galton, 22 May 1882, BL Add.Mss 45765, ff.115-17.

75. Mary Carpenter, *Six Months In India* (2 vols., London, 1868), vol. I, p.150; Miss C.G. Loch to F.N., 28 Jan. 1889, BL Add.Mss 45809, ff.99-100.

76. Dr E.A. Parkes to F.N., 1 Dec 1861, BL Add.Mss 45773, f.42.

77. *Transactions of National Association for . . . Social Science, 1863*, p.505.

78. F.N. to Hathaway, 18 June 1864, BL Add.Mss 45782, f.155.

79. John Strachey and J. McClelland, *Memorandum on Cholera*, 23 Mar. 1863, [Bombay]; Walker to F.N., 9 Aug. 1864, BL Add.Mss 45781, f.227.

80. India Office, *Imperial Gazetteer of India* (Oxford, 1907), vol. I, p.521.

81. F.N. to Frere, (draft) 27-8 Aug. 1867, BL Add.Mss 45752, f.222.

82. F.N. to Walker, 18 Oct. 1865, GLRO HI/ST/NCI/65/19.

83. F.N. to Galton, 13 Jan. 1866, 15 Jan. 1866, BL Add.Mss 45763, ff.141-3.

84. Farr to F.N., 2 Aug. 1866, BL Add.Mss 59786, f.27; Hewlett to F.N., 28 Sept. 1867, BL Add.Mss 45782, f.8.

85. F.N. to Frere (draft) 30 Mar. 1869, BL Add.Mss 45780, ff.150-6; F.N. to de Grey, 11 Feb. 1869, BL Add.Mss 43546, ff.130-1; F.N. Memorandum of interview with Napier, 4 Dec. 1869, BL Add.Mss 45754, ff.41-2.

86. Sutherland to F.N., 8 Nov. 1870, BL Add.Mss 45755, f.90; F.N. Notes of interview with Cunningham, 18 Feb. 1870, BL Add.Mss 45754, ff.79-83; 'Report of Army Sanitary Commission on Dr Brydon's report on Cholera in India, 20 May 1870, BL Add.Mss 43397, f.60.

87. F.N. 'Letter on Cholera', *New York Herald* [1883?] undated cutting in Chadwick Papers, University College, London CP 66; Galton, 'On Sanitary

Progress in India', *Journal of Society of Arts*, 28 Apr. 1876, p.528; Sutherland to F.N., 15 Mar. 1873, BL Add.Mss 45757, ff.75-6; Edwin Chadwick, *The Precautions To Be Taken Against Cholera, (Principles of Central Action)* (London, 1871, reprinted in part, 1883); Golaub Sing, *Hindu View Of Cholera* (London, 1871).

88. F.N. to Galton, 30 Oct. 1865, 7 Dec. 1865, BL Add.Mss 45763, ff.87-9, 106; F.N. to Walker, 18 Dec. 1865, GLRO HI/ST/NCI/65/27; Sutherland to F.N., 6 Dec. 1870, BL Add.Mss 45755, f.134.

89. Rawlinson to F.N., 30 Dec. 1862, BL Add.Mss 45769, ff.90-1.

90. F.N. to [Stanley?] (draft), [late Nov. 1863?] BL Add.Mss 45781, ff.106-9.

91. F.N. to Walker, 'Private' (copy) 18 June 1864, BL Add.Mss 45781, f.225; Hector Tulloch, *Report on . . . the Drainage Of . . . Madras* (Madras, 1865).

92. Napier to F.N., 22 Sept. 1867, 'Burn it!' 8 July 1868, BL Add.Mss 45779, ff.199-202, 219-20.

93. Sutherland to Chadwick, 27 Jan. 1875; Tulloch to Chadwick, 6 Feb. 1869; [5 Nov.? 1869] Chadwick Papers, University College, London, CP, 1920, 1998; Rawlinson to Acland, 24 Feb. 1868, Acland Papers, Bodleian Library, Oxford, d.66.

94. F.N. to W. Clark [an engineer in Calcutta?], 3 Nov. 1871, GLRO HI/ST/SU/71/12.

95. Colonel Playfair to Frere, 30 Nov. 1866, Mss EUR. F 90/45. India Office Library.

96. F.N. to Chadwick [draft – early 1865?] BL Add.Mss 45771, f.65. Francis William Fox, 'On Indian Railways and Indian Finance', *Report of British Association . . . 1875*, p.210; Lieut-General McMurdo, 'Settlement and Military Colonisation in India', *Journal of Society of Arts*, 22 Mar. 1878, pp.344-7.

97. Major Malleson, Memorandum on F.N.'s letter to Lawrence, 2 June 1866, BL Add.Mss 45782, ff.212-6; F.N. to Lawrence [draft Oct. 1868?], BL Add.Mss 45777, f.173; Napier to F.N., 13 Dec. 1868, BL Add.Mss 45779, ff.228-9.

98. Napier to F.N. [28 April. 1874?], BL Add.Mss 45779, ff.244-7; Frere to F.N., 14 Jan. 1875; F.N. to Frere [draft Jan. 1875?], BL Add.Mss 45780, ff.279-87, 292; Salisbury to F.N., 19 Sept. 1877; F.N. to Sutherland, 23 Sept. 1877, BL Add.Mss 45758, ff.64-71.

99. F.N. to Louis Mallet [draft Feb. 1878?], BL Add.Mss 45779, ff.148-55; F.N. to W.R. Robertson (Superintendent-General of Farms in Madras Presidency), 7 Mar. 1879, Mss EUR B.263, f.122, India Office Library; F.N. to Gladstone, 7 July 1879, BL Add.Mss 44460, ff.242-8. G.H.R. Hart, Memorandum on Monts de Piété and a National Bank for India, [Aug.-Sept. 1879?] Mss EUR F86/27, India Office Library.

100. Frere to F.N., 7 Sept. 1867, BL Add.Mss 45780, f.66; F.N., Memorandum of conversation with Galton and Dr Poore, [Nov.-Dec. 1888?], BL Add.Mss 45766, f.207; F.N. to Galton, 16 Dec. 1893, 23 Jan. 1894, BL Add.Mss 45767, ff.106-22; F.N. to Arnold Toynbee, (copy) 20 Oct. 1882, BL Add.Mss 45807, f.14; Jowett to F.N., 26 Feb. 1886, Jowett Papers, vol. VII, Balliol College, Oxford.

101. Sutherland to Chadwick, 10 Dec. 1887, Chadwick Papers, University College, London, CP 1920; F.N. 'Memorandum on Indian Sanitary Executive Boards', 18 July 1889, BL Add.Mss 45836, f.73; Memoranda of conversations with Sir Thomas Crawford, 6 Dec. 1889, 7 Mar. 1890, BL Add.Mss 45772, ff.104-15; F.N. to Galton, 2 Aug. 1888, 28 Aug. 1888, 31 Aug. 1888, 9 Sept. 1888, 16 Jan. 1889, BL Add.Mss 45766, ff.118-214; J.A. Godley, India Office, to Stanhope, 13 Feb. 1889, PRO WO 32/6069.

102. John and Richard Strachey, *The Finances and Public Works of India*

From 1869 to 1881 (London, 1882), pp.6-9; Richard Temple, *The Statistics of the Indian Empire* (London, 1881), pp.4, 15.

103. F.N., Memorandum of conversation with Prince Aga Khan, 5 July 1898, BL Add.Mss 45827, ff.192-3.

5 NURSING

Miss Nightingale's gift to nursing was to identify it in the public mind with sanctified duty. Contrary to nursing folklore, she neither invented modern nursing behaviour nor even the idea of nursing as a calling. But by bestowing her *imprimatur* upon secular vocational nursing she gave it standing in Victorian Britain and throughout the world. And, of course, she secured the benison of female nursing in army hospitals.

The regimen of sexual purity, punctuality, cleanliness and obedience to matron's orders coupled with skills in directing scrubbers and porters, surveillance and control of patients, applying dressings, leeching and administering enemas to both females and males, had been developed by the Anglican nursing orders in the London voluntary hospitals during the later 1850s, although expectations about hospital nurses' conduct had been rising in many hospitals, especially St Thomas's, since at least the 1830s.[1] Miss Nightingale assimilated and published as her own the knowledge supplied her by several very able, unsung women. Mrs Jane Shaw Stewart possessed considerable continental experience. She was a searching judge of hospital design and practice and did the detailed investigations of the Lariboisière which later, unacknowledged, served Miss Nightingale when advocating the pavilion system. Mrs Shaw Stewart was also, Miss Nightingale told Uncle Sam privately, the source of 'most of the ideas' on female military nursing.[2] Mrs Roberts, Miss Nightingale's stalwart in the Crimea, had been working to improve nursing at St Thomas's since 1830. Rev. Mother Clare, Rev. Mother Bridgeman and above all Mrs S.E. Wardroper also educated her in nursing matters. Mrs Wardroper, matron at St Thomas's between 1854 and 1887, was the main progenitor of the matron's role as manager of nurses, with a distinct sphere of authority within the hospital in contrast with the older role of housekeeper subject to the governors and steward; thereby she developed the type of quiet, stiffly humane, ladylike efficiency with due obedience to matron and the doctors that constituted 'Nightingale' nursing.[3] Miss Nightingale's famous *Notes on Nursing*, first published in 1859, is full of pithy good sense and vivid anecdotes about quiet, food, light and reassurance for patients and percipience in nurses. But it is wholly directed to home, not hospital, nursing. Miss Nightingale never produced a comparable guide for hospital work. She later supported district nursing, as an

155

extension of domestic nursing, but she showed no interest in advancing other kinds of specialised nursing, of children, for example, or the insane.

Indeed, the practice of nursing was never among Miss Nightingale's prime concerns. As the history of the Nightingale Fund demonstrates, she preferred patronage, and surveillance of nurses' lives, to guiding their professional work. The Fund was opened as a thanks offering in November 1855. When it closed two years later about £44,000 had been collected, £9,000 of it by compulsory levy on the troops at the Crimea, although as General Codrington assured the Secretary of War, the authorities had made it 'appear voluntary'.[4] The money was transferred to Miss Nightingale without strings, upon the understanding that the Heroine Nurse was to use it to fulfil her professed intention of opening a nursing school. The Romish renegade, Mary Stanley, had proposed such a school in her *Hospitals and Sisterhoods* (1854) and her advocacy of nurses under Christian vows and gushing eulogy of the Catholic and Anglican sisterhoods in the Crimea was, to those who knew, a rebuke to Miss Nightingale. But Mary Stanley had no money and her chances were spiked by the announcement of Miss Nightingale's plan in November 1857.[5] This achieved, Miss Nightingale returned to her main interest of defending her role in the Crimea and hounding Drs Hall, Smith and other enemies.

She had sought confirmation of her envisaged nursing plan from Mrs Shaw Stewart and Dr Sutherland, both of whom took the hint although the former, outspoken as ever, remarked that Miss Nightingale possessed neither the experience nor the staying power to conduct such an institution − a damaging comment on Miss Nightingale's pretensions, given Mrs Shaw Stewart's authority in nursing matters.[6] Miss Nightingale appears to have never afterwards sought Mrs Shaw Stewart's opinions on anything. Instead she launched many ill-substantiated (though not wholly unfounded) anecdotes about Mrs Shaw Stewart's cantankerousness and evaded a specific request to return her letter.[7] Nightingale biographers have repeated these rumours while ignoring the lady's estimate of their heroine. The Fund then lay idle for eighteen months during which time Miss Nightingale pondered various ways of spending it including building a model barracks, bequeathing it to St Thomas's Hospital as a private fund for training nurses, and salting it away for the posthumous publication of her 'Suggestions For Thought'.[8] After this flurry, the Fund lay unused and unconsidered for another eighteen months. Early in 1859, over two years after the Fund had opened, Sidney Herbert, one of the trustees, had become embarrassed by the delay and moved to use the Fund to underwrite a nurse training agreement between the St John's nursing institution and King's College Hospital. But when Miss Nightingale flared at his impertinence, he apologised and dropped the matter.[9] The decision which she finally took in late 1859 was hastened by yet another challenge, this time from the redoubtable Mrs M.A. Baines of the Leeds Nonconformist Liberal clan who was prominent in the Ladies Sanitary Association. They also wanted to create a nurse training scheme but had been hampered by lack of money. Mrs Baines privately sought cash from the Fund and threatened to ask again publicly if she was refused. Miss Nightingale instructed Aunt Mai to answer this 'impudent woman' and drafted a savage reply for either her or Uncle Sam to sign. Mrs Baines hoped she might 'be pardoned'. Miss Nightingale told Aunt Mai: 'Certainly Not', and added that she was to tell the lady that she would publish her ignorant, intruding letter if she persisted. Mrs Baines gave up.[10]

Herbert was right to be concerned because the press was beginning to question the trustees' inactivity. Miss Nightingale had initially demanded the establishment of a board to manage the Fund because she was too 'ill' to do it. Yet she chose the members of the board. It was a distinguished group. They included, in addition to Herbert, Sir James Clark, the Queen's physician, General Sir Joshua Jebb, the prison builder and the ubiquitous Mr Bracebridge. Unbeknownst to the public, clause 13 of the trust deed, drafted by Miss Nightingale, permitted her to define her powers in relation to the trustees, while the remainder of the deed bound the trustees 'to handle money as I direct'.[11] Criticisms of the board finally prompted them in May 1859 to issue an ultimatum to her, through her father-figure, Sir John McNeill, to start something. She riposted by creating an inner executive of three members and appointing Arthur Hugh Clough, her cousin by marriage, now broken in health and unemployed, secretary at £100 a year.[12] A further delay of six months ensued while Miss Nightingale havered about the Fund. The trustees' attempts to hurry her were met with the reply that she was too ill to act. Suddenly, in December 1859 she plumped for a nurse training scheme at St Thomas's Hospital. Sidney Herbert and Elizabeth Blackwell, who had had their plan for King's College Hospital ready for almost a year, were ignored, and thereby rebuked for their officiousness. St Thomas's had been under consideration since at least April 1859, but no full arrangement had been worked out and the trustees of the Fund apparently preferred the King's College Hospital plan. The Board of Governors of St Thomas's Hospital accepted willy-nilly into the hospital the cuckoo of the Nightingale Fund for Nurses. Indeed, it was only McNeill's last minute advice which stopped Miss Nightingale from commandeering the whole hospital.[13] The scheme was to be implemented in the hospital, conducted by their matron and the house surgeon, Mr Whitfield. But the Governors were to be excluded from the selection of Nightingale probationers, (Miss Nightingale's careful choice of noun — she did not want 'novice' with its overtone of religious orders.) The Governors were to have no disciplinary powers over them, the wards in which the Nightingales trained were to be wholly given over to them and the money which sustained them was to remain separate from the Hospital accounts. A less sacrosanct, less combative cuckoo would have been turned away.

Officially, Miss Nightingale had no standing in the arrangements. Privately, she made the rules. She apparently dictated them from her sickbed to McNeill who conveyed them to the Fund committee for their unconditional assent. Like the regime at the Harley Street Institution, Miss Nightingale's ordinances were about power, her power, and they are silent about what the probationers might learn or do. All pupils were to be registered, with a detailed physical description of each, 'as may afford the means of identifying them at a future time'. All were to live in at the Hospital and

> be subject to such ... regulations as to dress — hours of attendance on the sick — hours of attendance at lectures — hours of relaxation — hours of repose — etc as may be established by Miss Nightingale — The Matron to be responsible for the strict observance of all the rules which shall have been established for her pupils ... The Matron to keep a ... Discipline book in which shall be entered daily every instance of misconduct or act in omission calling for punishment or serious reprimand ... with the consequent proceedings of the Matron thereupon.

Each nurse was to record in a daily 'ward book' her duties and her observations of patients. These were to be sent monthly to Miss Nightingale. The 'ward books' together with the entries in the discipline register were to be reviewed before any certificate was issued by the Fund committee, that is, Miss Nightingale. She managed to inspect each set of reports and each probationer until at least 1881, when she was 61 and failing in health. The monthly discipline returns unnervingly display Miss Nightingale's steely, precise grasp of indirect control. Each printed sheet is divided into two main sections, the first covers, amongst other qualities, 'Trustworthiness', 'Personal Neatness', 'Quietness' and 'Ward Management' with spaces for marks specified between 'Excellent, good, moderate, imperfect and O'; the second section includes 'Sobriety', 'Honesty' and 'Truthfulness'. Here Miss Nightingale ruled 'no degree admissible . . . first dereliction ensures dismissal'. As an addendum to this initial formulation Miss Nightingale also required Matron Wardroper 'to furnish confidentially' to her 'a list of nurses to be dismissed to make way for the Nightingale Fund Nurses'.[14] She was not going to allow her probationers to suffer possible moral contamination from matron's old cronies. Equally secretly, patients had to be ousted to make room for the Nightingales. The Fund committee was uneasy and doubltess the St Thomas's governors were perplexed but Miss Nightingale went to bed, seemingly 'badly failing' and demanded immediate acceptance of her terms as requisite for her survival. The parties agreed immediately.[15]

The lady probationers were to be selected by Mrs Wardroper, subject to vetting by Miss Nightingale should she so decide. They were to be aged between 25 and 35 and to have character testimonials from their family physicians. Deserted wives, who had often turned to nursing, and had formed a valuable part of the Crimean contingent, were excluded. Their training was to last one year and be completed within that year. Each successful candidate was to receive a certificate. Probationers were to receive £10 during training; £2 at the end of the first quarter, £2 10s 0d at the ends of the two next quarters and £3 at the conclusion. The Fund was to supply them with lodging, including tea and sugar, washing and their outer uniform. The uniform was brown [like the Crimean uniform] with white cap and apron. Each Nightingale was to have her own sleeping cubicle, although all had to pray together, twice every day, eat together and collectively attend the service of the Established Church at 11 a.m. on Sundays. (Presumably the patients were left unwatched.) But there were to be no religious tests for admission. They were not to scrub floors, set fires or clean grates. This was work for the underclass of women scrubbers. Miss Nightingale was determined that nursing should be honourable. The income from the Fund permitted a recruitment of 15 pupils each year. They could expect hospital appointments at the end of their training at £20 to £25 per year plus board and lodging.[16]

Miss Nightingale's other ambition for the Fund was to train midwifery nurses. She had trouble in settling upon an acceptable training institution but in 1862 she finally arranged with the council of St John's House to train Nightingale midwives under St John's auspices in King's College Hospital. This course was for women who 'intend to pursue the calling as a business' as distinct from 'ladies'. They were to receive full board, and £10 per six months' course, in advance. Each applicant had to produce a 'certificate of health' and 'strict references as to character'. Trainees were subject to instant dismissal for 'misconduct', an all-encompassing term; the dismissal notice was to be forwarded to the offender's referees and the £10 was to be repaid. The twelve vacancies each year were rarely filled. Midwives in practice did not want the qualification and intending midwives neither could nor would delay gaining an income for six months. The scheme languished until 1867 when it finally closed, after an unusually severe outbreak of puerperal fever in the Nightingale training annex. Miss Nightingale, after years of procrastination, had plunged into the arrangement with the hospital. She ignored the hospital sanitation rules she had made famous in 'Notes on ... Hospitals' (1858) by permitting the authorities to designate as the lying-in ward a third floor section immediately above surgical wards which housed endemic erysipelas. A hospital rule forbade students engaged in the surgical wards or in dissection from entering the lying-in ward but the rule was disregarded and puerperal fever soon infested the third floor.[17] The doctors were helpless and thought that the miasma of the disease travelled up the ventilator shafts. By the time the Nightingale project ceased in the autumn of 1867 it had killed about 28 mothers, or about 1 in 28 of the inmates. Evidence is scarce about the number of midwives trained between 1862 and 1867, but in 1864 £60 was spent. Extrapolating from that, the Fund produced about 30.[18]

Miss Nightingale privately acknowledged that she had known about the heavy maternal death rate since early 1866, and very likely she knew of it long before that. Yet she did not stop the project until late November 1867. She announced then that she had intervened 'immediately' upon discovering the mortality rate.[19] Sir Edward Cook accepted this explanation, although he characteristically planted a clue to the real sequence of causes in a stray, allusive footnote (vol. I, p.159). Later writers repeat Cook's explanation, yet they compress the time-gaps in a half-conscious attempt to make it fit their heroine's concern with nursing and death rates.[20] But the King's College Hospital scheme really collapsed because of the spiritual tribulations of Miss Mary Jones.

Miss Jones had been lady superior of St John's House in 1854 when Miss Nightingale had been collecting nurses for the Crimea. They formed an effusive, intimate friendship, with Mary Jones as the adulatory dependent partner. Miss Nightingale sent her 'Dearest Friend' nosegays. Miss Jones assured her 'beloved Friend and Mistress' that she treasured them so much that she could not 'part with one flower even'. Her visits to Miss Nightingale were her 'one indulgence and greatest pleasure'. Miss Jones was one of the very few persons admitted to the presence during Miss Nightingale's days of illness and work in the 1860s.[21] In 1856 Miss Jones led the group of St John's nurses who took over King's College Hospital, and it was her incumbency that persuaded Miss Nightingale to locate her midwives' training scheme there. A High Church devotee, Miss Jones had decided by the summer of 1867 that her six nurses should take open vows, that she should become their acknowledged spiritual head, and that the High Church hospital chaplain, Mr Giraud, should set up an altar in her hospital room and expose the sacrament on it. Protests by Evangelicals prompted Tait, the Bishop of London, to forbid these proceedings. The embarrassed hospital authorities sided with the Bishop and asked Miss Jones to desist. She countered by offering to sever her connection with St John's House, to which the Bishop was both Visitor and Chairman of the Committee, and thereby remove herself and her sisters from his jurisdiction. She argued that fuller participation in the sacraments would make her sisters better nurses.[22]

Miss Nightingale let her heart rule her head and backed Mary Jones. Against her experience at Harley Street and Scutari, and against her known opposition to professed sisterhoods she denounced — to herself — 'ecclesiastics [who] always oppose women who do anything well', which was not the point of the dispute. Against even her private advice to her 'Dearest Friend' not to succumb to the Roman Catholic iniquity of subjecting women to their confessors, she publicly upheld Mary Jones's claims to govern her sisters' relations with their chaplain in her own way. Secretly through her intermediary, Sir Harry Verney, she warned the Bishop that 'if Miss Jones goes — I'll take our midwifery school away & bestow it wherever she goes'.[23] The Bishop and hospital authorities held firm and Miss Jones and her sisters withdrew in November 1867. Miss Jones subsequently opened a private nursing home. Miss Nightingale was surprised and upset that her friend should have persisted, against her advice, with her Romanising follies. She cut Miss Jones for most of the following year and only permitted a resumption of their intimacy after that lady humbly pleaded for it.[24]

The hospital authorities first considered approaching the High Church Clewer sisterhood to replace the St Johnites, but Miss Nightingale vetoed that. The Clewer women were associated with the formidable Louisa Twining and Miss Nightingale sensed trouble from her. Bishop Tait proposed what Miss Nightingale dismissed as 'those idiotic Deaconesses' led by their obstreperous founder, Rev. Thomas Pelham Dale. Miss Nightingale wanted them even less than the Twining lot. The prospect of Pelham Dale, who had fomented the Jones trouble, backed by Tait and the Hospital surgeons, was particularly daunting: 'How I wish there were no men', she lamented. After her two vetoes the hospital council, without telling Miss Nightingale, turned to the All Saints' sisters who were ensconced in University College Hospital, and their lady superior accepted. They came, despite Miss Nightingale's threat to remove her Fund.[25] Outmatched, Miss Nightingale withdrew, and began to talk about the puerperal fever death rate. When Mary Jones died in June 1887, Miss Nightingale memorialised her to herself:

> She is my oldest friend in the Nursing Cause. When dying & apparently speechless, she said in all at once in a distinct voice to her two oldest Sisters, kneeling by her: 'Little Children, keep yourselves from idols.'[26]

Miss Nightingale's failure with midwives' training impelled her to thwart the plans of others. In 1869 she opposed a move by the Ladies' Medical College to train 'skilled Lady Midwives'. The college's proposed tuition was elaborate and thorough. Miss Nightingale, who hitherto had urged such thoroughness, now denounced the scheme because it would produce over-trained women who would evolve into lady doctors and forsake ordinary midwifery. Her Fund could have saved the project; her authoritative opposition certainly helped to destroy it.[27] She also rejected as impractical and restrictive a contrasting take-over bid by the Obstetrical Society to register midwives, limit their ministrations to 'natural labours' and compel their attendance at 25 deliveries before registration, that is, more than four times the number required of medical students.[28] This scheme foundered too. Meanwhile coroners continued to report the sad outcomes of the ministrations of incompetent, grimy midwives. In 1873 the General Medical Council was asked to back a revised plan by the Obstetrical Society to register practising midwives after they had received some minimal instruction in cleanliness, anatomy, obstetrics and nursing at London and provincial hospitals. The teachers were to be volunteer medical men and hospital matrons; the tuition was to be free and given at times to suit the midwives. Proponents of the scheme on the Medical Council, such as the well-meaning Professor W.D. Acland, knew from the difficulties that the Nightingale Fund and Ladies Medical College had experienced that the main problem was to attract midwives to the courses. Miss Nightingale, having condemned the Ladies' Medical College plan for being too elaborate, now condemned this course for being too rudimentary. She specially sought evidence from Berlin and Vienna to prove that five months was the minimum period of instruction required in advanced nations. Throughout 1872-3 Acland, her spy on the General Medical Council, sent her the confidential minutes and drafts of the Council under the illusion that he and she were allies in the cause of improving midwives. Most of the Council were opposed to becoming involved with the midwives' question. They were able to demolish the proposal after Miss Nightingale, having refused to return to Acland some illicitly supplied documents, leaked information that she was privy to the Council's deliberations and disapproved them. She even scolded Acland for carelessness after the Council inadvertently included in a printed report some abusive marginalia which she and Bonham Carter had added to one of the purloined papers.[29] At this point Acland gave up. Had Miss Nightingale lent her authority to a midwives' training scheme, however elementary in its inception, a worthwhile system of instruction and registration would have emerged long before it finally did in 1902. There was widespread support for such a scheme among middle-class women, medical men, parliamentarians, and some midwives. Partly thanks to Miss Nightingale's obduracy, thousands more parturient women were to endure needlessly prolonged pain, mismanagement and death before the midwife situation began to be remedied.

However, Miss Nightingale did attempt to mend the hospital puerperal fever death rate, if for the wrong reason. In 1871 she and Sutherland belatedly published a trenchant survey of maternal mortality rates in lying-in and general hospitals. With their usual verve they covered a wide range of institutions, reproduced plans of wards to demonstrate overcrowding and bad ventilation, and concluded with sets of model plans and rules for hospital procedures. Their statistics were defective, but they got the general proportions right: women were safest when delivered at home and most at risk when confined in lying-in hospitals. Similarly, the Nightingale-Sutherland rules about cleansing wards and changing bed linen are sensible and practicable, despite their dependence upon the maxim, under challenge by 1871, that 'The smallest transference of putrescing miasm from a locality where such miasm exists to the bedside of a lying-in patient is most dangerous.' Yet again Miss Nightingale had founded right practice on wrong principles. Behind the scenes she was still working to stop the introduction of carbolic acid antiseptic procedures into hospitals, on the grounds that they made doctors careless and scrubbers lazy. The disturbing feature of *Notes on Lying-In Institutions* is the casual way in which five years of bad results at King's College Hospital are reported. It is indicative of Miss Nightingale's small concern with nursing and the operation of the Fund that she appears to have remained complacent about the hospital reports or even to have ignored them completely. In 1866 she had asserted that confinement at home was twice as safe as delivery in hospital yet she did nothing to apply the lessons of this to the Fund's ward at King's College Hospital.[30] But it is also fair to say that *Notes on Lying-In Institutions* provoked interest in its subject and accelerated the improvements in cleansing, rebuilding and antiseptic procedures that were beginning in maternity hospitals and wards about 1870. Yet the lethargy Miss Nightingale and Sutherland showed when writing the book, the nonchalance she displayed at its slow publication, and their unwontedly cool tone when handling horrifying statistics indicate that she at least regarded the *Notes* as a cover-up for her blundering connection with King's College Hospital and as a screen for her real reason in breaking with the hospital. None the less, her devious pursuit of self-satisfaction happened to issue, as it commonly did with Miss Nightingale, in public good.

The Fund's production of trained lady nurses was also modest, measured against the acclaim which the scheme received. Dropouts and expellees seem to have constituted a third of each year's intake and in some years, 1864 for example, as few as four survived. The annual reports of the Fund are uninformative and there were at least two major attacks upon its management. During the 1860s, at least, the unfilled places meant that income from the Fund was simply reinvested. Cynical contemporaries like the journalists on the *Pall Mall Gazette* asked publicly where the money went, and received no answer.[31]

But the money which was spent was well spent. The Fund sustained about 100 working nurses over the first decade and certified about 1900 all told between 1860 and 1903. Possibly because their numbers were small and Mrs Wardroper and Miss Nightingale constituted such a formidable duo of teacher and inquisitor, their quality was superb. The Nightingales carried with them throughout the world Mrs Wardroper's concern with cleanliness, exactitude, neatness and personal solicitude for every patient, reinforced by secure self-esteem based on confidence in their skills and status, and backed by the cachet of association with the national nursing heroine and the dedication she evoked. Miss Nightingale ensured, too, that the dedication was maintained: her nurses were directed to posts by the Fund and were subject to secret reports to the Fund from their employers. They were forbidden 'for a certain number of years' (which had become three by the 1880s) to take situations for themselves.

On the other hand, the widows, the religious seekers, the searchers for satisfying employment, the spinsters by choice and the unloved found a home in St Thomas's, a family in living and praying and working together, and parents in Mrs Wardroper and Miss Nightingale. Sister Sybil Airy, who went to nurse British troops in Alexandria during the Sudan campaign of 1884, is an example. With great courage she nursed a smallpox case and enteric fever cases in a makeshift hospital. On Easter Day 1884 she wrote to 'Dearest Miss Nightingale' describing the day's work and religious services:

We had our little Easter Service this evening at 5.30 with Holy Communion. I am *organist* (but only a very poor one) so I had the privilege of playing the dear *old* Easter Hymn 'Jesus Christ is risen to-day' . . . We decorated the Church a little with Palm branches, and exquisitely *sweet Roses* − eight pink, and eight yellow. While thus occupied my thoughts flew to dear old St Thomas's, and I wondered if Mrs Wardroper had decorated the Chapel there as beautifully as she used to in days gone by . . .

In 1887 Nurse Airy lost her baggage and personal possessions when the *Tasmania*, which was carrying her and the other nurses home, foundered on the south coast of Corsica. She took charge of the shipwrecked party, men and women, organised them to find shelter on the shore, built a fire, and obtained provisions by using sovereigns she had sewn into her stays. Miss Nightingale replaced the watch she lost in the wreck; once back at St Thomas's Miss Airy led the probationers in special prayers of thanks to Miss Nightingale.[32]

A large proportion of the Nightingales, perhaps even the majority, were not 'ladies'. Too few of these offered themselves, and Miss Nightingale and Miss Wardroper were obliged to take 'women' from the respectable lower-middle and working classes. Observers considered them to be physically stronger than the 'ladies', more obedient and readier to do unpleasant tasks and less flighty and 'tall-talk' especially in religious matters. They were also said to get on better with the working-class under nurses, who did most of the washing and feeding of patients, and with the scrubbers.[33] But anyone who stayed the course must have possessed determination, resilience and self-control. Before the 1860s were out the Nightingales had carried the evangel to Netley, Edinburgh, Liverpool, Salisbury, Lincoln, Leeds, to St Mary's and the Westminster among the London hospitals, and to Sydney.[34] Before she died, Miss Nightingale had the satisfaction of seeing 'her' standards introduced into Scandinavia, Italy, Russia, the United States and throughout the Empire. Rarely can such a beneficial revolution in the lives of so many people — patients and women — have been wrought on the basis of sheer reputation. Mrs Wardroper's young women, and the young women they trained in turn, made possible the modern curing, caring hospital and the modern district nursing service. Doubtless Miss Wardroper, even without Miss Nightingale's patronage, would have produced disciples to spread the ideal of effective nursing but the Nightingale money meant that there were more of them, and the Nightingale name ensured that they rose rapidly to matronships and to acknowledged domains of authority and expertise within the hospitals.

Snobbish, genteel rivals such as Elizabeth Garrett — later Dr Garrett Anderson — saw Miss Nightingale's elevation of 'women' as a capitulation to lower standards and as yet another disappointing closure of a promising field for employment of middle-class ladies. Miss Garrett, insecure *nouveau riche* like many of her sisters, argued that all probationers should pay premiums and that the salaries of superintending nurses should be low enough to discourage interlopers from below the 'governess' level. Her plea was taken up by Dr A.P. Stewart, a spokesman for the doctors, and hospital administrators hopefully echoed it. Miss Nightingale, *nouveau riche* too, but patrician in her values, rejected their arguments as 'disgraceful to . . . common sense'. She wanted good nurses regardless of their origins, and with a patrician grasp of financial realities she declared that *all* nurses should be 'highly paid' because they performed duties which required special skills. Besides, premiums and lower salaries would only diminish the already inadequate supply of recruits.[35] The genteel critics' vision of broods of well-born would-be nurses being elbowed aside by upstarts was destructive fantasy. Still, Miss Nightingale feared that a public debate would harm the nursing cause and while she fumed privately she left it to Farr and others to spread her message at dinner tables. We commonly blame Florence Nightingale for the traditional low pay for nurses, but some of the guilt should fall elsewhere. But it must be added that Miss Nightingale took no positive action to raise nurses' salaries and, indeed, was so ill-informed about them that she regularly overstated them publicly by about 10 per cent. Of course this might also have had the effect of raising the going rate in hospitals controlled by governors unversed in the matter.[36]

The publicity won by the Fund confirmed Miss Nightingale's standing as the national authority on nursing and women's work. Between 1860 and 1890 she was involved, welcome or not, in every major controversy over nursing in Britain and she had to be invoked, even consulted, on almost every major question about women's rights.

Other London and provincial hospitals soon developed training schemes in emulation of St Thomas's. Their nurses were beyond Miss Nightingale's control. From the late 1860s, as their numbers grew, these nurses combined with some restive spirits among the Nightingales to press for the creation of an autonomous nursing college to grant certificates, to bind the emergent 'profession', control entry and salary scales and, most important, inaugurate a superannuation scheme. Acland and the reformers on the General Medical Council realised that general standards had to be set and he undertook to persuade the Council to back a nursing college. All these proposals directly challenged Miss Nightingale's suzerainty and she fought them like a tigress.

She seized on the suggestion that general certification entailed formal examinations. These, she asserted, could never prove fitness to nurse. Doctors would set questions which inculcated 'contagion theory', and thereby blind nurses to the 'real causes' of disease. Moreover, lectures could never develop 'character', which came only from 'practical training'. Examinations could never replace the 'continuous assessment, weekly record, notices of character progress, practical work in ward' and matron's monthly reports which made for Nightingale conditioning. After all, musicians and painters were accepted for their 'work', not their examinable, theoretical knowledge. But behind these persuasive arguments lurked Miss Nightingale's real antipathy to examination schemes: they would 'fatally interfere with discipline'.[37]

During the next twenty years she used these arguments to beat back a succession of registration proposals. Public acceptance of the lady nurses and the associated emergence of the new curative hospital enabled royal ladies to busy themselves as patronesses. Naturally they consulted Miss Nightingale, who used them to repel the would-be certifiers. In 1877 Elizabeth, Princess of Roumania, sought advice about forming a nursing service for her country's soldiers. Miss Nightingale told her to select only persons of character and not mere examination nurses. She warned the Grand Duchess of Baden in 1883 that nursing attracted 'many apples, few good ones', but then she consoled the Duchess with the observation that Germany contained many women who retained the 'moral discipline' and 'Devotion to home duties' which was the 'best preparation for high devotion to Hospital life'. These worthy middle-class souls compensated for Germany's want of ladies, by comparison with Britain where primogeniture and inequality of fortunes within the family induced many ladies to turn to nursing to support themselves, but not, Miss Nightingale added, 'from the highest motives or from any great fitness'.[38]

Despite her rearguard activity her control gradually slipped away. In 1881 the Ratcliffe Infirmary, as Miss Nightingale chose to call it, had the temerity to reject for their superintendent's post the lady dispatched to them by Miss Nightingale and Mrs Wardroper (Miss Airy, later of Alexandria – the shipwreck heroine) and instead to 'select . . . a woman who knew absolutely nothing'.[39] Also in that year Miss Nightingale was not consulted when a District Nursing Association, backed by the Duke of Westminster, was established to train nurses to work with local provident dispensaries.[40] Six years later, her former ally William Rathbone, the nursing reformer from Liverpool and Sir Henry Ponsonby, the Queen's private secretary, combined to stop her getting hold of the Queen's Jubilee Fund in order to underwrite her plan for training district nurses. They intended instead to use the money as the basis for a superannuation fund. Her response was that 'nursing is a duty – not a reward'. Rather than be excluded, she then espoused the idea and began to suggest extremely shrewd ways of making it work – under her aegis. Rathbone was inclined to admit her to the organising junta, but Ponsonby would have none of her. After this final rebuff she dismissed it – the first substantial advance in providing effective superannuation – as 'another mischief-making & pauperizing charity'.[41]

The Queen's Jubilee Fund inspired the creation of other nursing bodies to bid for the spoils. A committee of matrons, about which Miss Nightingale had not been consulted, began to meet to discuss nursing matters and to seek money. Miss Nightingale was against it: the gatherings would 'only breed spite'.[42] But they continued. A more ominous challenge came from the proposed British Nursing Association.

This body was created by a committee comprising doctors' wives — a remarkable instance of their new respectability — hospital matrons and insurance promoters, under the patronage of Princess Christian. Their object was to make nursing 'a legally constituted profession', that is, to obtain a charter to enable the BNA to create a register of certificated nurses, set standards and control entry.[43] Miss Nightingale did not fight the BNA openly. But she let it be known that she disapproved and drafted pamphlets against the proposal, to be signed by her acolyte, Henry Bonham Carter. 'I'm staying out of the fray', she told Acland confidentially, 'but I send a pamphlet against the BNA scheme.' With a remarkable assumption that Acland might dismiss from his mind his knowledge of its origins at South Street, she added, 'We agree with this pamphlet.'[44] But Acland was disposed, timidly, to support the BNA. So did many Nightingales. Its professional advantages were too obvious to be denied. Marie C. Redpath wrote in 1889 to her 'old chief' from Kimberley in South Africa, to confess that she had joined the BNA 'with a view (to setting up a private nursing Home and School here) . . . and I think it will be useful (if the Charter is obtained) . . . but I am afraid you don't approve of the movement as I see no St Thomas's names on the Committee nor your own among the Patrons, and gathered so from Mr Bonham Carter's pamphlet', which Miss Nightingale had sent to her in common with all the Nightingales.[45]

Divisions among the sponsors of the BNA and the creation of a rival body, together with Miss Nightingale's known opposition, allowed the government to stall on granting the charter until 1893, two years after Miss Nightingale had lost interest in the affair. Thereafter she steadfastly refused invitations, even from Princess Christian and Louisa, Grand Duchess of Baden, to become a patroness of the Royal British Nurses Association.[46] Ironically, the bitterly won charter turned out to be full of loopholes and sadly disappointed its patient begetters. Even more ironically, most nurses believe, despite the real story being told first by Cook and since in Professor Abel-Smith's authoritative *History of the Nursing Profession* (1960), that they owe their present chartered status to Miss Nightingale.

One particular nursing episode provides a vivid display of Miss Nightingale's annexational, secretarial prowess. In 1864 she learnt of two moves to introduce trained nurses into workhouse infirmaries. In London Dr E.H. Sieveking, who had been concerned with the problem for almost a decade, made yet another attempt to develop a training system for poor and pauper women to equip them to nurse in the infirmaries and among outdoor paupers. In Liverpool, William Rathbone, the philanthropist, anonymously offered £700 to create a training scheme in the town's workhouses. Miss Nightingale, using Sutherland to write the letters, approached both men with advice and offers to supply the lady superintendents. Sieveking abandoned his project rather than have her take it over. Rathbone accepted her offer of a lady superintendent, but only that.[47] Even so, it was a slack period for the Nightingale Fund scheme and Miss Nightingale had no nurses available. By the autumn of 1864 negotiations were suspended. But in December a pauper in the Holborn Union, Timothy Daly, died in sufficiently public and horrifying circumstances to cause a scandal that could not be hushed up.[48] Miss Nightingale struck. She told C.P. Villiers, the president of the Poor Law Board, that 'poor Daly's' death made imperative a full inquiry into workhouse nursing. She promised to help the inquiry with all her strength. They could begin by emulating Liverpool where 'one noble man [was] putting up £1,200 [sic]'. Villiers, a wily old politician, smoothly rebuffed her. He informed her that the only inquiry envisaged was a departmental one into the immediate circumstances of Daly's death. The nursing issue was ignored. However, in deference to the great lady he added an ill-considered postscript: 'I'll see you about a possible enquiry if you want.' She hooked him by return mail:

From the PS to your letter it appears that you desire to have personal communication with me on the subject. I am hardly able to see anyone, but I consider the case of such importance that I would make an effort to see you if you should happen to desire it.

She concluded her letter with the heads of discussion for his visit: nursing as 'an acquired art' and not 'a natural gift' and the 'Liverpool experiment'. Villiers came to South Street in January 1865 and was complaisant.[49] By February when it became clear that Villiers had not acted to his promises and was evading her, Miss Nightingale turned yet again to Harriet Martineau to revive the flagging workhouse reform campaign in the *Daily News* and the quarterlies.

I have also had to see Mr Villiers and, at Mr Villier's desire, Mr Farnall [a poor law board inspector] to confer about introducing Trained Nursing into London Workhouse Infirmaries. They are much more frightened at the death from the Holborn Union than they 'let on'. I was so much obliged to that poor man for dying.

Villiers needed reminding, Miss Nightingale added, that he must attend
to powerful representatives of opinion outside Parliament, lest they join
his enemies inside the House of Commons.[50] Through H.B. Farnall,
sickened by the misery he observed but could not alleviate, she received
a secret flow of documents from within the Poor Law Office detailing
frightful overcrowding, privation, cruelty and filth in London
workhouses. She also obtained secret intelligence from Douglas Galton,
whom the Poor Law Board consulted about the design and fabric of
workhouses. This information she passed on to Harriet Martineau, to
the *Saturday Review* and, through Jowett, to G.C. Brodrick, a Balliol
man then on *The Times* staff.[51] They used these reports to add
substance to their editorials and news items as a succession of horrifying cases similar to Timothy Daly's came to light.

In the short run this campaign failed. The *Daily News, The Times*
and *The Saturday Review* had not mobilised public opinion and Villiers
was secure in the knowledge that the great majority of MPs remained
uninterested in radical reform of the Poor Law. Miss Nightingale had
provided him with the heads of a bill that would have transformed
the Poor Law and the management of the sick poor and which, indeed,
prefigured developments for the next 60 years. She proposed the
establishment of a new central authority, separate from the Poor Law,
to levy and spend a general metropolitan rate for the sick poor. All
workhouse infirmaries and suburban hospitals were to be transferred
to the new authority. These steps were to inaugurate a dismantling of
the workhouse system, the abolition of labour tests, and the ending of
outdoor relief for the able-bodied poor.[52] Her plan was not original.
Its elements and general shape were similar to various schemes for
'state medicine' promulgated by radical medical men since the 1840s.
Her distinctive contribution was to put the elements, medical
attendance, non-parochial taxation and central control together in a
particularly simple-looking, coherent way. None the less it was too
much for Villiers. He knew that any proposal to destroy local control
of taxation and spending on the poor would create violent opposition.
Miss Nightingale was in touch with at least one MP interested in radical
reform of the system, Arthur Mills, a paternalist Tory; but Villiers
adroitly delayed the committee stages of his bill until after midnight
and thus easily outflanked the tiny clutch of disunited critics in a
near-empty House of Commons. Miss Nightingale's admirably drafted
motion prepared for her brother-in-law, Sir Harry Verney, never came on.

Her motion is a lucid summary of her concerns as an improver and vividly expresses her disregard both of sentiment and political realities:

That inasmuch as the question of the due care of the sick poor in the metropolis is neither one of local rating nor of local management but of administration it is expedient that for the sake of economy, uniformity and efficiency that there should be one central and responsible administration to undertake the entire medical relief of the sick poor.[53]

Although she ignored immediate political realities, her motion went to the heart of the matter: about three-quarters of the 168,000 inmates of London workhouses were there because they were sick and their condition would remain scandalous until more money was spent upon classifying them, nursing them and building infirmaries for them — which was exactly the point that Villiers and his fellow MPs would not face. Even Farnall was frightened by the implications of Miss Nightingale's proposals. Without telling her, he and his fellow officials delegated to investigate workhouse conditions settled for improved ventilation, and dodged the rating and nursing questions. She was furious when she learned of his treachery from Villiers, who now was in Opposition and ready to make trouble for his Tory successor.[54] (Villiers used Miss Nightingale to see the papers Farnall was removing from the Office.) She was the more angry because Farnall, Villiers and the new president of the Poor Law Board, Gathorne Hardy, misunderstood her intentions. She wanted a reallocation and eventual reduction of expenditure, not an increase. The extra money that was to be spent on the sick poor was to be provided by a reduced expenditure on malingerers and the non-incapacitated sick, who would be discovered and declared ineligible for relief by a centralised, efficient medical authority bent on economy.

'FoolHardy' (Villier's name for his supplanter when writing to Miss Nightingale) was 'pompous . . . & foggy' as his subordinate, Farnall, said.[55] His Metropolitan Poor Bill of 1867 tinkered with the rating provisions and created opportunities for local unions to co-operate in building ventures. But 'foolHardy' remained deaf to suggestions from Sir Harry Verney, J.S. Mill, Villiers, Farnall, and the British Medical Association that he extend his bill to create a central building fund and provide for nursing. He transferred Farnall to Yorkshire and midst the MPs' preoccupation with parliamentary reform ignored Verney and Mill.[56] When it became clear that the bill would pass unaltered Miss

Nightingale, desperate but still carefully negotiating through an intermediary, begged Gathorne Hardy to permit the Nightingale Fund to train lady nurses in workhouses. He rejected her offer and deepened the humiliation by entertaining a rival bid from Miss Louisa Twining and her Workhouse Visiting Society to train pauper nurses. But this too came to nothing.[57]

Just when Miss Nightingale seemed relegated to impotent officiousness on the workhouse question a chance event enabled her to reassert her pre-eminence as nursing heroine and thereby compel attention from important people. On 19 February 1868 Miss Agnes Jones died of typhus fever in the Liverpool workhouse. She had been the lady superintendent in charge of nurse training, installed and paid for by William Rathbone. Her death caused Miss Nightingale to change her attitude to Miss Jones from private contempt to opportunist public adoption, tinged throughout with puzzlement at such unrelenting self-abnegation.

Agnes Jones was born in 1832 into an evangelical Anglican military family. Her childhood was spent in Mauritius, where she decided to be a missionary when she grew up. She was given to hiding, and evincing 'silent hysterics'. By her fourteenth birthday her family were back in England. She recorded in her diary: 'When I look back at the past year, I see nothing but sin, depravity and unhappiness.' At sixteen she 'blossomed' when she became 'greatly attached' to one of her teachers, Miss Mason, who with her particular friend, Miss Bellingham, had been Protestant missionaries in Ireland. Under Miss Mason's influence Agnes became a teacher at a Dublin ragged school. Two years later in 1853, she visited Kaiserswerth, that magnet for British Protestant *devotes*, and then returned to Ireland to take up visiting the sick. This lasted until 1859, when she was caught up in the Evangelical revival and became a full-time 'home visitor', tract distributor and Bible reader. After the revival ebbed in 1860 she retreated to Kaiserswerth.[58]

In 1861 Miss Jones sought admission as a Nightingale pupil at St Thomas's. Miss Nightingale opposed her entry, but was outflanked by Miss Jones, who surreptitiously gathered support from other members of the Fund committee. Miss Nightingale told her confidante Mary Jones that Agnes Jones's

> peculiar character . . . is want of character. She is always under some one's meridian . . . I told . . . Mr Rathbone . . . that I thought Miss A. Jones, with many excellent & even endearing qualities, would never

have the moral authority necessary for his purpose – & would get herself into ludicrous scrapes.[59]

At the end of her training Agnes Jones nursed in at least three London hospitals within three years: her 'low state of general health' and 'partial nervous deafness' apparently prevented her from securing a continuing appointment.[60] In mid-1864 she seems to have been the only applicant for Rathbone's Liverpool workhouse post. The Liverpool board of guardians had hedged Rathbone's initiative with crippling conditions. They made the lady superintendent subject to the workhouse master in all disciplinary matters relating to nursing and gave her no standing in the workhouse on matters deemed separate from nursing. But it was Dr Sutherland who worried about Miss Jones's mental and physical unfitness for the appointment and her acceptance of rules which breached Miss Nightingale's code giving hospital matrons clear authority in the nursing sphere. Miss Nightingale expected only failure from the experiment and held aloof from it.[61]

The Liverpool workhouse infirmary at the time of Miss Jones's arrival in early 1865 was a typical large urban pauper infirmary of its period. It contained between 1,200 and 1,500 inmates crowded into wards built to house many less, sleeping three to a bed. Violence was common, cross infections were endemic and deaths were frequent. The staff comprised 50 pauper nurses, mostly wholly untrained, and 150 scrubbers.[62] The workhouse master resisted Miss Jones from the outset and the guardians gave her no support. Every day she finally got to bed at 1 a.m. and rose again at 5.15 a.m. Her tearful entreaties and prayer sessions made little impact on hard-boiled, resentful nurses and she soon found herself doing much of the routine toil herself. Even after contracting typhus in early February 1868 she continued to work herself to exhaustion and succumbed within a fortnight.[63]

Within hours of learning of the death Miss Nightingale was busy: 'Of course a good many arrangements fall upon me', she answered Mary Jones's letter of condolence. 'It is something like saving from a wreck . . . Please return thanks for her – as you have prayed for her. You can't think how much good your letter of divine sympathy for her did me.'[64] Miss Nightingale wrote a eulogy of Miss Jones and employed a firm of advertising agents to foist it on every major newspaper and weekly in Great Britain. At first only the *Daily News* accepted it – although that paper did not normally carry obituaries – but the agents 'got an influential man on the job' and the obituary subsequently appeared ubiquitously.[65]

Before any request arrived from Liverpool Miss Nightingale had begun to interview likely replacements for Miss Jones. She and Mrs Wardroper finally agreed upon Mrs Kidd. As before, their choice was limited. One of Miss Jones's workhouse visiting friends in Liverpool found Mrs Kidd to be 'energetic ... but not superior', and predicted that she could not succeed where even the saintly Miss Jones had been 'overwhelmed'.[66] And indeed Mrs Kidd failed. She was dismissed in March 1869 for drunkenness and it soon emerged that she had been a drunkard long before her appointment. Miss Nightingale privately blamed Mrs Wardroper for the disaster. The Liverpool authorities pointedly ignored Miss Nightingale when choosing Mrs Kidd's successor and let it be known that their future nurse training would not be on the St Thomas's pattern. Miss Nightingale indignantly predicted that this would bring catastrophe. With marvellous inconsistency she declared: 'We believe that vice cannot exist without discovery among our trainees.'[67]

Miss Nightingale's obituary of the 'workhouse saint' quickly brought her the reverence she craved. Dr Bowman told her that he knew 'she [Agnes Jones] was one of the very few who enjoyed your full confidence, & whom you looked to for carrying on your system for the future ... you have heavy blows'. Henrietta Walker, a nurse at the Liverpool workhouse, filled several pages with incoherent grief and religiosity and ended by 'consider[ing] you ... the highest lady in the land, next to the Queen'.[68] Miss Nightingale published an expanded version of the obituary, entitled 'Una and the Lion', in *Good Words*, the Edinburgh Presbyterian monthly, in June 1868. She sent offprints to numerous friends, including her old Indian ally, Dr J.P. Walker. Her covering letter to him began with a long recital of her illnesses and administrative trials, and continued:

this very year has seen the death of the best & dearest of my pupils, my 'Una' [Miss Nightingale reduced Agnes Jones into an anonymous, mythical *Faerie Queen* 'being' in the *Good Words* article] ... Now my 'Una' is gone, I cannot think how I could ever be unhappy when she was doing God's work so gallantly at Liverpool Workhouse ... I don't know that I ever wrote so much about my own things before — But your kindness encourages me.[69]

The article in *Good Words* is a remarkable piece of autobiographical wish-fulfilment, half-conscious projection of herself, outright mendacity and calculated pleading. The autobiographical wish-fulfilment dwells on sainthood:

> One woman has died ... attractive and rich, and young and witty
> [Agnes had none of these attributes]; yet a veiled and silent woman,
> distinguished by no other genius but the divine genius – working
> hard to train herself in order to train others to walk in the footsteps
> of Him ... She overworked because others underwork ... She lived
> for life, and died the death, of the saints and martyrs.

The projection focuses upon concealment of self:

> I do not give her name! were she alive, she would beg me not ...
> Of all human beings I have ever known, she was the most free from
> desire of the praise of men ... she preferred being unknown to all
> but God; she did not let her right hand know what her left hand
> did ...

And lies:

> In under three years she brought 'discipline' to one of the most
> disorderly hospital populations in the world ... At St. Thomas's
> she was our best pupil ...

Completed with calculated pleading: 'there is no "amateur nursing"
[a blow at Louisa Twining and her pauper nursing schemes]. We need
more women to train as nurses ... we challenge England ...'[70]
'Una' caused a sensation. Ladies of 'a far higher class' flocked to
St Thomas's and within the year Miss Nightingale had sufficient
Nightingales to 'occupy' the St Pancras workhouse and Netley Hospital
and, subsequently, Highgate workhouse.[71] Harriet Beecher Stowe,
a correspondent of Miss Nightingale's since Crimean days, also received
an offprint. According to Miss Nightingale, she publicised 'Una' in the
United States and undertook to launch a poorhouse nursing scheme.
If she did, I could not trace it. Miss Nightingale also claimed that Henry
Ward Beecher, Mrs Stowe's brother, reissued 'Una' as a pamphlet with
a preface by himself, extolling Miss Nightingale. This appears to have
been wishful thinking by Miss Nightingale: there is no record of such a
pamphlet. Meanwhile she revelled in interviewing, choosing and drafting
her newly augmented following. 'I cannot think of her even now
[1870] without tears, which I have no time to shed.'[72]
This euphoria was broken in 1871 when a memoir of Agnes Jones by

her sister was announced, prefaced by Miss Nightingale's 'Una' and incorporating her name on the title-page. She secretly threatened the publisher, Alexander Strachan, with heavy punishment if he used her name or reproduced 'Una', or even issued the book. It does seem true that 'Una' and Miss Nightingale's name were used without her knowledge or permission; although, as Strachan was also the publisher of *Good Words* and presumably held copyright in 'Una', the position is not clear-cut. But she really wanted the withdrawal of the whole book and legally she had no case. Her vanity prevented her from doing what was possible, that is, ensuring that her name and 'Una' were deleted. Her real fear was that, having appropriated Agnes Jones and depersonalised her − 'I do not give her name; were she alive she would beg me not' − and absorbed her into her own reputation, she would lose her to this interloping sister. Strachan ignored her protests. She made Sutherland issue further threats − 'It is so hard to make me write another letter And I have no one to act for me' − but the book emerged unaltered.[73] The *Memorials* did indeed restore Agnes Jones as a saint in her own right. Thereafter Miss Nightingale kept silent about her and Miss Jones slipped from public memory.

The celebrity Miss Nightingale achieved with 'Una' also served to re-establish her links with government. The new president of the Poor Law Board, G.J. Goschen, an innate economiser and more active than Gathorne Hardy, was looking for ways to reduce Poor Law expenditure and he readily responded to an invitation in December 1869 from Miss Nightingale to visit her to be coached on the problem. She summed him up, present and future, in one unsparing, accurate paragraph:

> I don't think he will ever do much. He is a man of considerable mind, great power of getting up statistical information and Pol. Econ. but with no practical insight. It is an awkward mind − like a pudding in lumps. He is like a man who has been Senior Wrangler and never anything afterwards.[74]

She produced a scheme partly new, partly old, calculated to appeal to such a clever-simple politician. The new element envisaged the removal of able-bodied paupers to the provinces and the Colonies under a state subsidised emigration plan. Those who refused to go should be 'offered help to support themselves. Everybody ... women and children ... can produce to some extent'. The children were to be trained in state supported industrial schools. The old part was her familiar project of reclassifying the sick to reduce their numbers. Those with families were to be redefined out of pauperdom and made the responsibility of their families. The residuum were to be centrally redistributed through a metropolitan system of specialist institutions maintained by a metropolitan rate.[75]

Goschen recoiled from the emigration proposal: it was 'semi-communistic'. He argued that whatever the state did for the poor they would not do for themselves and thereby the state sapped 'the power of self-help'. He also betrayed Miss Nightingale's hopes by procrastinating on the metropolitan rate and the new system of pauper infirmaries. Miss Nightingale hated Goschen's 'stupid brutal cry for economy'. He and the Liberal government, she told Jowett, 'know no more of what the people of England are, or of what they ought to be, than the Man in the Moon'.[76] But the general reclassification and reduction of paupers could be quickly effected and win ratepayers' applause. During 1870 and then to 1874 under Goschen's successor, James Stansfeld, the number of paupers in England and Wales was cut by 18.5 per cent, or 194,000. They turned up again as 'unemployed' and in the queues at hospital out-patient halls, but in the short run Goschen and Stansfeld appeared to have conducted a triumphant piece of Liberal reform.[77] Miss Nightingale was not solely responsible for such a grotesque scheme but by encouraging Goschen, in particular, she shares responsibility for its implementation and its cruel results.

In nursing, as in all her enterprises, Miss Nightingale's achievement was mixed. She gave nursing a public standing and independence within the medical hierarchy that it would otherwise have taken much longer to consolidate. Her emphasis upon common sense care, pithily expressed in *Notes on Nursing*, was invaluable and she greatly strengthened the vocational aura of nursing by her posturing, but she added nothing to the details of technical proficiency required in a nurse's daily tasks. In workhouse nursing she had far-sighted ideas but she proved ready to abandon them for the immediate satisfaction of petty intrigues with Poor Law Board officials, and the practical results of her advice were malign. But then, she was less interested in the workhouse question, indeed in general nursing, as her delays with the Nightingale Fund prove, than her contemporaries and later biographers have believed. Miss Nightingale served the cause of nursing less than it served her.

Notes

1. Edward James Edwards, *Nursing Association For The Diocese Of Lichfield* (London, 1867), p.39; (Mary Stanley) *Hospitals and Sisterhoods* (London, 1854), pp.1-2.

2. Jane Shaw Stewart to F.N., 27 July 1858, 10 Nov. 1858, GLRO HI/ST/V2/58; F.N. to Uncle Sam Smith, 11 Nov. 1857, BL Add.Mss 45792, f.74.

3. Brian Abel-Smith, *A History Of The Nursing Profession* (London, 1960), pp.20-1.

4. *Lancet*, 4 July 1857, p.15; Codrington to Panmure, 1 Feb. 1856, PRO WO1/381, f.959.

5. Sir Edward Cook, *The Life of Florence Nightingale* (2 vols., London, 1913), vol. I, p.443.

6. Shaw Stewart to F.N., 13 July 1857, GLRO HI/ST/NC2/V35/57; Sutherland to F.N., 25 Aug. 1856, BL Add.Mss 45751, f.1.

7. F.N. to 'Dearest Friend' (Mary Jones) n.d. [early 1865?], 23 Sept. 1866, GLRO HI/ST/NC1/64/24; 66/15; F.N. to Sutherland [16 July 1861?] BL Add.Mss 45751, f.195.

8. F.N. to Uncle Sam Smith [6 Nov. 1857?], 11 Nov. 1857, BL Add.Mss 45792, ff.68-9, 72.

9. Herbert to F.N., 22 Mar. 1858, BL Add.Mss 43394, f.21; *Lancet* 3 Apr. 1858, p.346.

10. F.N. to Aunt Mai [19 Dec. 1859?], M.A. Baines to F.N., 19 Dec. 1859, BL Add.Mss 45793, ff.194-9.

11. 'Proper Trust Deed' of Nightingale Fund, Houghton Mss 18/120, Trinity College, Cambridge.

12. McNeill to F.N., 25 May 1859, BL Add.Mss 45768, f.100; McNeill to Herbert, 25 May 1859, GLRO HI/ST/SU/117; Herbert to McNeill, 15 Dec. 1859, 19 Dec. 1859, GLRO HI/ST/SU/121, 122.

13. McNeill to F.N., 11 Apr. 1859, BL Add.Mss 45768, f.94.

14. McNeill, 'Notes for service of Nightingale Fund nurses at St Thomas's', [19 Dec. 1859?] GLRO HI/ST/NCI/SU/123; Nurses Monthly Record Sheets – Nightingale Papers, 'Miscellaneous Photographs and Pamphlets' – BL; A.L. Pringle 'Some Recollections of Miss Nightingale . . .', GLRO HI/ST/NC12/4, p.76; (Mrs Ellis) 'Something Of What Florence Nightingale . . . Is Doing', *St. James's Magazine,* vol. I, 1861, pp.38-9.

15. Herbert to McNeill, (copy) 15 Dec. 1859, BL Add.Mss 45768, f.106.

16. F.N. to Mary Jones, 15 May 1860, GLRO HI/ST/NCI/60/3; Sir Joshua Jebb, 'Statement of the Appropriation of the Nightingale Fund', *Transactions of National Association for . . . Social Science, 1862,* pp.642-7; *Lancet,* 23 June 1860, p.626.

17. Jebb, 'Nightingale Fund', pp.644-5; F.N., 'Notes on the Sanitary Conditions of Hospitals . . .' *Transactions of the National Association for . . . Social Science,* 1858; *Lancet,* 13 Dec. 1862, p.662.

18. *Lancet,* 31 Mar. 1866, p.353, 4 Apr. 1868, pp.437-8, 1 Aug. 1868, p.154; *Pall Mall Gazette,* 23 Mar. 1866, pp.5-6, 11.

19. Nathaniel Powell to F.N. 29 Jan. 1868; F.N. to Powell, [draft 1 Feb. 1868?] BL Add.Mss 45800, ff.213-6; F.N. to Sutherland, [12 Mar. 1867?] BL Add.Mss 45752, f.252; F.N. to [Acland?] [draft, early Feb. 1868?] BL Add.Mss 45800, f.219.

20. cf. Cecil Woodham-Smith, *Florence Nightingale* (London, 1950), pp.473-4.

21. F.N. to [Mary Jones], 23 Sept. 1866, GLRO HI/ST/NCI/66/15; Cook, *Nightingale,* vol. i, pp.448, 502.

22. F.N., Memorandum on King's College Hospital dispute [Sept. 1867?], BL Add.Mss 45752, f.237.

23. F.N. to Mary Jones, 7 Nov. 1866, GLRO HI/ST/NCI/66/17; F.N., Memorandum [13 Oct. 1867], BL Add.Mss 45752, f.240; F.N. to Harry Verney, 15 Feb. 1867, BL Add.Mss 45791, ff.70-1.

24. F.N. to Sutherland, BL Add.Mss 45753, f.1; F.N. to Mary Jones, 19 Oct. 1868, GLRO HI/ST/NCI/68/12.

25. F.N., Memorandum, 12 Oct. 1862; F.N. to Sutherland [12 Nov. 1867?], BL Add.Mss 45752, ff.239, 253-5.

26. F.N. Memorandum, 3 June 1887, BL Add.Mss 52427, f.43.

27. F.N. to Acland, 20 July 1869, Acland Papers, d.70 ff.15-20, Bodleian Library, Oxford; Jean Donnison, *Midwives And Medical Men* (London, 1977), pp.76-7.

28. F.N. to Braxton Hicks, 23 Jan. 1872, GLRO HI/ST/SU 72/1; Donnison, *Midwives*, p.78.

29. F.N. to Dr Gottwald (copy), 26 Apr. 1872; Frau Littra to F.N., 24 May 1872, GLRO HI/ST/NCI/SU72/4, 8; Acland to F.N., 28 Mar. 1873, BL Add.Mss 45786, ff.30-2; F.N. to Acland, 31 Mar. 1873, Acland Papers, d.70, ff.41-57, Bodleian Library, Oxford.

30. F.N. *Introductory Notes on Lying-In Institutions* (London, 1871); F.N. to Sutherland [20 July 1870?] BL Add.Mss 45754, f.244; F.N. to Acland [25 Nov. 1865?] GLRO HI/ST/N4/66/20.

31. *Pall Mall Gazette*, 23 Mar. 1866, pp.5-6; *Lancet*, 25 Aug. 1883, p.343, 14 July 1884, p.81.

32. Sybil Airy to F.N., 13 Apr. 1884; 15 June 1887, BL Add.Mss 45775, ff.149-50, 173; *The Times*, 19 Apr. 1887.

33. A.P. Stewart, 'Hospital Nursing', *Transactions of the National Association for ... Social Science, 1866*, p.591; F.N., 'Notes for Dr Stewart' [Oct. 1866?] BL Add.Mss 45818, f.31; F.N. to Sutherland, 12 Sept. 1870, BL Add.Mss 45755, f.47.

34. J.S. Bristowe, *How Far Should Our Hospitals Be Training Schools?* (London, [1884?]), p.12.

34. Elizabeth Garrett, 'Hospital Nursing' *Transactions of the National Association for ... Social Science, 1866*, pp.473-4; F.N. to Farr, 13 Oct. 1866, BL Add.Mss 43400, f.111.

36. 'A Lover of Truth & An Old Nurse' to F.N. [June 1868?]; William Heathcote [Governor? of Hampshire Hospital] to F.N., 11 Apr. 1868, BL Add.Mss 45801, ff.8, 86-7.

37. F.N. to Acland, 'Private & Confidential', 20 July 1869, Acland Papers, d.70, ff.9-14, Bodleian Library, Oxford.

38. E.B. Mawer to F.N., 5 June 1877, BL Add.Mss 45750, ff.192-4; F.N. to Grand Duchess of Baden, (draft), 26 May-9 June 1883, GLRO HI/ST/SU83/2.

39. F.N. to Galton, 6 June 1881, BL Add.Mss 45765, f.13.

40. G.R. Trevelyan to F.N., 25 Feb. 1881, BL Add.Mss 59786, ff.52-3.

41. F.N. to Rathbone, 14 Aug. 1887, 1 Sept. 1887, 13 Oct. 1887, 14 Oct. 1887, 10 Dec. 1887, Henry F. Ponsonby to Rathbone (copy), 6 Oct. 1887, BL Add.Mss 49625, ff.5-21.

42. F.N. to Pringle, 21 Oct. 1887, GLRO HI/ST/NCI/SU/87/47.

43. Ethel Fenwick to F.N., 11 Feb. 1888, BL Add.Mss 45808, f.33.

44. F.N. to Acland, 7 July 1889, Acland Papers, d.70, f.127, Bodleian Library, Oxford; Henry Bonham-Carter 'Secretary of the Nightingale Fund', *Is a General Register for Nurses Desirable?* (London, 1888).

45. Marie C. Redpath to F.N., 12 Mar. 1889, GLRO HI/ST/NCI/V6/89.

46. F.N. to Rathbone, 3 June 1891, 5 June 1891, 27 Jan. 1891, 4 July 1891,

GLRO HI/ST/NCI/SU/91/3-13; F.N. to Acland, '6 a.m. confidential' 22 July 1893, 25 Mar. 1894, GLRO HI/ST/NCI/SU93/6; 94/2. F.N. to HRH Helena, Princess Christian . . ., 17 May 1894; F.N. to Louisa, Grand Duchess of Baden, 14 Apr. 1896, BL Add.Mss 45750, ff.98-100, 187-8.

47. E.H. Sieveking to F.N., 31 Dec. 1864, BL Add.Mss 45799, ff.68-70; Rathbone to F.N., 25 Feb. 1864, GLRO HI/ST/NCI/SU/151; F.N. to Rathbone (draft in Sutherland's hand) 30 July 1865, BL Add.Mss 45752, f.41; Louisa Twining, *Recollections of Workhouse Visiting and Management* (London, 1880), pp.17-19.

48. *The Times*, 4, 16 Feb. 1865.

49. F.N. to C.P. Villiers [draft 30 Dec. 1864?] [draft, early 1865?] Memorandum for discussion with Villiers [Jan. 1865?]; Villiers to F.N. 31 Dec. 1865, BL Add.Mss 45787, ff.54-66; Cook, *Nightingale*, vol. II, pp.130-1.

50. F.N. to Martineau, 12 Feb. 1865, BL Add.Mss 45788, f.280.

51. Sutherland, 'Notes for Conversation with Farnall', April 1865; F.N., 'Notes of Conversation with Farnall' [late April-early May 1865?], BL Add.Mss 45752, ff.11-34; F.N. to Farnall [drafts May 1865? early 1866?] BL Add.Mss 45786, ff.180, 197; F.N. to Galton 'Private & Confidential Burn' 17 Aug. 1866, BL Add.Mss 45763, ff.221-33; Jowett to F.N., 5 Dec. 1865, Jowett Papers, Balliol College, Oxford, vol. I; *Pall Mall Gazette*, 14 Feb. 1867.

52. F.N. to [?] draft [May 1865?], BL Add.Mss 45752, ff.1-2.

53. A. Mills to F.N., 15 June 1865; F.N., draft of motion on Poor Law [early June 1865?], BL Add.Mss 45799, ff.119-21.

54. F.N. to Galton, 20 Oct., 31 Oct., 9 Nov., 14 Nov. 1866, BL Add.Mss 45763, ff.234-56.

55. C.P. Villiers to F.N., 30 Jan. [1867?], BL Add.Mss 45787, f.72; Farnall to F.N., 27 Jan. 1867, BL Add.Mss 45786, ff.212.

56. Verney to F.N., 11 Mar. 1867; Verney to Gathorne Hardy, 12 Mar. 1867; Gathorne Hardy to Verney, 12 Mar. [1867?] BL Add.Mss 45791, ff.77-81; Mill to Chadwick, 5 Mar. 1867, Chadwick Papers, University College London, CP1401; Farnall to F.N., 6 Mar., 11 June 1867, BL Add.Mss 45786, ff.239-43.

57. F.N. to Gathorne Hardy, [draft Mar. 1867?] has read his bill 'with much satisfaction'; F.N. to Villiers [draft, Mar. 1867?] the Bill 'is a disaster', BL Add.Mss 45787, ff.132-41.

58. J. Jones, *Memorials of Agnes Elizabeth Jones, By her Sister* (London, 1871), pp.2-100.

59. F.N. to [Mary Jones?], 24 May 1861, GLRO HI/ST/NCI/61/3.

60. Sutherland to F.N. [early July 1864?] BL Add.Mss 45751, f.241.

61. Sutherland to F.N. [June 1864?] BL Add.Mss 45751, f.242.

62. Margaret E. Tabor, *Pioneer Women* (London, 1927), pp.112-4.

63. Sutherland 'Notes on Liverpool Workhouse', 13-17 Sept. 1865, BL Add.Mss 45752, ff.50-2; E. Gilpin to F.N., 8 Feb. [19 Feb.?] [1868?] BL Add.Mss 45800, ff.220, 243.

64. F.N. to 'Dearest Friend' (Mary Jones), 20 Feb. [1868?], GLRO HI/ST/NCI/68/3.

65. Rathbone Bros. and Co. to Verney; Rathbone Bros. to F.N., 25 Feb. 1868, BL Add.Mss 45791, ff.102; 45800, f.254.

66. Thomas Henry Satchell to F.N., 24 Feb. 1868; F.N. to Satchell [draft 25 Feb. 1868?]; Gilpin to F.N. 2 Mar. [1868?] BL Add.Mss 45800, ff.252-7, 270-3.

67. F.N. to Sutherland [late Mar. or early Apr. 1869?], BL Add.Mss 45753, f.230.

68. Bowman to F.N., 3 Mar. 1868; Henrietta Walker to F.N. 19 Mar. [1868], BL Add.Mss 45800, ff.261-3.

69. F.N. to Walker, 10 Aug. 1868, GLRO HI/ST/NU/68/8.

70. F.N. 'Una And The Lion', *Good Words,* June 1868, pp.360-3, reprinted in Jones, *Memorials of Agnes . . . Jones.*

71. F.N. to 'Dearest Friend' (Mary Jones), 5 Feb. 1870, GLRO HI/ST/NCI/70/3; F.N. to Sutherland [21 Dec. 1869?] BL Add.Mss 45754, f.43.

72. F.N. to Verney, 3 May 1872, BL Add.Mss 45791, f.142; F.N. to Mary Jones, 5 Feb. 1870, GLRO HI/ST/NCI/70/3.

73. F.N. to Sutherland, 24 Mar. 1871, BL Add.Mss 45755, f.183.

74. Thomas J. Spinner, Jr., *George Joachim Goschen* (Cambridge, 1973), pp.31-2.

75. F.N. to G.J. Goschen (draft) Dec. 1869, F.N. Memorandum on Poor Law [early 1871?], BL Add.Mss 45802, ff.94, 271; F.N., Memorandum of interview with Goschen [29 Dec. 1869?] BL Add.Mss 45754, f.52.

76. Spinner, *Goschen*, p.32; F.N. to Jowett [Dec. 1869?], BL Add.Mss 45783, f.147; Jowett to F.N., 26 Dec. 1869, Jowett Papers, Balliol College, Oxford, vol. III.

77. F.B. Smith, *The People's Health* (London, 1979), pp.383-4.

6 REPUTATION AND POWER

In August 1866 when her Indian and Poor Law pursuits were faltering Miss Nightingale was visited again by God. 'What has thou to do with rest & ease', He asked in good Authorised Version style. Her account does not record an answer. Instead, Miss Nightingale's next sentence reports her apparently addressing herself: 'It may be that they [official hindrances] only came as messengers – that it is really <u>God who has need of you</u>.' Her report of His appearance on 7 May 1867 also ends in tangled syntax. The day was, she recalled mistakenly, the fifteenth anniversary of His summoning her 'to the perfection of my service (to be a Saviour)'. When He came a third time at 6.30 p.m. on 28 July 1867 He reminded her, quite incorrectly, that she had, like Him, spent three unrequited years each at Harley Street and Scutari. Her vision of His head, crowned with thorns and bathed in light, merged with hers: 'I think that I am another Himself . . . another *en état de victime*.' A picture of Christ crowned with thorns hung in her bedroom.[1]

These reported experiences are the more strange because Miss Nightingale did not pray, did not attend divine worship, and only took the sacrament when Jowett brought it. She read the Christian mystics, only to disagree with their passivity, although she esteemed St Teresa of Avila. She did not believe, in any orthodox sense, in the Incarnation, the Atonement, Revelation, or Salvation through faith or works. She twice declared that she believed in an existence after death but that she had no concern with it because her business was with this world. Her future state existed, she affirmed, independently of her wishes and of any covenant with God. She reserved to herself a half-flippant, Whiggish scepticism. She jotted on a scrap of paper probably about 1866-7; 'I should like above all Eternities, to work in Hell . . . "to save the puir burning bodies". But to be shut up with Dean Scott etc etc. & Bishop etc etc . . . for 1000 years . . . the spirit shrinks appalled.'[2]

Her beliefs, in so far as she recorded them, have an Arian, Unitarian core. She wavered between regarding God as person and as idea. Generally she inclined to the latter, having decided in about 1850 that she preferred the 'Egyptian' system of belief which revered the attributes of God to the 'Greek' system deifying the faculties of man.[3] Her *Suggestion for Thought* are a jumbled, repetitive attempt over three volumes of print to develop two linked arguments: that 'God' exists as 'idea' in advanced civilisations like that of nineteenth century Britain, and that the proof of His existence and perfection lies in His creation of those natural laws by which man, using his intelligence to discover and free will to adopt, could work out his own happiness and advance towards perfection. Miss Nightingale, like many other Victorian improvers, was deeply worried by the impasse to good action presented by inexorable laws of human behaviour and the incidence of disease as revealed by statistical data. 'Free will', defined as the capacity to learn from the data and contrive adjustments, was her way, in common with other Victorians, of surmounting that impasse.

> Crime, disease and death, by God's law, always go together. Therefore, insensible but immense progress has been made through Dr. Farr's branding of a certain class of diseases with the word *'zymotic'* (and its association of 'preventible') towards the abolition of [these?] evils ... Man has power to realize all that is right and good, not by prayers to another Being to do *his* work, not by a mysterious 'self determining' power through which he shall 'will' to do it, but by taking God's appointed means.[4]

She knew the appointed means: 'It is a religious act to clean out a gutter and to prevent cholera, and ... it is not a religious act to pray (in the sense of asking).'[5] Moreover, she was divinely appointed to know. Ultimately, her faith was a sacralised egotism. She reminded Jowett that the 'most extraordinary' fact that she – a woman – should be uniquely possessed of 'all the practical knowledge of Army organization', united with the will to devote 'every instant' of life to it, proved that she was uniquely 'part of God's plan'. God had created her like Himself, 'a Trainer', in a world which was 'a training school'.[6] Her task was to declare God's laws of sanitation and virtue, and to aid and measure each person's adherence to those laws and thereby guide the world's slow march towards perfection. Her religious experiences and writings on religion – the *Suggestions* – are justifacatory exercises and corroborative arguments for her election as Trainer: they do not express her primary impulse to work in her chosen way. That impulse we can vaguely trace in her behaviour but its precise nature remains hidden in her psychopathology.

The 'Stuff' (her label for the *Suggestions*) occupied Miss Nightingale for thirty years. It is both a religious testament and a vindication of her rejection of her family. Her attacks on her family, as the quotations in Chapter 1 illustrate, are vivid and unfair. The disquisitions on metaphysics are clumsily argued, ill-informed and almost unreadable.

Jowett, whom along with several other great men she coerced into reading the 'Stuff', evaded direct criticism, but he privately told A.H. Clough that Miss Nightingale's arguments were thoroughly muddled, especially her various depictions of God as 'legislator', which were at once 'too vague' and too limiting because they rendered the 'universal God ... a finite entity'. Jowett subsequently dodged her repeated requests to edit the work. The material on the family is thrust into volume two, completely disrupting the discussion of religion in volumes one and three. As Jowett warned Clough, 'the book [is] ... too full of antagonisms'.[7] At its heart lay acute problems of personality that were alleviated only in work, deceit and paranoia.

Miss Nightingale also sent copies of the manuscript to her father, Sir John McNeill, John Stuart Mill, Monckton Milnes and Uncle Sam Smith, seeking their endorsement of her metaphysics and praise for her philosophical prowess. She hinted to each that he was the sole recipient of her confidence. She also supplied each with a pretext for the work. She told McNeill in May 1860, for instance, that in 1852 she had had

> a large and very curious acquaintance among the Operatives of the North of England, & amongst those ... called Holyoake's party [G.J.H. was a working class secularist] in London. The most thinking and conscientious of our enormous artisan population appeared ... to have no religion at all.
>
> I then wrote the first part of what I have ... [sent] you, without the least idea of every publishing it. And it was read in manuscript by some of them ... No one knows of it. And, till after my death, I would never have it published, certainly not in my name.[8]

She told Milnes that she 'had read' the manuscript 'to one or two', and Jowett that the 'artisans ... have implored me to publish something for them', with the implication that they had neither read nor heard it beforehand.[9] There is no evidence for any of these claims: some circumstantial evidence, indeed, suggests that they are false. Had she known Holyoake he would, as an assiduous tuft-hunter, have boasted of their acquaintance in his memoirs. But his own reference to her implies that he never met her. There are no letters from her among his papers and he would surely have preserved them had she written to him. Nor are there any Holyoake letters among her papers and had there been any it is uncharacteristic of her to have destroyed them. Furthermore, there is no evidence for any contact with artisans in the North of England even had she had time and opportunity.

Indeed, in August 1861 she told McNeill, having forgotten what she had told him fifteen months earlier, that she was considering a new venture teaching the *Suggestions* to the artisans of the East End of London. Altogether, it was an odd explanation to produce because there is nothing in the *Suggestions* about the working classes. It probably originated from Miss Nightingale's acquaintance with the wife of Edward Truelove, the Owenite free thought bookseller. Mrs Truelove made a hat for Miss Nightingale in 1867. Miss Nightingale had presented her with *Notes on Nursing* in 1860 and Stanley's *Life of Arnold* in 1861.[10]

Her correspondents were less gullible than her later biographers. Their responses offer insights into their characters and into the problem that, at one stage or another, afflicted many eminent Victorians – how to deal with a great national heroine who was also importunate and unbalanced. Her father was characteristically kind and flattering and, faced with the diatribe in volume two, embarrassed and defensive: 'Was ever sentence truer than yours? – "God's plan is that we make mistakes."' He then turned to tell her about the family cats. McNeill tactfully if unconsciously ambiguously – after a silence of four months – called the *Suggestions* 'a mine' and warned her off the working classes. They would find her arguments 'too abstruse'. Milnes, that radical friend of the working-men, suavely jibbed: 'Alas I have such a morbid horror of teaching on these subjects with what people call the lower classes'. Jowett, having condemned the *Suggestions* privately, humoured her. She must have informed him that she was already teaching in the East End because he replied that he was 'glad you see the Artizans'; her response that 'Elisha must have a new mantle', (II Kings 2) must have given him pause.[11]

Only good, grave John Stuart Mill – who had never met her – directly annotated Miss Nightingale's text. She asked him in September 1860 to read a 'religious work', adding the bait that it had been written years before for the 'irreligious artisans' but had not then been published because her 'health broke'. Her letter is in a laboured schoolgirl hand quite different from her usual flowing copperplate, on cheap ruled paper instead of her usual luxuriant headed wove. She added a dash of schoolgirlish flattery, too: 'Your "Logic" – especially as regards "Law" "Free Will" and "Necessity" – has been the forming influence of it and of "me".' A few weeks earlier she had used Chadwick to try and inveigle Mill to meet her at breakfast but he had refused and by way of apology had half-heartedly suggested that Miss Nightingale write to him direct. Now he was caught.[12]

Mill scrutinised her manuscript like an indulgent, careful but remote and very clever supervisor of a doctoral candidate. He noted small, and some great, errors of fact, logic and grammar, quibbled about matters of taste, but evaded quarrelling with her central propositions about the existence of God. He generally ignored her discussion of her family; although he appropriated for *The Subjection of Women* (1869), at the price of a delicately allusive compliment, several of her examples and ideas about women's trivialising duties within middle-class families, and women's relation to the arts and intellect. He is known to have begun his essay in 1860 and it seems likely that Miss Nightingale's sprawling, logically undisciplined effort spurred him to it.

Her text of the 'Stuff' and his marginalia comprise a fascinating serio-comic antiphon.

Nightingale: Some of those called the most highly cultivated of the human race, Descartes, Laplace, Hume, have not been able to conceive of a God at all.

Mill: There must, I think, be some mistake . . . about Descartes. He not only believed but thought he had proved the existence of God *a priori*.

Nightingale: Never let us give our belief unless our reason, feeling, conscience, are all satisfied; even though we cannot satisfy reason, feeling, conscience, by any other belief.

Mill: How do we know that the constitution of the world must be such as to satisfy our feelings and conscience?

Nightingale: between God and men there is no . . . agreement. Man did not ask to be born. God never asked man whether he would take charge of himself or not . . . But He is too good a Father to put it into His children's power to refuse it. If He were to do this, timid spirits would resign at once. According to the theory of responsibility, suicide would be justified. For a man may put an end to his service, if dissatisfied with it.

Mill: not if he has taken his wages.

Nightingale: That a man is blind implies some ignorance of physical law, either on his own part or on that of those who preceded him.

Mill: What if he is struck by lightning?[13]

After this encounter Mill never repeated his mistake. In 1867 he refused her plea to join the Indian Sanitary Commission.[14]

Mill's labours on the 'Stuff' and the adverse advice from her other correspondents went for nothing. Without waiting for their comments Miss Nightingale had an unrevised, anonymous version entitled *Suggestions For Thought to The Searchers After Truth among the Artizans Of England* privately printed in three volumes in blue book format by Eyre and Spottiswoode, the HMSO printers, early in 1860. Thomas Carlyle was one of the few to notice the work. He dismissed it as the bleating of a sheep lost in the wilderness.[15] Nearly seventy years later some of her mordant reflections on her relations with her family were reprinted as an appendix to *The Cause A Short History of the Women's Movement in Great Britain*, (1928) by Ray Strachey, a member by marriage of the clan with whom Florence Nightingale's reputation was to be linked over two generations. Miss Nightingale's piece, entitled *Cassandra*, has become the *locus classicus* of radical feminist opposition to the traditional family – a strange fate for an article by a woman who was but a lukewarm supporter of the emancipation of women in her lifetime and who believed in subordinating everybody else.

Miss Nightingale's was one of the first big names that campaigners for women's rights sought to add to their petitions and letterheads. Equally, the maintenance of her reputation as a great woman rested in part upon her association with such causes. But the relationship was always delicate and shifting: the campaigners wanted her name but not her interference. Their apprehensions were unfounded. When Miss Nightingale decided to move into an area of philanthropy already occupied, as in workhouse nursing in the mid 1860s, she preferred to mount a new distinct, rival operation, rather than try to capture the organisations already in the field. She rarely bestowed her name anyway. She had to be convinced that her association with an alien cause would enhance her reputation.

The crucial issue was women's suffrage. Miss Nightingale, like the Twining sisters and Mary Carpenter, could not afford to withhold her support but privately she was sceptical of the cause and disposed to belittle its campaigners. During the latter stages of the passing of the Second Reform Act in 1867 she boasted to Sutherland and to Mill that irrespective of the size of the male electorate she 'had more political power than if I had been a borough, returning two MPs'.[16] Indeed, she had one MP in her pocket: Sir Harry Verney, and therefore she was still much better off than the vast majority of her contemporaries, male and female. About this time John Stuart Mill asked her to support the movement to enfranchise women. Miss Nightingale was ingratiating, but evasive. She thanked him for his special invitation and continued:

> That women should have the suffrage I think no one can be more
> deeply convinced than I. It is so important for a woman to be a
> 'person' as you say . . .
> But it will be years before you obtain the suffrage for women. And
> in the meantime there are evils which press much more hardly on
> women than the want of the suffrage . . . Could not the existing
> disabilities as to property & influence of women be swept away by
> the legislature as it stands at present? [so far as property is concerned
> she proved right − the law was made more equal before women
> achieved the vote] . . . Is it possible that, if women suffrage is
> agitated as a means of removing these evils, the effect may be to
> prolong their existence? . . .
> As to my being on the Society you mention, you know there is
> scarcely anything which, if you were to tell me that it is right
> politically, I would not do. But I have no time. It is 14 years this
> very day that I entered upon work which has never left me 10
> minutes' leisure not even to be ill . . . If you will not think me
> egotistical, I will say why I have kept off the stage of these things.
> In the years that I have passed in Government offices, I have never
> felt the want of a vote . . . And I have thought that I could work
> better for others off the stage than on it. Added to which, I am an
> incurable invalid, entirely a prisoner to my room.[17]

In 1868 Miss Nightingale signed a petition for the suffrage, after 15,000
other women headed by Mary Somerville, the writer on science, had
already signed it.[18] But privately she refused to try to register as a
voter. In 1870 she subscribed to the National Society for Women's
Suffrage and allowed her name to be added to the General Committee
in 1871, but she remained inactive. In 1878 she permitted the
movement to print a brief statement by her supporting women's
suffrage on the Millite grounds that they were householders, ratepayers
and 'persons'. But she added that she did 'not expect much from it'
because women voters were unlikely to be any more enlightened or
progressive than men.[19] She had begun to swing against women's
suffrage, as others of her kind, Octavia Hill and Beatrice Potter among
them, were to do. In June 1889 she refused to sign a women's suffrage
petition. However, she also held aloof from the revolt of the female
Unitarian-Quaker-Positivist-Intellectual cousinhood that erupted into
print during that month. She did not join that high-minded galaxy −

Mrs Matthew Arnold, Mrs W. Bagehot, Mrs Russell Barrington, Mrs E.S.
Beesley, Mrs J.H. Bridges, Lucy Cavendish, Mrs W.E. Forster, Mrs T.H.
Green, Mrs Frederic Harrison, Mrs Courtenay Ilbert, Mrs Lynn Linton,
Miss Christina Rossetti, Mrs Leslie Stephen, Mrs Alma-Tadema, Mrs
Humphry Ward – who with 90 others declared their opposition to
women's suffrage in the *Nineteenth Century*. Miss Nightingale wrote,
probably after reading their protest, that women were 'too ignorant of
politics . . . look at Women Unionists and Home Rulers – furious and
ignorant'. They knew nothing of 'what is feasible, what has been done,
what has failed, what is historically true or historically false' – a just
observation on Mrs Lynn Linton, Mrs Humphry Ward and Mrs Russell
Barrington, at least.[20] Miss Nightingale found the ultimate proof of
women's political incapacity in the campaign to register nurses without
her consent, thereby demonstrating that women voters would be moral
wreckers. But beyond this disquiet, Miss Nightingale had presciently
glimpsed that women would not vote to further their special interest,
but would follow their husbands into party divisions that only hindered
the advancement of women.

Like most extra-parliamentary reformers, Miss Nightingale was
impatient with party politics. She understood and was well informed
about the daily parliamentary round but she remained disengaged. She
took a poor view of most politicians, especially when they crossed her.
In 1871 when Edward Cardwell, an efficient, reforming War Secretary,
blocked her access to his Office she attributed his action to simple
political malice and belittled him as a time-saver, with 'no type of
greatness in his mind'. She wanted what neither Cardwell nor anyone
else could accomplish against the colonels and the Horse Guards, a
wholesale reorganisation of the army, the cutting down of the Guards
regiments, elevation of the engineers and promotion by merit
throughout. She dismissed his Army Regulation Bill and the abolition
of purchase as 'toys'. Both his Liberal Party and the Tories existed only
'to register popular feeling, to satisfy popular ignorance, to make a
scene in effect before the pit', and in this they were abetted by the
press. They were forsaking 'solid practical administrative things for
glittering politics'.[21] Only the few, she wrote in another private
memorandum, probably in the late 1870s, could make the great
reforms. Yet the few were increasingly thwarted by the newly
augmented majority, who were inevitably 'fools'. The work of the
innovative few had become 'as difficult to reconcile with party government, as . . . the "survival of the fittest" with Christianity'. The few
were being driven even further into 'expediency'; although expediency

was morally justified 'when it is incarnating the eternal idea into the earthly form . . . of practical good'. She saw the minority as invariably right and the majority as invariably wrong, not because the minority was open-minded, creative and pluralistic and the majority was the reverse, but because the minority was ordained by God to lead.[22]

Her notion of the 'eternal idea' expressed in practical good meant that Miss Nightingale had no fear of the growth of the central state. Here she differed from philanthropists of inferior rank who had had to build their empires with less state aid. Mary Carpenter and Louisa Twining, for example, looked to the state to provide 'pecuniary support and coercive power' to their private philanthropic ventures. In this way, they argued, they actually contained the secular state by taking its money and using its police, while retaining for private middle-class Christian persons responsibility for the efficient, humane, immediate management of the lower orders, thereby enabling each individual to fulfil her ultimate Providential role. The central state was augmented in service but not enlarged in power.[23] Miss Nightingale, by contrast, sought to make the state coterminous with her private concerns. Her procedures aped the standard reform tactics of male parliamentarians. They sought select committees and Royal Commissions to investigate particular abuses and to produce evidence to back the legislation they envisaged. She contrived her own select Committees and Royal Commissions and, like her parliamentary counterparts, stage-managed the flow of evidence to fit the report she had commonly drafted beforehand. Like them, too, she looked to a central authority delegated by government to enforce the uniform rules she had devised, with the difference that she herself privately sought to control that statutory central authority, which she also endeavoured to keep independent of ministers, and superior to local units whether in hospitals or in Indian army barracks. Her peak period for such operations, the decade between the later 1850s and later 1860s, coincided with the peak period for more orthodox Royal Commissions. Reformers of prisons, schools, universities and trades unions proceeded in a similar way but none did it with so much finesse, confronted such formidable male bastions, or achieved such a widespread preservation of life.

Miss Nightingale's extraordinary ability to avoid public controversy yet win moral approval shows vividly in her dealings with the anti-Vaccination and anti-Contagious Diseases Acts agitations. Her guile in the latter, especially, is positively Gladstonian.

The campaign to end compulsory vaccination against smallpox

never engaged her. When the campaigners sought her public backing she delayed her replies but finally wrote privately agreeing with their allegations that vaccination occasionally harmed people, although only permitting herself to be quoted as saying that the problem needed further study. In the mid-1870s, however, when the Ladies Sanitary Association began to press for a Royal Commission Miss Nightingale could not resist supplying them with the right questions:

> does Vaccination retain its power against Smallpox?
> does compulsion under two years work?
> does Vaccination introduce disease?
> can the present system of employing and paying public Vaccinators be bettered?
> would pure cow lymph be better?

Miss Nightingale was not original in thinking these were the crucial issues but as usual she made them curt and clear and they were the questions ultimately addressed by the Royal Commission of 1889. Yet, having defined the questions, she refused to sign any petition for the Commission. Of course, she said, she agreed with the objects of the petition, but the overriding importance of her general sanitary aims was such that she could not risk offending 'those whose co-operation I desire [who] might hold different views'.[24] Fundamentally, she disliked vaccination because it was beyond her control and threatened her sanitary province.[25] She never supported it in India. In the mid-1890s, at the time of one of the recurring rows about compulsory vaccination in England, she told Sir William Wedderburn, the old India hand, that

> Vaccination (in India) I don't much care about — the greatest authorities in England believe that the diminution of smallpox has resulted more from Sanitation than from Vaccination (But I don't dare say anything about it).[26]

This is both an incorrect and wrong-headed comment on one of the signal successes of medical intervention in nineteenth century Britain. It is cruelly unfortunate for her reputation and for some of those who died that she did not lend her reputation to spreading vaccination, in India especially.

In common with many other Victorians Miss Nightingale was both fascinated and appalled by the moral questions raised by the Contagious

Diseases Acts. Female prostitution negated the ideal of chaste womanhood to which she and other Victorians subscribed. Her interest in the problems of prostitution and venereal diseases long predated the passing of the first Contagious Diseases Act in 1864. In about 1852, amidst one of the flurries about Anglican Sisterhoods and prostitute rescue work, she told Henry Edward Manning that poverty, not innate depravity, was the cause of prostitution and that rescue work had to include training in gainful skills, caring for silk worms, printing, weaving, farm work which would sustain a girl when she left the retreat and equip her for emigration. 'Anything' was 'better than needlework' which was underpaid and would 'take them back . . . to their old habits'. She was against continuously preaching at them, as the Clewer sisters and chaplains did. Instead she advised a 'variety of work, less food, especially meat, to "lower their tempers", and to compel them to "wash all over with soap" . . . [because] personal purity is so necessary to mental purity'.[27]

Late in 1857 some medical men and army officials began to work for legislation to protect soldiers against venereal diseases by inspecting prostitutes in garrison towns and controlling those found to be infected. A sensationalist, inaccurate book by Dr William Acton on prostitution was the pretext for, and indeed was possibly occasioned by, the campaign. It also seems a reasonable supposition that the move was intended as a diversionary counter-attack upon Miss Nightingale's revelations about the Crimea and army death dates from disease. By the end of 1860 the War Office and Sidney Herbert were ready to join the agitation.

Miss Nightingale was opposed to this Continental system of licensing immorality. It proved yet again that the authorities regarded common soldiers as 'unmanageable animals'.[28] She wanted positive inducements to the soldiers to forego vice: encouragement of marriage within the service, full support of army wives and children, and greater provision of rest-rooms and leisure activities for unmarried soldiers. Her arguments were rational and were proved right by events. She declared firstly that inspection had not diminished venereal disease in France and that there were no grounds for believing that it would diminish disease in the United Kingdom. In Gibraltar, the Ionian Islands and Malta where the system already obtained, there had been no measurable decrease in the incidence of disease among the soldiery. Secondly, she argued that the proposed legislation was unfair because it penalised the prostitute while exonerating her customer, and unnecessary because it would be simpler and more effective to enforce and strengthen local laws against brothel-keeping and living upon immoral earnings. Miss Nightingale was not lenient towards prostitutes but she did believe that the law should be equal in its incidence and that every individual should be protected against arbitrary arrest and degrading treatment by authority. Repressive though she wanted the law to be, she also admitted that prostitution could not be stopped − anymore, she said, than she could stop her cat lapping milk. Rather than spending public money upon punitive lock hospitals she preferred the establishment of more effective curative wards in general hospitals.[29] These persuasive arguments, however, were only embellishments to her fundamental conviction that inspection and control were the outcome of a wrong-headed belief in contagion. Throughout the later 1850s and early 1860s, as I remarked in Chapter 3, she was embattled on the smallpox and tuberculosis fronts and her resistence to every attempt to include venereal diseases among the contagions was part of that battle. 'There is no satisfactory evidence', she asserted, 'that syphilis is propagated only by contact with infected persons . . . It rests exactly on the same evidence as does the presumed origin of small-pox solely from contagion.' In fact it rested on much less. Nobody knew what syphilis was or how it was caused or cured. But the doctors were more right than she was when she scornfully dismissed their description of it as a 'specific poison', especially when she went on to assert that 'all evidence tends to show that venereal disease is generated by vice not . . . propagated by infection'. She justified this assertion by the example of 'demoralized' France where disease increased under the regulation system because 'demoralization' damaged bodily functions in the same way as physical miasma, and thereby induced disease 'between persons who have no disease'. Even her allies were apparently unimpressed with her claim that she knew 'more about it than most men'.[30]

Her boasts notwithstanding, Miss Nightingale's arguments were better than those of the regulationists. They had no evidence to support their claim that compulsory inspection had reduced the incidence of venereal disease in France and there was much circumstantial and anecdotal evidence to suggest that regulation was ineffectual as a sanitary measure. They had no sound evidence for their assertion that venereal disease had increased dramatically in the British army and navy about 1860, although there are plausible grounds for thinking that they might have been right. It is likely that the better care of the troops that followed the post-Crimean rows, thanks in part to Miss Nightingale, meant that fewer men died from other severe infections, while the increase in the number of European soldiers stationed in India might well have led to a sudden rise in venereal disease, or at least a better reported incidence because of the closer medical inspection that better care involved. The regulationists believed that the statistics − which with hindsight look worthless − made intervention imperative; and ironically their most powerful argument was derived from the lesson which they had learned from Miss Nightingale and her coadjutors, Chadwick and Farr. This was the assertion that venereal diseases intolerably lessened efficiency, and raised costs in the army and navy.[31]

In 1861 Herbert bowed to the Horse Guards and War Office in adding, without telling her, a lock ward to the Devonport Military Hospital in readiness for voluntary inspection and the incarceration of prostitutes. She unwisely turned to Lord de Grey, the new War Secretary, and W.E. Gladstone, 'at their own request', for support and even threatened them in 1862 with instigating Sir Harry Verney to raise the matter in the House of Commons. She was desperate because she apparently knew that a secret inter-departmental committee was studying the problem and she found herself unable to influence it. 'You are known to have seriously considered the growing evil in Civil life', she prompted Gladstone. De Grey, although he avoided giving Miss Nightingale a direct answer, favoured compulsion, while Gladstone, who for the next twenty years was to evade declaring himself on the Acts, dismayed Miss Nightingale by shilly-shallying and then admitting that he leaned, in her words, towards 'direct coercion'.[32] Miss Nightingale in common with almost every other Victorian reformer, female ones especially, persisted in the hopeless quest of enlisting Gladstone, and like her rivals she was always disappointed. His circuitous utterances always promised that he was for them, but never said he was with them.

The inter-departmental committee met during 1863 and reported early in 1864. It upset everyone's expectations with a majority report along Nightingale lines, recommending voluntary lock hospitals, improved barracks and recreation facilities for the soldiers and sailors and more strict enforcement of local laws against brothel-keeping and living from immoral earnings, and ended with a declaration that the Continental system was ineffective in France and inappropriate for the United Kingdom. Miss Nightingale, although she never claimed the honour, might well have assisted the majority to arrive at these conclusions by rehearsing her arguments in her anonymous *Notes on the Supposed Protection afforded against venereal disease, by recognizing Prostitution and putting it under Police Regulation*, privately printed in blue-book format early in 1863. She sent copies to important people including Sir George Lewis at the War Office. She put Sutherland's name on this copy and when he was reprimanded for attempting to browbeat his chief she left him to carry the blame. She also once more enlisted Harriet Martineau to reproduce her arguments and statistics in the *Daily News*.[33]

The committee's findings were suppressed and instead a dissenting report advocating regulation by Sir John Liddell, Director-General of the naval medical department, was leaked to the press as the full committee's report. The War Office reinforced this manoeuvre by planting letters supporting regulations in *The Times* and other newspapers.[34] Miss Nightingale was beaten at her own game. The Contagious Diseases Bill which ensued from Liddell's report was poorly considered and badly drafted. When it was referred to a Select Committee Sir Harry Verney succeeded in having its police powers better defined and limited, but the measure passed in Parliament without debate or public scrutiny in July 1864.

Almost immediately the authorities found it necessary to create a commission to implement the Act, although the Act did not provide for one. Miss Nightingale boasted to Miss Martineau that she had been 'asked to name the War Office member upon it . . . and to write the Instructions'. In fact, unasked, through Galton she nominated two men, Graham Balfour and Longmore, and attached a list of 'instructions' proving that regulation did not and could not succeed.[35] Balfour was included in the commission but it seems likely that he was chosen for his statistical expertise, despite Miss Nightingale's support. Longmore was ignored. However, Balfour justified her hopes by entering a dissenting report in October 1864 recommending the Nightingale-secret committee line of more certain implementation of existing laws curbing prostitution and closer inspection of soldiers. The majority report of the commission admitted that the Act was unworkable because it was almost impossible to detect and conclusively diagnose venereal disease in women. It too recommended enforcement of existing laws and more 'cheerful . . . camps and hulks' for the men, equipped with savings banks and libraries.[36] The legislation was amended in 1866 and 1869, but it never proved fully effective. There is no evidence that Miss Nightingale took much interest in these developments. She had abandoned the issue in 1864 when she realised that the first Bill could not be stopped.

The campaign to repeal the Acts also developed independently of her. She followed a policy towards it similar to the one she had taken towards women's suffrage. She permitted herself to be loftily associated with the cause and joined Harriet Martineau, Mary Carpenter and Josephine Butler and over 100 other women in signing a protest against the Acts on New Year's Day 1870. She also readily, if anonymously, fought in print her old enemies, the hard lady doctors such as Elizabeth

Garrett and Elizabeth Blackwell who supported the Acts.[37] But she held aloof from becoming identified with the daily round of theatrical agitation headed by the beautiful, charismatic Josephine Butler.

The organisation of which Mrs Butler was the luminary, the Ladies' National Association, first asked Miss Nightingale to become a Vice-President in August 1870. The LNA was a thoroughly expressive organisation. When the Government had offered a Royal Commission on the Acts as a compromise in May 1870, the LNA had pledged non-co-operation. Miss Nightingale was disposed to rebuff them but, as usual, she used Sutherland as a sounding board:

> What do you advise me to do about 'giving' 'my' name as Vice-President
> My feeling is this: My horror of this legislation is, if possible, yet stronger than ever, – there being ... scarcely a tittle of evidence in favour of its doing what it promises. But ... if anything could have supported the objectionable legislation, it is: the blunder of this Association – especially their public protest against an enquiry ... there is scarcely a person of the least weight among them ...
> I should not like to join them as Vice President. Yet I should not like to refuse to join them without telling them that I am unchanged in opposition to the C.D. Acts ... But above all, I don't want a correspondence with them. I have suffered too much from Mrs Butler.[38]

Sutherland duly gave her the advice she half wanted: to decline the Vice-Presidency – and say 'not from want of interest – but feeble health'. A fortnight later, she still had not done so and wrote again to Sutherland who was now himself seriously ill – 'I am sorry you are ill. But, I suppose, as I have not heard again, that you intend me to believe that you are either well or dead' – to confirm her view that she should refuse. The Butlerites were getting much publicity, she added wistfully. But she declined their invitation.[39]

Behind the scenes she continued to badger Home Secretaries and correspond with Mrs Butler. Occasionally she nearly got caught, as in November 1872, when the Council for the National (Repeal) Association sought her permission to publish a phrase she had unwisely used in a letter to Mrs Butler, 'that ... compulsory examination' was 'monstrous': 'As your influence is so great, we are very anxious to ... use ... this extract ... as showing that you are still as heartily opposed to the Acts as ever.' Miss Nightingale turned to Sutherland: 'Please say

– It was you who approved this sentiment.' Sutherland jibbed for once. He told her to tell the National Association that her opinion remained unchanged 'but that from your peculiar position you find that you must keep clear of controversy.'[40] She did not remark publicly upon the suspension of the Acts in 1883 or their repeal in 1886. But, as with women's suffrage, she gradually changed her opinion. In 1896, after sensational allegations of a rise in venereal disease in India with the ending of compulsory inspection the year before, doctors and army officers agitated for the reimposition of the Acts there. Miss Nightingale signed a ladies' memorial calling for regulation, although she added a reservation seeking an independent inquiry. Mrs Butler was back in the fray with a passionate pamphlet: *Truth before Everything*. Miss Nightingale privately dismissed her old rival: Mrs Butler was one of the 'shouting ladies'. 'She does not want to hear facts; she wants to be enthusiastic.'[41] Miss Nightingale always had the facts on her side.

From about 1871 Miss Nightingale ceased her pursuit of power. Occasionally, as with the battle about registration of nurses, or supplying female nurses for the campaign in the Sudan in 1882-5, or a succession of fights about architects' plans for hospitals and women's colleges, she revived as the tricky, dogmatic, wheedling manipulator of the 1850s and 1860s. But her efforts lacked their former drive and each was short-lived. Her compulsion to work was gone.

The death of her father and the decrepitude of her mother and Parthe seemed to ease her private difficulties. She had once described herself, when she was about 27, and yet to find her way, as 'the Moon' to her family, 'the Earth'. 'The Moon revolves round her, moves with her, never leaves her. Yet the Earth never sees but one side of her; the other side remains for ever unknown.'[42] Now the moon was preparing to reveal her unknown side to herself, at least. Her need to identify with other people, to enter and possess their minds, ebbed away. On 14 September 1877 she told herself in her diary that 'Everything henceforth shall be between God and me – no need to think other people's thoughts at all – No help from people'.[43]

None the less she remained dependent upon the effusive affection and admiration of women. During the 1880s she frequently invited to stay with her and sent presents to matron A.L. Pringle, her 'ever dearest "Little Sister"'. In 1888 Miss Nightingale was desolated when Miss Pringle went over to Rome. The 'Nightingale Fund' removed her from St Thomas's.[44] She also took up nurse Pirrie and felt bitterly

deceived when her 'un-friend' revealed that she intended to marry.[45]
In 1872 she had spent a whole fortnight trying to persuade matron
Torrance not to marry 'that wretched little Dowse'. She was furious
when Torrance finally told her to mind her own business.[46] Later,
she always made time, even when she was 'very ill' or had to 'put
off the other lady', to see 'my Goddess', matron Rachel Williams of
St Mary's Hospital. When Miss Williams volunteered as an ordinary
nurse for the Suakim Expedition in 1884 Miss Nightingale, unasked,
wangled her promotion to superintendent. Miss William's announcement
of her engagement during the following year shocked Miss Nightingale:
'O dearest Miss Williams this is bitter & grevious indeed.' Miss
Nightingale sought a meeting to talk her out of it, but Miss Williams
apparently refused to see her. Miss Nightingale was reduced to pleading:
'I crave to see you once more ... he will see you all his life', adding
the bait that Sir Harry Verney had 'gone straight to W.H. Smith' (the
War Secretary) with Miss Williams's complaints about the 'chaplain's
laxity in Egypt'; but there are no more mentions of Miss Williams.[47]

These rebuffs drove Miss Nightingale further back upon herself.
The unsparing appraisals she had formerly made of others she now
made of herself: 'You have never been "mother in chief" to St.
Thomas's. You take the Cross ... and you use it as a club to give
blows with.' 'I have never been Thy servant. I always seek my own
glory – not Thine.'[48] By late 1893 all her old male 'wives' as she called
them, with the exception of ailing Sir Harry Verney who was to die
in February 1894, had predeceased her. Her mother and Parthe were
dead. She had lost her 'dearest friends', Mary Jones, dead in 1887,
and nurses Pringle, Pirrie, Williams and Torrance. Belatedly, in
1893, she besought the Holy Spirit to 'make me learn sympathy with
them by my own troubles and illness – instead of making me think
that they should allow for me. I have never prayed for any of them
I only talked of them.'[49] Pondering the departed again in 1899, and her
own approaching translation, she asked herself, 'What is the language ...
spoken at the "Last Judgement"? What is the language or languages
spoken in Heaven?.'[50]

Heaven had to wait another eleven years. Meanwhile she made and
re-made her will, began numerous small, anonymous acts of
philanthropy and, perhaps, continued her rediscovery of her self. Miss
Nightingale was wealthy, although she continued to tell people that she
was poor. Apart from her minor share of the family estate she made
a lot of money from her books, especially *Notes on Nursing*. She was
to leave £36,127, £35,000 of it in personalty. She ate well and lived
comfortably, although she secretly skimped on the sanitary arrange-

ments of her own house. Her establishment at Number 10 South Street comprised a cook, four housemaids and a commissionaire.[51]

During lucid intervals she continued her practice of eliminating as beneficiaries under her will persons who offended her, and making them aware that she had done so. In 1872 she had struck out her main medical ally at St Thomas's, Mr Whitfield, for 'carrying on' with nurse Butler.[52] In 1897 she docked £2,000 from Francis Galton's portion which had been earmarked for a Nightingale Professorship of Applied Statistics — 'Social Physics' — at Oxford. She had discovered both that the amount was insufficient for a full professorship and that Galton had become untrustworthy because he admitted to a belief in germ theory. Poor matron Pringle's Romish perfidy was similarly penalised. The twenty pounds she was allotted to enable her to buy a 'small gold . . . cruxifix' was withdrawn in 1901.[53]

In her will of 1896 Miss Nightingale ordered that her private papers be 'destroyed without examination'. And in 1901 she revoked the order. Meanwhile, as she had done with Lizzie Herbert, she resolutely fobbed off seekers after letters in her possession and besought holders of her letters to destroy them. Her view seems to have remained unaltered from 1860 when she asked Monsignor Manning, 'Dear Sir or dear friend', to burn her letters to him. 'I have alas! met with such treachery in my poor life that any carelessness on the part of those whom I <u>know</u> to be friendly to me might easily be turned to bad account.'[54]

A generation later she rebuffed Mrs [T.H.?] Green who approached her on behalf of Evelyn Abbott, Jowett's biographer, seeking copies of Jowett's letters to her. Miss Nightingale was in top evasive form. The projected biography was 'so dear to my heart', but she had to select out the private unimportant letters which would only encumber Mr Abbott's researches. She would have liked to have accepted Mr Abbott's kind offer to call but unfortunately she was too ill to receive him. Moreover, the 'real difficulty' was that she had 'not the strength' to select out the private letters.[55] The biography appeared without them. Miss Nightingale's reply was not all evasion. Her manuscripts and papers were littered throughout the first floor of the house, inside piano stools, behind coal scuttles, under sofas, on bedroom wash-tables. Such order as had prevailed had been Sutherland's, and once he departed — nearly 80 and worn out — about 1887-8, her bundles of drafts of letters to various correspondents, packets of envelopes bearing pencilled or orange crayoned memoranda, sheafs of letters from correspondents around the world, boxes of annotated parliamentary papers, slipped into chaos. Time was when she knew where things were but by the 1880s she had lost control. Her careful drafts of letters and copies of memoranda were no longer available for reference and had become superfluous. The vertical filing cabinet would have been her salvation but it was developed in the 1890s, too late for her. Moreover that vivid sense of the sequence and particular thrill of past events which sustain hoarders of memorabilia had faded and the events had blurred and lost significance. Often she reverted to the Crimean days, oblivious of listeners, babbling and shouting incoherently about half-recalled conflicts.[56]

The puzzle remains why she did not effect the destruction of evidence that was so damaging to her reputation, and which she knew to be damaging, as we know from her correspondence with Mrs Green, Lizzie Herbert and Manning. Possibly her manuscripts survived intact because she never found criteria for distinguishing the 'public' – the successes, army sanitary reform, Indian sanitary reform, the development of hospital nursing – from the 'private' – the failures, her monstrously unfair depreciation of her family and her ingratitude for the support they lavished on their 'swan', her bigotry about cholera, her double-dealing with Dr Hall, Rev. Mother Brickbat and Agnes Jones, her duplicity about King's College Hospital and midwives' training. Beyond that we can only speculate that Florence Nightingale, like Mr Richard Nixon and his tapes or Donald Crowhurst and his false sailing records, was so possessed by the habit of deceit, the savouring of special private information against the world, and the conviction that the full, or near-full record would compel posterity to vindicate all her actions, however aspersed during her life, that she could not bring herself to destroy material which had become part of her identity. Having brazened out lies in life she would brazen them out in death.

After all she had successfully beaten back attacks on her reputation by Parthe in pre-Harley Street days, by Fanny Taylor, Mary Stanley and Elizabeth Davis in the 1850s and 1860s, by medical men such as Greenhow and Leith who had criticised her statistics and her dogmatism about contagion and Indian sanitary policy. She had been fortunate that those who possessed evidence which contradicted her claims, Rev. Mother Bridgeman, Sir John Hall, Lizzie Herbert, Cardinal Manning, Sir John Lawrence, the fifteenth Earl of Derby (Lord Stanley), held their peace, respectful of her national standing, fearful of her vindictiveness and mindful that each was implicated in the machinations by which her reputation had been built. Not until

Stanmore's *Memoir of Sidney Herbert* finally appeared in 1906 did anyone dare to describe her publicly as a little lower than the angels. Through E.T. Cook (1913) the family made an astutely ambiguous, effective response. In this study I have tried to construe that species of fallacy that Cook half exposed, but which later writers, excepting Lytton Strachey, have embraced and obscured again — that doers of good deeds must necessarily be good in themselves.

Perhaps Miss Nightingale hoped too that she might in old age by re-reading old letters and re-living old controversies find the key to the mystery of that divided self which had impelled her to fight, to cheat, to bully, to boast and to save lives. The text which hung in her bedroom must always have been at once a comfort, a warning and a conundrum to her, as it is to any reader of her papers: 'It is I; be not afraid.'[57]

Notes

1. F.N., Memoranda, 2 Apr. 1867, 28 July [1867?], BL Add.Mss 45844, ff.4-8.

2. F.N., Note, Nov. 1845, BL Add.Mss 43402, f.34; F.N. to Jowett, Oct. 1868, BL Add.Mss 45783, f.145; F.N., Note [late 1860s?] BL Add.Mss 45844, f.215.

3. F.N. to her parents, 29 Apr. 1850, BL Add.Mss 45790, f.23.

4. F.N. *Suggestions For Thought to The Searchers After Truth among The Artizans Of England* (3 vols., privately printed, 1860) (drafts — 1852-3, 1859-60) vol. I, p.172; Reba N. Soffer, *Ethics And Society In England* (Berkeley, 1978), p.96.

5. F.N. to Jowett [copy, 1 July 1862?], BL Add.Mss 45783, f.7.

6. F.N. to Jowett [draft, 1880s?] BL Add.Mss 45783, f.65.

7. Jowett to Clough, 22 July [1860?], 9 Aug. 1860, BL Add.Mss 45795, ff.19-24.

8. F.N. to McNeill, 17 May 1860, GLRO HI/ST/NCI/SU/130. The copy of this letter in the BL varies in some important details, BL Add.Mss 45768, f.112.

9. F.N. to Milnes [1860?] Houghton Mss 18/131, Trinity College, Cambridge; F.N. to Jowett [draft, early 1860?] BL Add.Mss 45785, ff.104-5.

10. F.N. to Mrs Truelove (copy), 5 Nov. 1860, BL Add.Mss 45979, f.147; F.N. to Mrs Truelove [1861?] BL Add.Mss 45798, f.44; F.N. to Mrs Truelove, 5 Sept. 1867 in Sue Goldie, *A Calendar of the Letters of Florence Nightingale* (London, 1980), number E.859.

11. Sir Edward Cook, *The Life of Florence Nightingale*, (2 vols., London, 1913), vol. I, p.504; McNeill to F.N., 31 Aug. 1860, BL Add.Mss 45768, ff.120-3. Milnes to F.N., Jan. 1860, Houghton Mss 18/121(2), Trinity College, Cambridge; Jowett to F.N. 17 Nov. [1859?] Jowett Papers, vol. I, Balliol College, Oxford; F.N. to Jowett [draft early 1860?] BL Add.Mss 45785, f.104.

12. F.N. to J.S. Mill, 'Private', 5 Sept. 1860, BL Add.Mss 45787, f.1-2; Mill to Chadwick, 7 Feb. 1860, F.N. to Chadwick, 31 July 1860, BL Add.Mss 45770, ff.128, 148-53.

13. 'Suggestions', BL Add.Mss 45840, ff.13, 35, 53, 34.

14. F.N. to Chadwick (copy), 30 May 1866, BL Add.Mss 45771, f.97; Stanley to F.N., 27 July 1865, BL Add.Mss 45781, ff.173-4.

15. W.J. Bishop and Sue Goldie, *A Bio-Bibliography of Florence Nightingale* (London, 1962), p.121.

16. Louisa Twining, *Thoughts On Some Social Questions* (London, 1903); J. Estlin Carpenter, *The Life and Work of Mary Carpenter* (reprinted Montclair, New Jersey, 1974), p.429; F.N. to Sutherland, [after 17 May 1867?] BL Add.Mss 45752, f.63; F.N. to Mill, drafts, 11 Aug. 1867, BL Add.Mss 39927, f.62.

17. F.N. to Mill, 11 Aug. [1867?], Cook, *Nightingale*, vol. II, pp.215-17.

18. Helen Taylor to F.N., 22 Apr. 1868, BL Add.Mss 45801, ff.37-8.

19. F.N. to Sutherland, 2 July 1868, BL Add.Mss 45753, f.46; Mentia Taylor to F.N., 26 Apr. [1870?], BL Add.Mss 45802, f.130; Cook, *Nightingale,* vol. II, pp.217, 451.

20. F.N. to [?] (draft), 30 June 1889, BL Add.Mss 45809, f.160; *Nineteenth Century*, June, July, Aug. 1889, pp.781-7, 104-5, 356-84.

21. C. Edmund Maurice (ed.), *Life Of Octavia Hill* (London, 1913), pp.262-5; F.N., Memorandum [May 1871?] BL Add.Mss 45843, ff.35-9; F.N. to Milnes, 18 May 1880, Houghton Mss 18/142/2, Trinity College, Cambridge.

22. F.N., Memorandum, 5 Nov [early 1870s?], BL Add.Mss 45844, f.234; F.N. to Jowett, (drafts mid-1880s), BL Add.Mss 45783, ff.203-6.

23. Carpenter to Chadwick, 26 Nov. 1860, Chadwick Papers, University College, London, C.P.445; Carpenter, 'The Education of Neglected Children', *Congrès International de Bienfaisance*, 1862, Tome II, pp.89-90. William Carpenter, (ed.), *Voices Of The Spirit and Spirit Pictures*, Bristol, 1877, p.ix; Louisa Twining, *Recollections of Workhouse Visiting and Management ...* (London, 1880), pp.29-39; Louisa Twining, *State Organisation And Voluntary Aid* (London, 1882), p.1.

24. H. de Noailles to F.N. [1876?], F.N., draft reply, n.d. GLRO HI/ST/NCI/V2/76.

25. F.N. to Sutherland, 6 Mar. 1872, BL Add.Mss 45756, f.162.

26. F.N. to Sir William Wedderburn, draft [Dec. 1896?] BL Add.Mss 45814, f.40.

27. F.N. to Manning [1852?] BL Add.Mss 45796, ff.2-7.

28. F.N. to Balfour, 10 Dec. 1860, BL Add.Mss 50134, ff.90-2.

29. (F.N.) 'Private and Confidential' *'Note on the Supposed Protection afforded against venereal disease, by recognizing Prostitution and putting it under Police Regulation*, [1863?]

30. *Note*, p.2; F.N. to Galton, 12 Apr. 1862, BL Add.Mss 45760, f.64; 25 June 1861, BL Add.Mss 45759, f.232.

31. Paul McHugh, *Prostitution and Victorian Social Reform* (London, 1980), pp.35-52; F.B. Smith, 'Ethics and Disease in the Later Nineteenth Century: The Contagious Diseases Acts', *Historical Studies*, vol. 15 (1971), pp.123, 132. Indeed, there is one set of superficially plausible figures which shows that reported venereal diseases were diminishing by about 7 per cent per year during the early 1860s, before the first Contagious Diseases Act in 1864, Benjamin Scott, *A State Iniquity* (London, 1890), p.13.

32. F.N. to Galton, 25 June 1861, BL Add.Mss 45759, f.235; F.N. to Martineau, 25 Aug. 1863, BL Add.Mss 45788, f.208; F.N. to Gladstone, 26 Apr., 4 May 1862, BL Add.Mss 44389, ff.213-14, 239-40; McHugh, *Prostitution*, pp.36, 48.

33. Report of a committee comprising Samuel Whitbread, J. Liddell, T.G. Logan, Tom Taylor, E.H.F. Pocklington, 15 Dec. 1862. PRO WO33/12/188; F.N. to Martineau, 25 Aug. 1863, BL Add.Mss 45788, ff.208-11.

34. *Lancet*, 19 Mar. 1864, pp.327-9; 'Report', p.4.

35. F.N. to Martineau, 31 Aug. 1864, BL Add.Mss 45788, f.275; F.N. to

Galton, 22 Aug. 1864, BL Add.Mss 45762, ff.184-5.

36. 'Report of a committee on the Contagious Diseases Act', October 1864, PRO WO33/17A.

37. McHugh, *Prostitution*, p.56; *Pall Mall Gazette,* 25 Jan., 3, 18 Mar. 1870.

38. F.N. to Sutherland, 22 Aug. 1870, BL Add.Mss 45755, ff.40-1.

39. F.N. to Sutherland, 12 Sept. 1870, BL Add.Mss 45755, f.46.

40. Mrs F. Pennington to F.N., 22 Nov. [1872?]; F.N. to Sutherland, 24 Nov. 1872; Sutherland to F.N., 25 Nov. 1872, BL Add.Mss 45757, ff.41-2.

41. *The Times,* 25 May 1897; George W. and Lucy A. Johnson (eds.), Josephine Butler, *An Autobiographical Memoir* (Bristol, 1913), pp.232-3; Cook, *Nightingale,* vol. II, p.408.

42. Cook, *Nightingale,* vol. I, p.59.

43. F.N., Diary, 14 Sept. 1877, BL Add.Mss 45847, f.84.

44. F.N. to Pringle, 21 Oct. 1887, GLRO HI/ST/NCI/87/47; Jowett to F.N., 31 Dec. 1888, BL Add.Mss 45785, ff.100-1; Lizzie Herbert to F.N., 9, 18 Mar. 1890, BL Add.Mss 43396, ff.230-8.

45. F.N. to Miss Pirrie, 21 Dec. 1885, GLRO HI/ST/NCI/85/13; F.N., 'Note', 31 Oct. 1897, BL Add.Mss 45844, f.190.

46. F.N. to Sutherland, 'Most private', 21 Oct. 1872, F.N. to Bonham Carter, 9 Nov. 1872, GLRO HI/ST/NCI/72/25, 44.

47. F.N. to Rachel Williams, 20 Mar. [1873?]; 11 Jan. 1885; 23 Sept. 1885, GLRO HI/ST/N3/SU180, 129, 149.

48. F.N., Notes, 1-2 Feb. 1890, 9 Jan. 1891, BL Add.Mss 45844, ff.44, 50.

49. F.N. Notes [Oct. 1893?] BL Add.Mss 45844, f.116.

50. F.N., Note, June 1899, BL Add.Mss 45844, f.196.

51. *The Times,* 31 Nov. 1910; *Westminster Gazette,* 2 Nov. 1910; F.N. to Galton, 26 July 1870, BL Add.Mss 45764, f.286; F.N. to Mrs A.E. Hawthorn, 23 Apr. 1890, BL Add.Mss 45776, f.273.

52. F.N. to Bonham Carter, 15 Oct. 1872, GLRO HI/ST/NCI/72/22.

53. F.N., Will, Somerset House; F.N. to [?] draft [Aug. 1897?], BL Add.Mss 45815, f.124.

54. F.N. to Manning, 25 Feb. 1860, BL Add.Mss 45797, f.103.

55. F.N. to Mrs [T.H.?] Green, 17 Oct. 1894, BL Add.Mss 45812, ff.200-1.

56. Helena Gleichen to Miss Lloyd Still (copy), 31 July 1930, GLRO HI/ST/NC5/4.

57. *The Times,* 13 Aug. 1937.

SELECT BIBLIOGRAPHY

Florence Nightingale was an indefatigable correspondent, recorder and hoarder. Two enormous collections of her letters and papers are held at the British Library and the Greater London Record Office. There is also a valuable collection, which includes copies of documents held elsewhere, at the Wellcome Institute for the History of Medicine, London. Her peculiar method of working upstairs, with her secretariat of Sutherland, Galton and other downstairs and at the War Office, resulted in the setting down of a vast amount of day-to-day business, then normally conducted by conversation and now handled by telephone. Moreover, her early universal fame and the ensuing correspondence with notables led to wholesale preservation of her letters; there can hardly be a large manuscript repository in the world which does not boast at least a handful of her beautiful copperplate autographs.

Her letters crop up among the papers of many other eminent Victorians, but most pertinently and/or plentifully in the following collections:

Acland Papers,	Bodleian Library, Oxford.
Carpenter Collection,	Bristol Archives Office.
Chadwick Papers,	University College, London.
Farr Papers,	British Library of Political and Economic Science, London.
Frere Papers,	India Office Library.
Gladstone Papers,	British Library.
Herbert Papers,	British Library.
Houghton Manuscripts	Trinity College, Cambridge.
Jowett Papers,	Balliol College, Oxford.
Lawrence Letters,	India Office Library.
Shaftesbury Diaries,	Broadlands Mss, National Register of Archives.

The two indispensable guides to Florence Nightingale's vast output are:

Goldie, Sue, *A Calendar Of The Letters Of Florence Nightingale* (London, 1980).

Bishop, W.J. and Sue Goldie, *A Bio-Bibliography of Florence Nightingale* (London, 1962).

Other printed sources and authorities include:
'Report upon the State of the Hospitals of the British Army in the Crimea and Scutari', *HC, 1854-55,* vol. XXXIII.
'Report of the Board of General Officers appointed to inquire into . . . the reports of Sir John McNeill and Colonel Tulloch . . .', *PP*, 1856, vol. XXI.

Allen, Donald R., 'Florence Nightingale: Toward a Psychohistorical Interpretation', *Journal of Interdisciplinary History* vol. VI, Number I, Summer 1975
Andrews, Mary Raymond Shipman, *A Lost Commander: Florence Nightingale* (Garden City, NY 1929).
Anon., *Addresses presented to Sir John McNeill . . . and Col. Tulloch* (Edinburgh, 1857)
Anon., *Proceedings of an ordinary meeting of the municipal corporation of Calcutta* (Calcutta, 1864)
Baylen, J.O., 'The Florence Nightingale/Mary Stanley Controversy: Some Unpublished Letters', *Medical History*, vol. 18, (1974)
Beddoe, John, *Memories of Eighty Years* (Bristol, 1910)
Bell, E. Moberly, *Octavia Hill* (London, 1942)
Bellis, H., *Florence Nightingale* (London, 1953)
Blackwood, Alicia, *Narrative of personal experiences . . . During a Residence on the Bosphorus throughout the Crimean War* (London, 1881)
Bolster, Evelyn, *The Sisters Of Mercy In The Crimean War* (Cork, 1964)
Bowd, D.G., *Lucy Osburn c.1836-1891; . . .* (Windsor, NSW, 1968)
Bryce, Charles, *England And France before Sepastopol, looked at From A Medical Point Of View* (London, 1857)
Carpenter, J. Estlin, *The Life And Work of Mary Carpenter*, 2nd edn. (1881), reprinted Montclair, New Jersey 1974.
Carpenter, Mary, *Six Months In India* (2 vols., London, 1868)
Carter, Henry Bonham, *Suggestions for Improving The Management of the Nursing Department in Large Hospitals* (London, 1867)
——, *Is A General Register for Nurses Desirable?* (London, 1888)
Carter, Victor Bonham, *In A Liberal Tradition* (London, 1960)
Chadwick, Edwin, *The Precautions To Be Taken Against Cholera, (Principles of Central Action)* (London, 1871)
——, *"Circulation or Stagnation"* (London, 1889)

Concannon, Helena, *The Irish Sisters of Mercy in the Crimean War* (Dublin, 1950)

Cook, Sir Edward, *The Life of Florence Nightingale* (2 vols., London, 1913)

Cope, Zachary, *Florence Nightingale and the Doctors* (London, 1958)

Davies, Celia (ed.), *Rewriting Nursing History* (London, 1980)

Davis, Elizabeth, *The Autobiography of . . ., a Crimean Nurse*, Jane Williams (ed.) (2 vols., London, 1857)

Davis, John, *Florence Nightingale, or the heroine of the east* (London, 1856)

Donnison, Jean, *Midwives And Medical Men* (London, 1977)

[Doyle] Sister Mary Aloysius, *Memories of the Crimea* (London, 1904)

Edwards, Edward James, *Nursing Association For The Diocese Of Lichfield, etc.* (London, 1865)

Eyler, John M., *Victorian Social Medicine* (Baltimore, 1979)

Faber, Geoffrey, *Jowett* (London, 1957)

Ffrench, Yvonne, *Florence Nightingale, 1820-1910* (London, 1954)

Finer, S.E., *The Life And Times Of Sir Edwin Chadwick* (London, 1952)

Fink, Leo Gregory, *Catholic Influences In The Life of Florence Nightingale* (St. Louis, Mo., 1934)

Fleming, Donald, review of C. Woodham-Smith's *Florence Nightingale, American Historical Review*, vol. 57 (1951-2)

Galton, Douglas, *Healthy Hospitals* (Oxford, 1893)

Garrett, Elizabeth, 'Hospital Nursing', *Transactions of the National Association for the Promotion of Social Science* (London, 1866)

Gaskell, Elizabeth, *The Letters . . .*, J.A.V. Chapple and Arthur Pollard (eds.) (Manchester, 1966)

Goldsmith, Margaret Leland, *Florence Nightingale. The woman and the legend* (London, 1937)

Goodman, Margaret, *Experiences of an English Sister Of Mercy* (London, 1862)

Goodman, Margaret, *Sisterhoods in the Church of England*, 3rd edn. (London, 1864)

Greenleaf, W.H., 'Biography and the "Amateur" Historian: Mrs. Woodham-Smith's "Florence Nightingale"', *Victorian Studies*, vol. II (Dec. 1959)

Gurney, Joseph John, *The 'Record' And Miss Nightingale* (London, 1855)

(Hall, Mrs S.C.), 'Something Of What Florence Nightingale Has Done And Is Doing, *St. James's Magazine*, vol. I (April-July 1861), pp.29-40

Hay, Ian (John Hay Beith), *One Hundred Years Of Army Nursing* (London, 1953)

Hennessy, James Pope-, *Monckton Milnes* (2 vols., London, 1949, 1951)

Holloway, S.W.F., 'The All Saints' Sisterhood at University College Hospital 1862-99', *Medical History*, vol. III, (1959)

Howe, Julia Ward, *Reminiscences 1819-1899* (Cambridge, Mass., 1900)

Hubble, Douglas, 'William Ogle of Derby and Florence Nightingale', *Medical History*, vol. 3 (1959)

Hutchinson, George, *Address . . . on the Treatment Of Criminals In The Punjab* (Bristol, 1866)

Huxley, Elspeth, *Florence Nightingale* (London, 1975)

'Hygiene' [Charles Hathaway?], *Calcutta and its Health Officer* (Calcutta, 1863)

Jones, J., *Memorials of Agnes Elizabeth Jones, By her Sister* (London, 1871)

[?Jones, Mary], *The Training Institution For Nurses St. John's House, Norfolk Street* (London, 1863)

Kinglake, A.W., *The Invasion Of The Crimea, . . .* (8 vols., Edinburgh & London 1863-87)

Kirby, Percival R., *Sir Andrew Smith, M.D., K.C.B.* (Capetown, 1965)

Kopf, Edwin W., 'Florence Nightingale as Statistician', *Publications of the American Statistical Association*, vol. XV (1916-17)

Lambert, Royston, *Sir John Simon 1816-1904* (London, 1963)

Lammond, D., *Florence Nightingale* (London, 1935)

(Lawson, George), *Surgeon in the Crimea*, Victor Bonham-Carter (ed.) . . . (London, 1968)

Longmore, Thomas, *The Sanitary Contrasts of the British And French Armies during the Crimean War* (London, 1883)

Lückes, Eva C.E., *What will Trained Nurses gain by joining the British Nurses Association?* (London, 1889)

———, *How Far Should Our Hospitals Be Training Schools For Nurses* (London, [c.1890])

Macalister, Florence, *Memoir of the right hon. Sir John McNeill . . .* (London, 1910)

Mackerness, E.D., 'Frances Parthenope, Lady Verney (1819-1890)', *Journal of Modern History*, vol. XXX, no. 2, June (1958)

MacMunn, George Fletcher, *The Crimea In Perspective*, (London, 1935)

Mahājana Dharmapāla, *The Administration of Sir John Lawrence in India, 1864-1869* (Simla, 1952)

Manton, Jo, *Mary Carpenter And The Children Of The Streets* (London, 1976)

Martineau, Harriet, *England And Her Soldiers* (London, 1859)

Martineau, John, *Life and Correspondence of Sir Bartle Frere* (2 vols., London, 1895)

Mills, John Saxon, *Sir Edward Cook K.B.E. A Biography* (London, 1921)

Mitra, S.M., *The Life and Letters of Sir John Hall* (London, 1911)

Moore, R.J., *Sir Charles Wood's Indian Policy 1853-66* (Manchester, 1966)

Nash, Rosalind (ed.), *Florence Nightingale to her Nurses* (London, 1914)

O'Malley, I.B., *Florence Nightingale, 1820-1856. A Study of her life down to the end of the Crimean War* (London, 1931)

Osborne, Sidney Godolphin, *Scutari and Its Hospitals* (London, 1855)

Panmure Papers, George Douglas and George Dalhousie Ramsay, (eds.) (2 vols., London, 1908)

Pickering, George, *Creative Malady: . . .* (London, 1974)

Pincoffs, Peter, *Experiences of a Civilian in Eastern Military Hospitals, . . .* (London, 1857)

Pitale, Balkrishna Nilaji (ed.), *The Speeches And addresses of Sir H.B.E. Frere* (Bombay, 1870)

Poole, Stanley Lane-, *The Life of . . . Stratford Canning* (2 vols., London, 1888)

Ramsay, Grace, *Thomas Grant, First Bishop of Southwark* (London, 1874)

Rathbone, Eleanor F., *William Rathbone. A Memoir* (London, 1905)

(Reid, Douglas A.), *Soldier-Surgeon; . . .* Joseph O. Baylen and Alan Conway (eds.) (Knoxville, Tenn., 1968)

Rickards, E.C., *Felicia Skene at Oxford* (London, 1902)

Rolt, L.T.C., *Isambard Kingdom Brunel* (London, 1970)

Rosenberg, Charles E., 'Florence Nightingale on Contagion: The Hospital as Moral Universe', in Charles E. Rosenberg (ed.), *Healing and History* (New York, 1979)

Sargant, N.C., 'Mary Carpenter . . . and her Connection with India . . .', *Indian Church History Review*, vol. XII (1978)

Saywell, Ruby Josephine, *Mary Carpenter Of Bristol* (Bristol, 1964)

Scharlieb, Mary, *Reminiscences* (London, 1924)

Seymer, Lucy Ridgely, *Florence Nightingale* (London, 1950)

Shrimpton, Charles, *La Guerre d'Orient. L'Armée Anglaise et Miss Nightingale* (Paris, 1864)

Skelley, Alan Ramsay *The Victorian Army At Home* (London, 1977)

Smith, Brian Abel-, *A History Of The Nursing Profession* (London, 1960)

Smith, Cecil Woodham-, *Florence Nightingale* (London, 1950)

Smith, F.B., *The People's Health* (London, 1979)

Smith, J.L. Clifford-, *A Manual for the Twenty-Fifth Anniversary of the National Association for the Promotion of Social Science* (London, 1882)

Smith, Reginald Bosworth, *Life of Lord Lawrence*, 6th edn. revised (2 vols., London, 1885)

Spiers, Edward M., *The Army and Society 1815-1914* (London, 1980)

Stanley, A.P., *Supplement to the second edition of the memoirs of Edward And Catherine Stanley* [1880?]

(Stanley, Mary) *Hospitals and Sisterhoods* (London, 1854)

Stanmore, Lord, *Sidney Herbert* (2 vols., London, 1906)

Stephen, Lady, 'The Real Florence Nightingale', in *The Woman's Leader*, 15 February 1929.

Sterling, Sir Anthony Coningham, *Letters from The Army In The Crimean*, London [1857?]

Strachey, John and McClelland, John, *Memoir on Cholera* ([Calcutta?], 23 March 1863)

Strachey, John and Strachey, Richard, *The Finances And Public Works Of India From 1869 to 1881* (London, 1882)

Strachey, Lytton, *Eminent Victorians*, first published 1918 (London, 1977)

Tabor, Margaret Emma, *Pioneer Women* (London, 1927)

A Lady Volunteer (Fanny Taylor), *Eastern Hospitals and English Nurses* (2 vols., London, 1856)

(Taylor, Fanny), *Religious Orders* (London, 1862)

——, *The Stoneleighs of Stoneleigh, and other Tales* (London, 1880)

Taylor, James S., *Alexis Soyer A Chivalrous Chef* (Washington, 1921)

Temple, Richard, *The Statistics of The Indian Empire* (London, 1881)

——, *Men And Events of My Time In India*, (London, 1882)

——, *Lord Lawrence* (London, 1889)

Terrot, Sarah Anne, *Reminiscences of Scutari Hospitals in winter 1854-55* (Edinburgh, 1898)

(Terrot, Sarah Anne), *Nurse Sarah Anne With Florence Nightingale at Scutari*, Robert G. Richardson (ed.) (London, 1977)

Trevelyan, Charles Edward, *The British Army in 1868*, (London, 1868)

Tulloch, Alexander Murray, *The Crimean Commission and the Chelsea Board* (London, 1857)

Twining, Elizabeth, *A Few Words on Social Science to Working People*

(London, 1862)

Twining, Louisa *Deaconesses for the Church of England* (London, 1860)

——, *Nurses For The Sick* (London, 1861)

——, *A Letter to the president of the Poor Law Board . . .* (London, 1866)

——, *Recollections of Workhouse Visiting and Management, . . .* (London, 1880)

Verney, Sir Harry, (ed.), *Florence Nightingale At Harley Street* (London, 1970)

(Vicars, Fanny), *Work in Brighton . . . or Woman's Mission to Wormen* (Preface by Florence Nightingale) (London, 1877)

Wedderburn, William, *Agricultural Banks For India*, (Bombay, n.d. [1880?])

——, *Octavian Hume, C.B., Father of the Indian National Congress* (London, 1913)

Whitcombe, Elizabeth, *Agrarian Conditions In Northern India*, vol. I (Berkeley, 1972)

Williams, Thomas Jay, *Priscilla Lydia Sellon* (London, 1965)

Wintle, W.J., *The Story of Florence Nightingale*, ([London ?] 1896)

Wood, Catherine Jane, *Boards Of Guardians and Nurses* (London, 1893)

Wrench, Edward M., 'The Lessons of the Crimean War', *British Medical Journal*, 22 July (1899)

INDEX

Abbott, Evelyn 200
Acland, Prof. H.W. 102, 162-3, 169
Acton, Dr W. 193
Airey, General Sir Richard 84
Airy, Sybil 165
Aitken, Dr W. 95
Albert, Prince 65, 73, 118
Alexander, Dr Thomas 67, 76, 77, 83, 115
Anderson, Dr A.54
anti-compulsory vaccination campaign 191-2
Army Medical Department 25, 76, 96, 102
army medical schools 63, 75, 76, 77, 81, 94-5, 102
Aspden, Richard 87

Baines, Mrs M.A. 157
Baker, W.E. 123
Balfour, Dr T.G. 67, 75, 83, 96, 100, 196
Barracks Improvement Commission 81, 93, 95-7, 104, 114
Barrett, Jerry 85
Barrington, Mrs Russell 190
Beecher, Henry Ward 176
Blackwell, Dr Elizabeth 90, 157, 197
Blackwood, Lady Alicia 43
Blomfield, Bishop C.J. 27-8
Bolster, Sister Evelyn 29, 68n9
Bowman, Dr William 175
Bracebridge, C. Holte 26-7, 33-4, 38, 40, 42, 45, 50, 53, 55, 61, 157
Bracebridge, Selina 26-7, 33, 38-9, 40, 42, 50, 52, 86
Bridgeman, Rev. Mother Mary Francis 29-32, 42-3, 45, 47-9, 56-67, 155, 201
British Nursing Association 168-9
Brodrick, G.C. 171
Brougham, Lord 132
Brunel, I.K. 102
Budd, Dr W. 143
Burgoyne, Sir John 101
Burns, – (Irish soldier) 51
Butler, Josephine 131, 196-8

Cambridge, Duke of 68, 88, 96, 102, 108
Canning, Lady Charlotte 11, 33
Carlyle, Thomas 188
Cardwell, Edward 95-6, 103, 108, 190
Carpenter, Mary 129-37, 139-40, 151n50, 188, 191, 196
Carter, Henry Bonham 135, 163, 169
Cautley, Sir Proby 115
Chadwick, Edwin 88, 90, 91, 97, 98, 99, 114-15, 134, 143, 186, 195
Chisholm, Mrs Caroline 84
cholera 16, 48, 56, 63, 127, 138, 141-3, 184
Christian, Princess 169
Clarendon, Lord 25
Clark, Sir James 76, 92, 157
Clarke, Mrs M. 36, 38-9, 40, 52
Clough, A.H. 157, 185
Clough, Miss 53
Codrington, General Sir William 62, 63, 156
Contagious Diseases Acts 191-8
Cook, Sir Edward xi, 17, 75, 86, 160, 202
Cotton, Sir Arthur 145, 147
Cox, C.L. Army-Surgeon 117
Coyle, Mary Ann 39
Cranborne, Lord (Third Marquess of Salisbury) 127, 128, 130, 146-7
Cranworth, Lady Laura 13, 66
Crimean Hospitals 53-4, 57, 59-61, 63, 65-6
Crowhurst, Donald 201
Cuffe, Rev. Fr Michael 47
Cumming, Dr A.J. 46-7, 79

Dale, Rev. T.P. 162
Daly, Timothy 170-1
Daughters of the Faithful Virgin (Norwood Sisters) 28, 30, 34, 47
Davis, Elizabeth (Nurse) 61, 201
Dean, Miss 57
Deeble, Mrs 94
DeGrey, Earl 118, 126-7, 130, 195
Delane, J.J. 123

Dickens, Charles 52
Disraeli, Benjamin 50
Dufferin, Lord 135
Duffy, Rev. Fr Michael 58, 66
Dunmore, Lady Catherine 106

Ebrington, Viscount 88, 132
Ethelreda, Sister 34
Ewart, Dr Joseph 117

Fagg, Emma 36
Faithful, Emily 133
Farnall, H.B. 170-2
Farr, Dr William 81, 96, 99, 114-15, 122, 123-4, 126, 132, 166, 184, 194
Filder, William 73, 82
Fitzgerald, David 63-5, 77
Forester, Lady Maria 25-6, 28
Forster, W.F. 102
Frederick, J.J. 124, 126
Frere, Sir Bartle 118, 127-9

Galton, Douglas 91, 93, 96, 99, 101, 107, 119-20, 123, 126, 127-30, 138, 143, 147, 171, 196
Galton, Francis 87, 199
Galton, Marianne 17
Garrett, Dr Elizabeth (Anderson) 166, 196-7
Gaskell, Mrs Elizabeth 16, 17, 49-50, 91
Gibson, Dr J.B. 95
Gipps, Miss 39-40
Giraud, Rev. Mr 161
Gladstone, W.E. 91, 104-6, 120, 147, 194-5
Gleeson, Rev. Fr. Michael 66
Goldsmith, Margaret xi
Goschen, G.J. 177-8
Grant, Bishop Thomas 28
Grant, Sir Alexander 136
Green, Mrs [T.H.?] 190, 200, 201
Greenhow, Dr E. Headlam 98-9, 201
Gregg, Sam 49
Grey, Rear-Admiral F.W. 58-9
Grey, Third Earl 81-2

Hadley, Dr 56
Hall, Dr John 33, 56-67, 75-7, 79, 82, 84-5, 156, 201
Harding, Jane 46
Hardy, Gathorne, 172-3, 177
Hart, G.H.R. 147
Hastings, G.W. 132-5

Hathaway, Charles 137
Hawes, Sir Benjamin 63-4, 67, 101-3
Herbert, Mrs Sidney (Lizzie) 11, 25-7, 33, 37, 42, 50-1, 62, 90, 91, 100, 103-8, 200-1
Herbert, Sidney 23, 26-8, 30-3, 36-7, 41-5, 49-50, 52, 62-5, 67, 75-6, 78, 83-5, 86, 87-9, 90, 93-7, 99, 100-8, 114, 115, 119, 120, 127, 156-7, 193, 195
Hill, M.D. 132
Hill, Octavia 132, 189
Holyoake, G.J. 185
Hopkins, Ellice 132
Howell, T.G., Army Surgeon 117
Hume, Rev. Mr 25-7
Hunt, Mrs Maria 41

India
   army barracks 121
   army death rates 114-15, 122-6
   prison reform 130, 137-8
   sanitary reform 114-18, 120-1, 140-5, 148, 192
India Office 115, 117-19, 121, 124, 128-9, 135, 138
Inglis, Lady 11
Invalid Gentlewomen's Institution, 1 Harley St 11-17, 25, 35, 40, 46, 131, 158, 183

Jebb, General Sir Joshua 157
Jervoise, Dr J. Clarke 99
Johnson, Dr Walter 89
Jones, Agnes 173-7, 201
Jones, Dr Henry Bence 103
Jones, Mary 23, 38, 86, 160-2, 173-4, 199
Jowett, Benjamin 19, 23, 86, 87, 92, 100, 119, 127, 130, 147-8, 171, 178, 183, 184-6, 200

Kaiserswerth 21-2, 173
Kellett, Mrs Elizabeth 41
Kidd, Mrs 175
Kinglake, A.W. 52, 78, 82-3
King's College Hospital 16, 157, 160-2, 164

Lawfield, Mrs 38, 58, 67
Lawrence, Sir John 118, 120-2, 125-6, 128, 131, 137-40, 201
Lefroy, J.H. 63, 66, 75-7
Leith, Dr A.H. 124-6, 201
Lewis, Sir George Cornewall 97, 195

Liddell, Sir John 196
Linton, Mrs E. Lynn 190
Liverpool Workhouse Infirmary 174-5
Longmore, Dr T. 95, 196
Louisa, Grand Duchess of Baden 168-9
Lugard, Sir Edward 101

McNeill, Lady 89-90
McNeill, Sir John 53-5, 65-7, 73, 76,
    80, 82-5, 89-90, 97, 105-7,
    114-15, 117, 157-8, 185-6
Macpherson, Dr Duncan 117
Manning, Rev. Henry Edward 29-32,
    42, 47, 61, 65-6, 193, 200-1
Martin, Sir Ranald 91, 95, 115
Martineau, Harriet 92, 103, 119, 123,
    170-1, 195-6
Menzies, Dr Duncan 33, 36, 42, 79
Middlesex Hospital 16-17
Mill, John Stuart 20-1, 172, 185-9
Mills, Arthur 171
Milnes, Mrs Annabel Monckton 83,
    90
Milnes, Richard Monckton 18, 20,
    26-7, 50, 66, 185-6
Mohl, Madame 16, 20
Moore, Rev. Mother Mary Clare 27,
    29, 36, 39, 47-8, 92, 155
Mouat, Dr F.J. 138
Murray, Lord 74, 83

Nash, Rosalind 92-3
National Association for the Promotion
    of Social Science 99, 117, 130,
    132-5, 138
Neison, G.P. 99
Netley Hospital 76-7, 93-5, 176
Newcastle, Duke of 26, 35
Newman, Rev. John Henry 30
Newmarch, William 132
Nightingale, Florence
    ambitions 12, 16-17, 19, 68, 72-3,
        85, 118-19, 130, 132, 183-4,
        199
    and midwives' training 159-63, 201
    and moral welfare of troops 41,
        61, 121-2, 193, 195
    and nursing 15-16, 21-2, 27, 35-6,
        39-40, 42-4, 50, 155-6, 158-9,
        164-70, 178
    and Poor Law 170-3, 177-8
    and women's suffrage 188-90
    army sanitary reform 67-8, 74, 78,
        82, 89, 97-8, 117, 122, 140-2
    contagion theories 79, 96-100,
        116, 163, 167, 192, 194
    family background 18-20, 22-3,
        42, 49-50, 132, 198
    hospital design 93-4, 102, 119,
        128, 160, 163
    ill-health 54-6, 78, 89-93, 108,
        117, 136, 159, 186
    managerial qualities 14-15, 27,
        35-7, 38-40, 42-3, 49, 52-3,
        62-3, 66-7, 80, 117-19, 158-9
    manipulative impulse 11-13, 26-7,
        37-8, 44-7, 49, 53-4, 64-5,
        72-9, 81-3, 88-90, 103-6,
        114-15, 119, 123-6, 129, 169,
        176-7, 188, 191
    novelist's sense 12, 16-17, 55-6,
        64, 176
    political opinions 72, 177-8, 190-1
    private self 85-7, 176, 198-9,
        202
    religion 21-2, 23, 48, 183-5,
        187-8, 199
    reputation 42, 50-2, 67, 72, 201-2
    statistics 96, 98, 123, 163, 184
    Suggestions for Thought . . . 20,
        22-3, 156, 183-8
Nightingale, Mrs W. (Fanny, mother
    of F.N.) 13, 18-20, 22, 49, 91,
    198-9
Nightingale, Parthenope (sister of
    F.N.) 13, 16, 17, 18-19, 22,
    25-6, 49-51, 65-6, 86, 198-9, 201
Nightingale, William Edward (father
    of F.N.) 11-13, 18-19, 51, 185-6,
    198
Nightingale Fund 67, 72, 156-62,
    164, 167, 170, 178, 198
Nixon, Richard 201
Norman, H.R. 123, 126
Northcote, Sir Stafford 128-30, 138

Osborne, Rev. S.G. 51

Palmerston, Lord 25, 74-5, 93, 96-7
Panmure, Lord 52, 58, 63, 67, 73-8,
    81, 83, 87-9, 93, 97, 156
Parkes, Dr E.A. 67, 95
Pickering, Sir George 89
Pincoffs, Dr Peter 74-5, 77
Pirrie, Nurse 198-9
Ponsonby, Sir Henry 168
Poor Law 85, 92, 169-74, 177-8
Potter, Beatrice (Webb) 189
Prendergast, Joseph Samuel 51, 54-5
Pringle, Matron A.L. 86, 198-200

Prostitution 16-17, 192-8

Quarantine 100

Radcliffe Infirmary 168
Raglan, Lord 52-3, 55, 82
Rathbone, William 168, 170, 173-4
Rawlinson, Robert 53, 67, 83
Redpath, Marie C. 169
Rendle, Dr William 86
Roberts, Mrs 54, 155
Robinson, Robert 54
Robinson, Sarah 132
Roebuck, J.A. 52, 72
Ronan, Rev. Fr William 31, 46
Rose, Sir Hugh 124
Russell, W.H. 25, 51-2

St John's House Nurses 27-8, 33-4, 36, 38-40, 52-3, 56, 157, 159, 160-1
St Thomas's Hospital 86-7, 94, 98, 155-9, 165, 167, 169, 173, 175-6
Scutari Hospitals 35-8, 43, 47, 54, 56, 58, 79-80, 85
Sellon, Lydia Priscilla 27
Sen, Keshub Chunder 136
Shaftesbury, Lord 96-7, 131-2
Shepherd, Rev. C.P. 27-8, 32, 39
Sheridan (Nurse) 61
Shuttleworth, James Kay 132
Sieveking, Dr E.H. 169
Simon, Dr John 98-100, 132
Skene, Felicia 33
Smith, Brian Abel 169
Smith, Cecil Woodham xi, 17-18
Smith, Dr Andrew 25, 64, 75, 77, 79, 83, 85, 94, 156
Smith, Mai (aunt of F.N.) 11, 40, 42, 87, 89-90, 157
Smith, Samuel (uncle of F.N.) 26, 65-6, 90, 115, 155, 157, 185
Somerville, Mary 189
Soyer, Alexis 53-4
Sprey, Sister Mary Winifred 62
Stafford, Augustus 52, 72
Stanley, A.P. 31, 186
Stanley, Lord (15th Earl of Derby) 115, 119-20, 123-7, 132, 138, 201
Stanley, Mary 31-2, 43, 45-7, 73, 94, 100, 156, 201
Stanmore, Lord, *Life of Sidney Herbert* 26, 108, 201
Stansfeld, James 178

Sterling, Sir Anthony 69n40
Stewart, Dr A.P. 166
Stewart, Mrs Jane Shaw 94, 155-6
Storks, General Sir Henry 58-60, 75, 83
Stowe, Harriet Beecher 176
Strachan, Alexander 177
Strachey, Lytton xi, 17, 18, 26, 202
Strachey, Ray 188
Strachey, Sir John 121
Strachey, Sir Richard 138
Stratford de Redcliffe, Lady 27, 37
Stratford de Redcliffe, Lord 25, 37, 46, 58, 59-60
Strzelecki, Count Paul 124
Sutherland, Dr John 20, 53-4, 67, 73, 75-7, 83-4, 86-7, 91, 96, 99, 101, 114-15, 118-20, 124-5, 127-9, 137, 143, 147, 156, 163-4, 170, 174, 177, 188, 195, 197-8, 200

Tait, A.C. (Bishop of London) 161
Taylor, Dr A.H. 65
Taylor, Fanny 54, 201
Temple, Richard 145
Terrot, Sister Sarah Anne 49
Torrance, Matron Elizabeth 199
Truelove, Mrs 186
Tulloch, Alexander 53, 67, 73, 75-7, 83, 97
Twining, Elizabeth 188
Twining, Louisa 162, 173, 176, 188, 191

University College Hospital 162

Verney, Sir Harry 161, 171, 188, 195-6, 199
Victoria, Queen 50, 55, 65, 67, 72, 73-6, 78, 83, 85, 86, 117, 147
Villiers, C.P. 170-2
Vivian, Sir Robert 115

Walker, Dr J.P. 125, 138-41, 175
Walker, Henriett 175
Ward, L. (purveyor) 36
Ward, Lord William 55-6
Ward, Mrs Humphry 190
Wardroper, Mrs S.E. 155, 159, 164-6, 168, 175
War Office 25-6, 29-30, 32, 53, 58-60, 63-4, 67, 72, 75, 77-8, 80-2, 88, 91, 93, 95-7, 101-5, 107-8, 114-15, 118, 121-4, 129,

135, 193, 195
Wear, Mary 53-4, 57-61
Wells, H.G. 37
Whitfield, R.G. 158, 200
Williams, Dr C.B. 106
Williams, Miss Rachel 199
Winkworth, Catherine 16

Wood, Sir Charles 115, 119, 123-6, 130, 138
Woollett, Rev. Fr J.S. 57
Wyatt, Matthew Digby 119
Wynter, Dr Andrew 114-15

Youl, Rev. Dr 29

APR   '86

DATE DUE			
FEB 04 1993			
FEB 25 1993			
RO JSC			
MAR 16 2001			
MAR 14 2001			
APR 09 2001			